SAFE
Overseas
Travel

Maximizing Enjoyment
by Minimizing Risk

BRIAN JOHNSON
BRIAN KINGSHOTT

43-08 162nd Street
Flushing, NY 11358
www.LooseleafLaw.com
800-647-5547

Library of Congress Publication Data

Johnson, Brian R.
    Safe overseas travel : maximizing enjoyment by minimizing risk / Brian R. Johnson, Brian F. Kingshott.
        p. cm.
    Includes bibliographical references and index.
    ISBN 978-1-932777-78-9 (alk. paper)
    1. Travel--Safety measures. I. Kingshott, Brian F. II. Title.
    G151.J64 2008
    613.6'8--dc22

                                                    2008046466

Cover design by: *Sans Serif, Inc.*, Saline, Michigan

Table of Contents

Dedication

To my wife, Shari

— Brian Johnson

To my wife, Mavis and
our two sons, Jan and Matthew

— Brian Kinghsott

ABOUT THE AUTHORS

B rian R. Johnson is a Professor of Criminal Justice at the University of North Alabama, Florence, AL. Johnson holds a Ph.D. and Masters Degrees in Criminal Justice and Labor and Industrial Relations from Michigan State University. Johnson served as a police officer and as the Assistant Director and Interim Director of a regional police academy in Michigan and worked several years in both proprietary and contract security firms. He is also a security consultant and trainer for companies and organizations, and has a broad background in the design and delivery of security training and education programs. As a Professor, he has also taught several security-related courses. He is currently the Chair of the Security and Crime Prevention section of the Academy of Criminal Justice Sciences (ACJS), an international association that fosters professional and scholarly activities in the field of criminal justice. He is the author of two texts: *The Management of Security Personnel*, and *Crucial Elements of Police Firearms Training*. He has also published several articles, writing on issues related to crime prevention and safety, policing, and private security. Besides his domestic travels, he has also traveled throughout the UK and the European Continent on several occasions.

B rian F. Kingshott is an Associate Professor of Criminal Justice at Grand Valley State University, Grand Rapids, Michigan. He obtained his MA and Ph.D. at the University of Exeter, (England) in Police Studies. His areas of specialty include: terrorism and counterterrorism, law enforcement, community policing, criminal investigation, Human Rights Auditor and Ethicist. He has written extensively in these fields. He is a former member of the United Kingdom Cadre of International Hostage Negotiators. Kingshott retired from the Devon and Cornwall Constabulary after 32 years of service in 2001. For his work on personal and organizational ethics he was elected Fellow of the Royal Society of Arts (London). He has also published extensively in the field of policing and security. As a former British Merchant Navy Officer, Kingshott has traveled the world.

PREFACE

Most travel books are either generic in nature or, alternatively, they are specific to a country or region of the world. The result is that the information contained in these texts is often dated or irrelevant. In many cases these books are so large and intimidating in size that they actually discourage the potential traveler from reading them! The purpose of this book is different: our goal is to provide up-to-date, concise, and relevant information for the traveler. It provides general and pertinent information related to the key components of ensuring a safe and enjoyable experience overseas. Within this context, it is geared toward all travelers, highlighting the most relevant and significant scholarship that exists regarding safe travel.

This book was specifically designed to be a practical workbook. The design allows for the traveler, alone or in groups, to assess their vulnerabilities to various types of risk that exist, based on their travel destination and activities. In addition, it includes ancillary information, such as links to various government websites to encourage further research on safe travel. This book also incorporates the experiences of the authors. Both authors are criminal justice academicians and have extensive personal experience in traveling abroad. These experiences are incorporated into the text and shared with the reader.

1
INTRODUCTION

Traveling to a foreign country can be an exciting, exhilarating, and an extraordinary life experience. Dreams can be realized; cultures and customs experienced, and places and people, previously seen only as photographic images, become enduring memories. However, before the euphoria of travel can be experienced, it must be planned out. This task, however, can be overwhelming for the novice or even the most seasoned foreign traveler. For example, there are the health and financial-related issues that have to be identified and dealt with. Additionally, history has proven that a traveler could become the target of theft, kidnapping, terrorism, and other crimes including sexual assault and robbery. Of course, travelers are also at risk for a variety of accidents while vacationing. Consider the following real-life incidents:

- Local criminals kidnapped a college student on spring break in Mexico. He was held for ransom until his friend (who was not abducted) could come up with the $250 ransom.

- An entire tour group traveling to Russia had their passports stolen from them by a man posing as a police official.

- A bear attacked a group of U.S. tourists on a remote trail in the Carpathian Mountains in Romania, killing a woman and injuring two others.[1]

- Chinese officials reported the arrest of a taxi gang in Shanghai that allegedly had scammed more than a dozen foreigners out of $7,000 in less than two months.[2]

- Two Canadian tourists in Belfast were robbed by four youths who were armed with screwdrivers and knives.[3]

---

[1] *U.S. tourists attacked by bear in Romania: 1 dead* (June 24, 2007). Associated Press.

[2] *Foreigners grapple with crime in China* (March 17, 2008). Associated Press.

[3] *Four teenagers arrested after tourist attack in Belfast* (December 30, 2007). Belfast Telegraph.

- Two 16-year-old students from London were arrested in Ghana allegedly carrying £300,000 of cocaine. Ghanaian Narcotic Control Board officials found the drugs on the girls while trying to board an aircraft at Accra Airport. They were unaware of the fact that the package that they were carrying for a "friend" contained drugs.[4]

A quick review of additional newspaper headlines and Internet websites provides further insight into the risks that travelers face when venturing not only to foreign countries but even within the confines of the U.S. Of interest, is that the above examples and other events that the reader knows about could have most likely been mitigated and/or avoided if the travelers had better prepared for, and understood the dangers of, foreign travel.

The purpose of this book is to assist travelers in making themselves safe. To be a safe traveler, there will be a myriad of questions that will have to be answered. Those questions are often prefaced by "What if...?", "How do I...?", "Where do I...?" and/or "Who do I contact if...?" These are very important issues that have to be dealt with before, during, and after the travel experience.

The underlying theme of this book is that safe travel is a practice and a mindset. Planning for travel requires identifying potential problems. More importantly, it also requires finding the solution to the problems. Therefore, the individual traveler has to first anticipate problems they may encounter. Next, the traveler will need to train their mind in the context of thinking about every minute detail of their travels and the risks associated with it. Finally, safety needs to become a habit and a lifestyle choice, but this does not minimize the enjoyment of the travel experience. In this context, the traveler needs to always plan ahead and ask: "What are the risks?" and, "How can I avoid or mitigate risk?"

Avoiding and planning for risk is quite easy. Oftentimes, it doesn't require major changes or modifications to a person's travel plans. Instead, it only requires some common sense

---

[4]   *UK girls in Ghana: Drug arrests* (July 12, 2007). BBC News.

practices on how a person plans for and engages in their travels in order to make him or herself safer.

It is possible that the previous paragraphs have made the traveler apprehensive, but this need not be the case. This book is structured in a manner where it can be used in preparing and planning for a safe trip. Additionally, the information in this book can also serve as a ready-reference while traveling.

These concerns are addressed within the text because the main topics of this book include, but are not limited to:

- Getting Ready
- The Passport
- Visas
- Healthy Travel/Medical Issues
- Luggage Tips/Traveling Light
- The Airport

- Aircraft Security
- Lodging Security
- Street Smarts
- Using Public Transportation/Getting Around
- Getting Out
- Culture
- Safety and Security Resources

Although much of the content of this book relates to "foreign" travel, a traveler should keep in mind that many of the risks and strategies identified in this book are applicable globally. Therefore, domestic travel does not mean a traveler is safe – travel risks should be considered universal in nature.

While some of these chapters may not appear specifically related to safe travel, they nevertheless are. In fact, every component of travel can somehow be traced to safety. Consider for example, the forthcoming chapter on Luggage Tips. Having too much luggage to a traveler may not be considered a safety issue, per se. At a minimum, too much luggage could be considered a burden. However, traveling with too much luggage can slow a person down. It may also serve to alert would-be criminals that a novice traveler and target is present, relative to other proficient travelers in the same area. Remember: In crime the victim is targeted, so travelers need to minimize their profile as a target.

THE CRIME TRIANGLE

Figure 1-1
The Crime Triangle

Before venturing into specific topics of safe travel, becoming a safe traveler first requires insight into what causes a person to become a victim of crime. According to Marcus Felson,[5] a noted criminologist, crime and criminal activities can be explained through the crime triangle that is shown in Figure 1-1. On the inner triangle are the: 1) Offender; 2) Place; and, 3) Target. On the outer triangle are control agents that include: 1) Handlers; 2) Managers; and, 3) Guardians.

First, it can be safely assumed that the world is full of motivated and likely offenders. At any time and place a person can become a victim of crime. At the same time, there are certain places in the world (and society in general) that are more dangerous than others (places). These can be specific regions of the world, certain countries, and even locales within countries. Of course, there are the targets. In the context of travel, the target could be the traveler or their possessions. Handlers (the offender's parents, family members, or peers), meanwhile, look after or supervise potential offenders, and the lack of these handlers could lead to the potential offender committing crimes. Guardians, meanwhile, focus on the crime targets (i.e., a traveler looking after their luggage; travelers looking after one another). In addition, managers look after certain places (i.e., hotels, terminals). The point here is that the lack of these control agents can lead to increased opportunities for the motivated offender.

In the examples provided in the beginning of this chapter, the reader can see the crime triangle at work. First, the traveler(s) and/or their possessions were the targets. They unfortunately were "in the wrong place at the wrong time" where offenders targeted the travelers for a host of reasons that this book will

---

[5]   Felson, M. (2006). *Crime and nature.* Thousand Oaks, CA: Sage.

cover in detail. All these examples also share the common theme that control agents (i.e., handlers and guardians) were minimal, lacking or even supporting criminal activities in some way.

Based on this model of crime and crime prevention, the traveler is always a target for motivated offenders. Naturally, the environment (what country they are traveling to, airports, hotels, and other locales) can also make a person more vulnerable to becoming a victim of crime. Additionally, the nature, quality and quantity of the control agents – handlers, guardians and place managers will vary in quality and quantity. Therefore, a traveler needs to gain an understanding of how and to what degree these elements of crime exist in order to reduce the chances and/or prevent themselves from becoming a victim of crime.

Of interest is the fact that this same crime prevention triangle can be applied to other non-human threats. Consider, for example, viruses that a traveler could be exposed to during their trip. Now, the offender is a microbe, and the health issues are caused by the lack of control agents – improper sanitation, food preparation, etc. in the destination country.

When it comes to travel, a wise assumption to take is that control agents are lacking. Therefore, the traveler needs to be fully responsible for their own safety; any other existing control agents should only be considered to be a "bonus" for the traveler's own well-designed security and safety program. This requires careful and detailed advanced planning in a variety of subject areas, allowing the traveler to make well-informed decisions on whether, when, and where to travel.

Oftentimes, however, this component of the trip is overlooked. This can be the result of the traveler preoccupied with preparing for other components of their trip. Or, they may take the position that "it can't happen to me," but the safe traveler will always be aware.

UNDERSTANDING RISK

Preparing for any trip begins with a great amount of self-reflection and study. This self-reflection and study first begins with understanding risk. Risk is anything that could cause damage, loss, or any other undesirable outcome. *The Oxford English Dictionary*[6] defines risk as a "hazard, danger; exposure to mischance or peril." Therefore, to put oneself "at risk" means to participate voluntarily or involuntarily in an activity or event that could lead to injury, damage, or loss.

Risks can be divided into specific types that are listed in Box 1-1.[7] Within each of these large categories, there are also some subcomponents related to the type of risk that may cause property or personal harm. In the context of travel, all of these risks (and their sub-risks) exist.

Box 1-1
Types of Risk

- □ **Reputational** – How will your exposure to a threat/peril impact your reputation?
- □ **Financial** – How will the risk impact your financial health (both long and short term impacts)
- □ **Dynamic** – Risk where there is some tangible or intangible benefit

---

Risk has both short and long-term effects. For example, if one's wallet is stolen while traveling, this could be considered to be a short-term problem – the traveler needs to get some money, cancel their credit cards and obtain new identification cards. At the same time, it may have some long-term ramifications ranging from identity theft to the traveler's credit score being affected. In the context of risk, meanwhile, this incident could also affect the traveler's reputation (i.e., credit history). This incident is also an example of dynamic risk. In this example, even though there were problems on the trip, the traveler (hopefully) still had some good experiences to recollect.

Risk, meanwhile, is caused by perils. Perils are the way or means by which damage or loss occurs. Perils can be human, such as pickpockets. Or, they can be natural, such as a tropical storm or a virus. Perils are also called hazards. As this book will stress, it is very important for the traveler to identify those particular

---

[6] *Oxford University Press*, 1971.
[7] Broder, J.F.(1999). *Risk analysis and the security survey*. Burlington, MA: Elsiver.

hazards that they are likely to encounter prior to travel. It is also important to continually reevaluate the presence of hazards during one's travel. In many cases hazards are dynamic in nature, constantly changing based on a variety of situational characteristics during one's travels. Nevertheless, they can easily be identified if a traveler remains alert and aware.

VULNERABILITY

Vulnerability deals with the inherent characteristics of the person that creates the potential for harm. They are independent of the probability of risk. For example, the risk of kidnapping exists for all foreign travelers. American tourists, because of world events as well as the perception that all Americans must be wealthy, make them more vulnerable to such attacks, independent of those actions they engage in to reduce their exposure to such crimes. Therefore, all Americans face a certain probability for theft. However, in the context of individual attributes and practices while traveling, the traveler may make themselves more vulnerable to the risk of theft.

MANAGING RISK

All of the examples given so far in this chapter can be prevented or mitigated (the effects of the incident reduced to a controllable level). Therefore, the key to safe travel is to manage risk. Travel risk can be managed through risk avoidance, transfer, spreading and acceptance.[8]

Risk Avoidance

The concept of risk avoidance is simply avoiding certain locations or activities while traveling, based on the inherent risks associated with the travel. The U.S. State Department, for example, provides a list of countries that a traveler should avoid. At the same time, there are locations within certain countries that travelers should avoid. Depending upon the information at hand, a traveler, for example, may consider avoiding locations where there are large concentrations of tourists. These locations

---

[8] Ibid

may make a traveler more vulnerable to a variety of criminal activities.

Risk Transfer

Risk transfer is a strategy used to remove the risk from the owner to a third party. Risk transfer occurs when a traveler takes out insurance (i.e., travel, health, and kidnap/ransom). The insurance company assumes some of the risk in exchange for a fee. One of the more common insurance policies that a traveler may take out includes supplemental health insurance.

Risk Spreading

Risk spreading is a strategy to move or divide assets. The goal behind risk spreading is simple: if one asset is compromised, then there is still another asset elsewhere. Perhaps the best example of risk spreading while traveling is to not carry all of one's money and credit cards in the same location. If, for example, a traveler carries all of their money and financial instruments in their wallet and it is then stolen, they are facing a far more serious situation than if they had their money and credit cards "spread" or stored in other locations on their body.

Risk Acceptance

Risk acceptance occurs where the traveler assumes some level of risk, after reducing the risk level to an acceptable level. In any activity, a person accepts a certain amount of risk, regardless of what activities they are involved in. For example, simply walking down the street exposes a person to a certain level of risk, such as getting struck by a car. Nevertheless, the person accepts the fact that there is a low probability of the risk of occurrence. To reduce that risk even more, the person engages in a variety of simple activities (i.e., risk reduction), such as being aware of their surroundings and looking both ways before crossing a street.

As is the case with travel, no matter how safe a person is, there is always a certain degree of risk that they may be exposed to. Risk acceptance, however, does not call for the traveler to be passive and accept the fact that they may be exposed to many different perils. Instead, a traveler must understand and be prepared for a wide variety of issues that arise, that need to be addressed while traveling.

What often makes the management of risk difficult is the fact that risk will vary based on the nature of the travel (the where, what, when, and how of travel). It also deals with the specific attributes of the traveler, as well as their travel companions. Consider, for example, a traveler's gender. Female travelers are usually more affected by the religious, social beliefs, and norms of some countries, relative to male travelers. Therefore, females need to better prepare themselves for the differing norms and attitudes that may exist in other countries and the increased vulnerability to certain risks that males may not have. Other personal attributes that could increase or decrease one's vulnerability may include, but are not limited to: age, race, appearance, height, weight, and even health, which the forthcoming chapters of this book will cover in detail.

ABOUT THIS BOOK

Travelers obviously do not always act in ways that serve their own best interests, even as defined by them. Sometimes, they underestimate the risk of particular actions or behaviors. It is possible, indeed likely, that some travelers engage in risky behaviors because of a perception of invulnerability. In other cases it can be attributed to the fact that the traveler is uninformed of the hazards and subsequent risks that exist in foreign travel.

The forthcoming chapters in this book will provide the reader with a wealth of information on how to eliminate, minimize and then manage and control the many risks that they may face when traveling to foreign countries. While the reader may find the contents of many of these chapters overwhelming, the purpose is not to deter a person from engaging in foreign travel. On the contrary, it is designed to enhance the travel experience by making the reader more safety-conscious and an informed traveler. This, in turn, will lead to an enjoyable overseas experience.

2
GETTING READY

Y ou have chosen your destination(s) and the next stage is planning your dream vacation. It is at this stage where the traveler can start to minimize their exposure to risk. This chapter will expand upon the concept of risk introduced in Chapter 1 by examining specific issues in order to get the reader to start considering the vast array of pre-departure activities that have an impact on travel safety.

This chapter is designed to be a workbook. Throughout this chapter, the reader will have the opportunity to stop and examine what they have learned along the way through questions included in the text. It is encouraged that the traveler write his thoughts and answers to these questions before proceeding. The reader should also keep in mind that the forthcoming chapters will then provide detailed points on specific issues related to safe travel.

BASIC THOUGHTS AND CONCEPTS

First, one needs to consider the risks by critically examining the "who, what, when, where, why and how" of their travels.

How Safe is the Country and Region?

Travelers from westernized and/or industrialized nations may not be well-liked and/or received in some countries. These countries may like the tourism dollars that a traveler brings in and that is all! Therefore, one of the most important pre-departure planning activities is to research the safety of the region and destination country in order to make a well-informed decision on whether, when and where to travel. An evaluation form to list safety-related issues is shown in Box 2-1 (an additional copy of this form can be found in Appendix A). This research includes issues related to personal safety (i.e., overall crime, terrorist threats) as well as health conditions including the presence of, or outbreaks of various diseases. In order to do this, a traveler has many resources available to them.

Travel Warnings

Travel warnings are issued when the State Department (or another consular office) recommends that travelers avoid a certain country, for a variety of legitimate reasons. Each country has a government department tasked to assess the safety of its citizens in other countries. Often this is linked to foreign policy and other diplomatic assessments. Therefore, it may be that a citizen of country "A" is safe to travel to country "C," but a citizen from country "B" may be at risk traveling to country "C."

For a citizen of the United States, travel warnings can be found on the U.S. State Department's web page (http://www.state.gov). Information on this site is updated regularly and it provides advice and/or recommendations on whether or not to travel, based on the threat analysis or profile of that particular country or region of the world. Some of the information in these travel warnings may include:

- Overall Security – Terrorism, civil unrest, overall crime rates, etc.
- Disease/Epidemics – Includes existing and potential outbreaks.
- Demonstrations – Could impede and endanger travelers.

To ensure accuracy in travel warnings, it is also recommended that the traveler check similar web pages. Perhaps one of the best ways to verify the authenticity and timeliness of travel information and warnings from the State Department's web page is to compare it to the contents of other western nation consular websites, such as Canada and Great Britain. There are also many fee-based companies and consultants that provide up-to-date risk assessments for certain countries or regions of the world. Some of these sources are listed in Appendix M.

Another source for travel information and advisories is to research the destination country's website. Some caution, however, should be exercised when using the destination country's web page. Some travel experts, for example, have questioned the validity of some country's sites in the context that they may not report or under-report crime, etc., in order to maintain their tourism industry and their reputation as a "safe" country. In some cases, the last thing these countries want to do is to have a bad reputation that affects the tourist trade, which brings a great amount of hard currency into their country.[9]

Consular Information

In addition to travel warnings, the U.S. State Department also publishes safety and travel-related information for every country of the world on its website. These publications include facts about the land, people, history, health conditions, and the type of government. They also include information on political and economic conditions as well as foreign relations-related issues. The State Department also provides maps of the country and region and links to other pages that provide additional information on the destination country.

Trip Registration

A traveler should also consider registering with the U.S. Embassy or Consulate in the country that they are visiting. Registration makes the traveler's presence and whereabouts known, in case it is necessary for a consular officer to contact them in an emergency. During a disaster overseas, for example, American consular officers can assist in an evacuation if that were to become necessary. However, officers cannot assist if they do not know where the traveler is.

According to the State Department, registration is particularly important for travelers who plan to stay in a country longer than one month, or who will travel to:

- A country that is experiencing civil unrest, has an unstable political climate, or is undergoing a natural disaster, such as an earthquake or a hurricane.

---

[9] Hagedorn-Auerbach, A. (1998). *Ransom*. New York: Henry Holt

- A country where there are no U.S. officials. In such cases, a traveler should register at the U.S. embassy or consulate in an adjacent country, leave an itinerary with the Consular Section, and ask about conditions in the country that they will visit.

Box 2-1
Country Safety Issues

Information from Travel Warnings:
- _____
- _____
- _____

- _____
- _____
- _____

Information from Consular Sheets:
- _____
- _____
- _____

- _____
- _____
- _____

Other Relevant Information on Country:
_____
_____
_____
_____
_____
_____
_____
_____
_____
_____
_____
_____
_____

Travelers can register on-line through the State Department's Travel Registration Website. In cases when traveling with a tour group, the traveler should check with the travel agent to make sure the trip has been registered on the State Department's travel registration website. If not, then the travelers should register themselves.

Who Am I Traveling With?

Who a person is traveling with has a great bearing on their safety. The actions and activities that a person's travel partner(s) engage in could put the traveler in danger at times. In fact, traveling with certain individuals and/or a tour group is like luggage – some individuals may be cumbersome, difficult to be with, and they may slow other travelers down. Therefore, a key component to group travel is to obtain information about one's companions *prior* to the trip. Perhaps one of the best ways to assess the strengths and weaknesses of whom a person is traveling with is to have a simple, but candid discussion with them, addressing the following questions.

- *What is the nature and extent of their travel experience?*
- *How do they handle stress?*
- *What is their level of emotional maturity?*
- *What are their strengths?*
- *What are their weaknesses?*
- *How will they ensure the success of the trip?*
- *Are they a leader or follower?*
- *What are some of their greatest concerns with this trip?*

Shown in Box 2-2 is a traveler assessment form to assist a traveler in determining their strengths, weaknesses, and abilities prior to travel. An additional form is provided in Appendix B. This form can be used individually or in a group setting where individuals can pair up and assess one another.

Any weaknesses (i.e., vulnerabilities) identified through this process can often be corrected before departure. For example, if a traveler cannot read a map or train timetable, this issue can be readily fixed by simply reading this book. In other situations where the weakness or issue cannot be readily corrected, by simply being aware of the situation, those in the group can assist one another (i.e., translating for a group member that does not speak the language).

Box 2-2
Traveler Assessment Form

Questions	Answers
What is the nature and extent of their travel experience?	
How do they handle stress?	
What is their level of emotional maturity?	
What are their strengths?	
What are their weaknesses?	
How will they correct these weaknesses?	
Are they a leader or follower?	
What are some of their greatest concerns with this trip?	
How will they ensure the success of the trip?	
Other Points......	

Besides these general preparatory questions, another important issue to consider is if the traveler shares the same interests with the balance of the tour group. As an example, many structured tours or programs are geared toward families, certain age groups, and/or interests. If the traveler does not have the same interests, etc., they may stray away from the group, and perhaps increase their exposure to certain risks. Even if they appear to be the same, other issues should be considered.

They may include:

- *Are their lifestyle choices/activities the same as mine?*
- *Do we share the same moral and ethical values?*
- *Do we share the same socio-economic status?*
- *Do we have similar interests?*

In other situations, if the majority of travelers want to engage in certain activities that the traveler should consider risky, they may participate in them nevertheless, increasing their vulnerability to the risk.

Structured Trips with Guides

Because a trip is structured or endorsed by an organization, company, or university and comes complete with a guide, this does not mean that a traveler will be any safer in the context of the exposure to risk. For example, in many cases, large groups may attract unnecessary and unwanted attention. Guides, meanwhile, may be knowledgeable of the area, but many types of risk that exist while traveling are beyond the control of the guide; therefore, it is always important to know the guide's abilities. It is also vital that the traveler never yield their personal safety to the responsibilities of others. If a decision is made to take a guided trip, it is important to make sure that the person or tour group has experience in that country or region of the world. It is also important to verify the qualifications of the guide(s) by asking for the names of previous travelers in order to obtain their opinions about the quality of the guides. If a company is hesitant about providing this type of information, it could be an indicator that the overall quality and competency levels of the staff may be substandard.

Who Are My Emergency Contacts?

Emergencies can happen while traveling. They can happen to the traveler while they are overseas. Or, they can happen at the traveler's home, resulting in the need for them to be located or contacted in a timely manner.

Prior to traveling, a detailed itinerary should be left with a dependable family member or friend in case of such emergencies. This person should be told in advance that they are the emergency liaison person so they are prepared for such events, if they should occur. A sample emergency information form is shown in Box 2-3. An additional copy of this form can be found in Appendix C.

Some of the information that should be on this form includes the traveler's:

- Itinerary
- Known Medical Conditions and Prescriptions
- Name of Primary Care Physician
- Overseas Contact Names and Numbers
- Passport Number
- Social Security Number
- Health and Dental Insurance Information
- Other Personal Information (i.e., employer, friends, acquaintances)

The information on this form can serve many purposes. Consider, for example, if there is an emergency in the U.S. that necessitates finding and notifying the traveler. Through the use of this information on this form, the traveler could be located at the airport, in the country, or even at a certain location in the country, if necessary.

In addition to the information on the form, the traveler should also include photocopies of important documents. Copies should be left with the designated emergency liaison person. The traveler should also consider carrying a copy of this information with them in a safe and secure location and/or scan copies of this information onto a flash drive or a .pdf file that can be retrieved from an e-mail account.

Travelers should also make sure that personal matters are in good order before traveling. An up-to-date will, and even granting power of attorney to a person to ensure access to bank accounts, are just a couple issues that should be considered.

What Am I Doing?

In this context, a person needs to ask: "What Am I Doing," by engaging in foreign travel. As already pointed out, travel can be taxing. Therefore, the traveler needs to ask the crucial question: "Am I up to the challenge?" Being up for the challenge includes both the physical and mental requirements of travel.

To see if one is "up to the challenge," it is important to talk with friends and family to get their candid opinions. Talking to other travelers who have experience with the same kind of travel may also be useful. During these discussions it is important to ask them what they think some of the greatest challenges, frustrations, etc. during the trip will be, based on their personal knowledge of the traveler's abilities and disposition. Additionally, the travelers should compare themselves to other known travelers and ask: "Am I honestly up for the challenge?" This self-assessment process should include the completion of the Traveler Assessment Form found in Box 2-2.

One of the most common mistakes made by travelers is having too much confidence in their abilities, thereby underestimating the danger or risks associated with travel. Not only could this place a traveler in greater danger, but it could also cause undue stress for loved ones. If a traveler is unprepared (or gives the impression of being unprepared) this could stress loved ones prior to and during the trip, as they sit at home and worry. Subsequent incidents on account of being unprepared will also naturally stress these individuals out even more, as the traveler may have to rely upon them in some manner. The traveler also needs to be considerate of their travel partners, too. Being unprepared will lead to stress and strife with those they are traveling with. In addition, being unprepared could also expose travel companions to increased levels of danger.

Box 2-3
Emergency Information Form*

Traveler Information:
Full Name   _____
D.O.B   _____
SSN: _____
Passport #   _____

U.S. Emergency Contact:
Name   _____
Address   _____
City, State   _____
Telephone   _____
E-mail   _____
Relationship   _____

Health Insurance
Policy #   _____
Name   _____
Address   _____
City, State   _____
Telephone   _____
E-mail   _____

Overseas Contact:
Name   _____
Address   _____
City, State   _____
Telephone   _____
E-mail   _____
Relationship   _____

Flight Information:
Airlines: _____
Flight #'s   _____
                   _____

Primary Care Physician:
Name   _____
Address   _____
City, State   _____
Telephone   _____
E-mail   _____

Dental Insurance
Policy #   _____
Name   _____
Address   _____
City, State   _____
Telephone   _____
E-mail   _____

Known Medical Conditions:
                   _____
                   _____
                   _____

Prescriptions
                   _____
                   _____

Detailed Daily Itinerary:
_____
_____
_____
_____
_____
_____
_____
_____
_____
_____
_____
_____

---

* Be sure to leave copies of your passport and any other travel documents with your emergency contacts.

What Are the Entry and Exit Requirements?

For authoritative information on a country's entry and exit requirements, travelers should also contact the host country's embassy or consulate. When making inquiries, the traveler should ask about/research:

- Where to obtain a tourist card or visa;
- Visa price, length of validity, and number of entries;
- Financial requirements: proof of sufficient funds, proof of onward or return ticket;
- Special requirements for children traveling alone or with only one parent;
- Health requirements;
- Currency regulations: how much local or other currency can be brought in or out;
- Export/import restrictions; and,
- Departure tax: how much and who must pay.

This information can often be obtained from the U.S. State Department website, and other Internet sites. Nevertheless, it is still a good idea to establish contact with individuals in or from that country. Usually, these individuals can provide more detailed information and additional insight into the destination country.

What is the Language?

Language barriers can make a trip frustrating. In order to reduce the problems associated with language barriers, travelers should consider taking language lessons before leaving. Travelers do not have to be fluent in that particular language. Instead, learning some of the common phrases that will be used on a daily basis would be beneficial. Besides common phrases, learning emergency phrases is important, too. Attempting to speak the language instead of assuming that individuals will speak English may also go a long way in establishing good will with the citizens of that country.

Besides learning the language, a traveler should also construct and carry a card that contains some of the normal phrases that will be used (exercise some caution in displaying this card when overseas). Of course, a small translation phrase book (or perhaps an electronic language translator as reviewed in Chapter 9) may be quite useful, too.

What Documents Do I Need?

The traveler also needs to make sure that their documents are in order. The most important document a traveler will need is the passport. Depending upon the destination, the traveler may also need to apply for a visa. Issues regarding the passport and visa will be reviewed in the forthcoming chapters.

In some cases, the traveler may need other documents for travel and for their activities within the destination country, where they will have to prove the authentication of these documents. The U.S. Department of State's Authentications Office is responsible for signing and issuing certificates under the Seal of the U.S. Department of State. This office receives a variety of documents from commercial organizations, private citizens, and officials of the federal and state governments. Documents include but are not limited to: company bylaws, powers of attorney, trademarks, diplomas, transcripts, and letters of reference.

When Am I Traveling?

The *"when"* of traveling also deals with significant dates and even the seasons. Travelers could be at greater risk during certain times of the year due to religious festivals, political unrest or instability, and war. Certain dates or anniversaries (i.e.,, 9/11) may also be more dangerous days to travel, too. Besides increased dangers, travelers could also experience delays because of increased security measures during these times.

Traveling as an American to certain countries in the Middle East may not be wise because of resentment of U.S. foreign policy toward Middle Eastern countries following the first Gulf War (in the early 1990's) and the current war in Afghanistan and Iraq.

Instead, it may be a better alternative to postpone travel to a later time when the political, social, and economic climate improves. In other cases, individuals may travel during peak travel times. In the context of crime and safety, this may not be the safest alternative. Airports and lodging establishments, public transportation and other public places may be extremely crowded with tourists. Criminals could consider this "open season" and be out in force at these times.

Where Am I Going?

In many cases, a traveler has limited knowledge on where exactly they are going in the context of geography. Therefore, it is important to get a map and study the region in order to become familiar with the customs, history, and geography of the destination country. As is the case in the *"when,"* travelers should also seriously consider the political, economic and social conditions in the destination country including local holidays. Even though the destination country might be safe, it is important to keep in mind that the majority of borders can be easily penetrated. Therefore, the problems from neighboring countries can easily spill into the destination country. And, in some instances, it could be sudden.

Information of this nature can be gleaned from a variety of sources. The State Department and other country-specific websites have already been indicated as some good sources. Additionally, the prospective traveler may want to visit the following sites:

- CIA World Factbook: https://www.cia.gov
- Center for Disease Control: http://www.cdc.gov
- The World Bank: http://www.worldbank.org
- The United Nations: http://www.un.org
- The World Health Organization: http://www.who.int/en/

Some questions to consider are:

- What is its culture and how does it differ from mine?
- What are some of the customs?
- What are some regulations and laws that exist in my destination country? Remember: when traveling abroad, you are subject to the laws of that country.
- What limitations are there in relation to gender issues?
- Who are the neighboring countries? Will they impact upon my travel?
- Are there any specific health risks?
- What is the food like?

To gain additional knowledge on the destination country, a traveler can also purchase some up-to-date guidebooks that can provide further insight into a country, its customs, and history. Books of this nature will also provide some additional ideas for places to visit, etc. This information should then be recorded in a Country Characteristics Form, as shown in Box 2-4. An additional copy of this form can be found in Appendix D.

Why Am I Traveling?

The question "why am I traveling" can be as simple as because "I have to" or because "I want to." This mindset, however, can have a great bearing on the traveler's attitude and preparedness for travel. In the "because I have to" mindset, the traveler may take a passive, dependent role in travel, and perhaps in preparing for a safe journey. On the other hand, if a traveler adopts the position "because I want to," they may be more proactive in the planning process.

An individual may also be traveling for business or pleasure or a combination of the two. This fact alone will dictate those activities that the traveler will be engaged in. It may also dictate the degree of control they have over their schedule, who they are traveling with, and the type and quantity of clothing that will be needed for the trip.

Box 2-4
Country Characteristics Form

Destination Country: _____

Region of the World: _____

Characteristics of
Neighboring Countries: _____

Form of Government: _____

Location of
Embassy/Consulate: _____

Major Religion(s): _____

Health Risks? _____

Size: _____

Population Density: _____

Overall Stability of Region: _____

Overall Stability of Country: _____

Other Points: _____

_____

How Am I Going?

Methods of travel vary from person to person. Consider the fact that the way a person travels (i.e., aircraft, cruise ships, buses, trains) could expose them to different threats, and therefore increase their risk levels. Additionally, the traveler also needs to consider how they are going to tour throughout the destination country. For example, backpacking alone or in small groups in a remote area of the world could expose a traveler to a greater number of threats than traveling alone on a train. As this book will point out, each form of travel carries its own risks that must be managed.

Like the traveler assessment form, it is also important to list all of the planned means of travel to and from, and within the destination country. After listing each form of transportation, it is also important to reflect upon their strengths and weaknesses in the context of safety and security. A transportation checklist is shown in Box 2-5. An additional copy of this checklist can also be found in Appendix E.

Box 2-5
Transportation Checklist

Form of Transportation	Risks
Walking	
Bicycle	
Vehicle Rentals (cars, scooters, etc.)	
Planes	
Trains	
Buses	
Taxis	
Others:	

How Much Money Will Be Spent?

Foreign travel can be expensive. Trip-related expenses can readily exceed what the traveler has budgeted. A traveler should have a realistic understanding of how much money they are going to spend and then multiply that amount by at least another 25%. "Going on the cheap" and running short on money can expose travelers to additional risks (i.e., sleeping in terminals, parks) and cause strife in group-based travels.

To prevent over-spending, the traveler must properly budget their money, based on those specific activities they are to perform. It is also recommended that the traveler prepare in advance for a financial issue and develop the proper arrangements to get additional money. That way, it is not necessary to rely upon others on the trip for financial help. The best way to accomplish this goal is to write down the complete travel itinerary and cost out each activity, as shown in Box 2-6. An additional form can be found in Appendix F.

In many cases, it is quite easy to calculate a travel budget. For example, if the traveler plans on touring a certain location, they can look up admission fees, etc. on the Internet and review tourist guidebooks for costs related to that particular activity.

Box 2-6
Travel Expenses

Nature of Activity	Cost
Pre-Departure Expenses	
Clothing Necessities	
Luggage	
Passport/Passport Photos	
Medical (Exams, Inoculations, etc.)	
Toiletries and Sundries	
Tickets	
Others (Itemize Accordingly)	
Destination-Related Expenses	
Room Rates x No. Days	
Breakfast x No. Days	
Lunch x No. Days	
Dinner x No. Days	
Snacks and Beverages x No. Days	
Souvenir/Gifts/Postcards x No. Days	
Entertainment x No. Days	
Tips x No. Days	
Other Travel Expenses x No. Days	
Activity Fees x No. Days	
Others (Itemize Accordingly)	
EXPENSE TOTAL	

CALCULATING TRAVEL VULNERABILITIES

Hopefully by now, the reader has started to think about safety and security issues related to their travels. The next stage is to begin "mind mapping" on all of the "what ifs" and then develop a plan of action to control or mitigate those risks.

First, a traveler should outline all of the activities that they plan to engage in. After identifying specific activities, the next step is to consider what perils they may be exposed to. A sample worksheet for calculating travel risk is shown in Box 2-7. The reader will soon find that a simple "mind mapping" session will produce a long list of risks that they could face. Combined with the information in the forthcoming chapters, this list will grow even longer.

Box 2-7
The Risk List

Activity	Risk(s)	Perils
Staying at Hostel	Theft of backpack	1. Other hostel guests 2. People I'm traveling with 3. Hostel Management

The next stage is to prioritize those risks.[10] One method of prioritizing vulnerabilities is to create a scale based on the criticality and probability of occurrence. Criticality deals with the question: "If it happens, how much damage will result?" Probability deals with the odds of something happening. Criticality and probability assessments are often subjective interpretations of an event. However, they can also be objective in nature, grounded in factual information from a variety of credible sources. Both types of information will assist the traveler in thinking and planning for various problems that might be encountered. Table 2-8 shows how to establish safety priorities based on the probability of occurrence and criticality.

---

[10] Johnson, B.R. (2005). *Principles of security management.* Upper Saddle River, NJ: Prentice-Hall.

Table 2-8
Prioritizing Risk[11]

	Value Level	Degree of Seriousness
Probability of Occurrence		
	4	Will occur, if not corrected
	3	Odds are better than 50/50 if not addressed/corrected
	2	Odds are approx 50/50 if not addressed/corrected
	1	Possible but unlikely (less than 50/50)
Criticality		
	4	Extreme physical injury, property and/or financial loss that would end the trip
	3	Serious financial, property or personal loss that would create a crisis during the trip (i.e., ending the trip short, long delays, etc.)
	2	Moderate and temporary injury, financial, property or personal injury that would create a moderate problem (i.e., time delays, changes in the travel schedule and certain activities)
	1	Slight impact on personal, personal or financial assets – can easily recover from the incident
Vulnerability Ranking = Probability + Criticality		

This form can be used for both short and long-term safety and security-related issues. Consider for example, traveling to a country that has a known health problem – malaria, which has both short and long-term health ramifications. If a traveler does not take precautions, the probability of occurrence is high that an infected mosquito will bite them. This health issue could affect them on their travels. Furthermore, it could later cause long-term health issues that could lead to extreme or serious physical illness (and even financial loss).

In order to make sense of all of the identified risks, the next stage in assessing risk is to add the probability of occurrence

---

[11] Ibid.

value with the determined criticality value. This generates a vulnerability ranking. As a general rule of thumb, a value of 6 or more is considered a high priority; a value of 5 is medium priority; and, a value of 4 or less is considered low priority. Those issues with the highest scores should be dealt with first, followed by those security and safety issues that received a lower vulnerability ranking or score.

This chart is often subjective in nature. That is, there are no hard and fast rules that exist on what point value an issue should be assessed. It is based on what factual evidence the traveler can obtain from a variety of sources as well as common sense predictions. If anything, it might be prudent to overestimate the risks involved with many travel activities. That way, the traveler may be better prepared for those events if they should occur. Furthermore, each issue can have a variety of strategies that can be rank-ordered. That way, the traveler can choose what they believe is the most appropriate way to manage the identified risks.

The next stage is to come up with some ways to control or mitigate the identified dangers. An example is shown in Table 2-9 on two hypothetical risks. The first risk, taking a side trip to Colombia from Ecuador was determined too risky by the traveler (a value of 8), based on the review of travel warnings, etc. Therefore, the fictitious traveler decided to avoid this country and activity. In the second example, losing a backpack to theft while in a hostel was also identified as a problem (value level 5) where the traveler came up with a variety of risk reduction strategies to deal with this issue. An additional form is located in Appendix G.

Table 2-9
Risk Management Checklist

Event	Risk Priority	Risk Reduction Strategies (reduction, avoidance, transfer, spreading)
Travel - Colombia	8	DON'T GO – TOO DANGEROUS
Theft of Pack @ Hostel	5	Purchase lock, Sleep with Pack, Rent Locker, Don't leave it unattended...

CONCLUSION

Travel safety and security begins prior to journeying. As identified within this chapter, some preliminary thoughts should include the *"who, why, when, where, and what"* of traveling, along with other issues ranging from the country's culture and language to financial issues. Getting ready for travel also requires a detailed analysis and anticipation of problems that a traveler may encounter. Based on this analysis, appropriate countermeasures to deal with these issues can then be created to ensure a safe and relaxing travel experience.

PASSPORTS

A passport is a "ticket" into a country and it is the ticket home. It can also be considered to be a key that unlocks borders. The passport is essentially the only universally accepted form of identification in the world. Therefore, it should be thought of as an international identification card. Without a passport, a person cannot travel. Simply put: "No Passport, No Travel."

MAKE SURE THE PASSPORT IS VALID

One of the first steps in preparing for a foreign trip is to make sure that the passport is valid by checking its expiration date. U.S. passports issued to adults are valid for a period of 10 years from their date of issuance. The expiration date is found on the first or second page of the passport.

Besides its expiration date, a traveler should also make sure that the passport is not close to its expiration date. Some countries, for example, require that the passport be valid at least six months beyond the dates of the trip and have two to four blank visa/stamp pages remaining. Furthermore, some airlines will not allow a traveler to board if these requirements are not met.

APPLYING FOR PASSPORTS

The U.S. Department of State is responsible for issuing passports. The State Department designates many post offices, clerks of court, public libraries and other state, county, township, and municipal government offices to accept passport applications on its behalf. These applications are then mailed to one of the State Department's

> **Travel Tip**
>
> Never destroy expired passports. Old passport numbers may be required when applying for visas. Make sure the expired passport is kept in a safe and secure location, since it contains personal data.

Persons intending to travel should not wait until the last minute to request a passport. Routine requests for the issuance or renewal of a passport usually takes 10 weeks. If a traveler should need one sooner, an expedited passport can be requested, at an additional cost. This usually takes two weeks.

If a traveler is in a real hurry for a passport, there are also passport expeditor companies that specialize in getting passports fast – for a fee. They can be found in the Yellow Pages and on the Internet.

When the passport is received from the State Department, it should always be reviewed for accuracy and signed in blue or black ink. The first few pages of the passport should also be reviewed. These pages contain additional travel safety information, restrictions, and other guidelines related to its use.

USING THE PASSPORT WHILE TRAVELING

The passport will be used a great deal when traveling. When departing from the United States, it will generally be examined at the airline check-in counter, at passenger screening, and often at the boarding gate. During the international flight, the traveler will be given a "landing card" by the airline crew just prior to landing. This landing card identifies the holder as a foreign national, requiring some personal information, including the traveler's passport number, to be entered on the form.

Upon arrival, the passport is the ticket of entry, where the traveler and their passport will be processed through a passport control area. At this passport control area, the traveler's identity will be verified and the passport will be stamped with the date of entry into the country. This may not be the last time the passport is used before flying home. A traveler may be required to present their passport at the hotel when checking in. A traveler might also be asked for their passport when exchanging currency or even using a credit card. While traveling on trains, a traveler may even be asked for their passport at border crossings or checkpoints. Finally, if the traveler is moving between countries, every time a new country is entered, the traveler could go through the departure/arrival scenario described above.

When using the passport, it is important that some level of confidence is displayed. A common mistake often seen in airports are travelers at the check-in or passport control areas bumbling and fumbling for their misplaced passports, to the point where they are unpacking their suitcases. Activities like this announce to all who can see that there is a novice traveler present. This, in turn, lets the would-be offender know that there is an easy target available. It would be much better to have the passport available without delay, so when the traveler approaches the counter, it can be readily shown and inspected, and readily re-secured.

Besides identification purposes, the passport also serves other functions. For example, the emergency information page in the passport can provide officials with an emergency contact name, if a crisis should arise. This page also has space available where the traveler can provide their address in the U.S. and abroad. While its completion is not required, it should nevertheless be completed for the traveler's protection. This information should be completed in pencil; some of the information may change from trip to trip.

SAFEGUARDING PASSPORTS

The passport must be protected at all times when traveling. Listed below are some ideas for safeguarding the passport.

- If traveling in a group, never have one person carry all of the passports. The Golden Rule for passports is to NEVER relinquish one's passport to another person.
- Never turn the passport over to a non-governmental official.

In some countries, the hotel front desk may request that they keep a traveler's passport. Oftentimes, this is so local police can check to see who is staying at the hotel. In other cases it is used as a guarantee that the traveler will pay their bill. In some cases, a traveler can politely refuse this request. Considering the fact that passports can be placed in a non-secure mail slot behind the front desk where a hotel employee (or essentially anyone else) has access to it for a variety of nefarious purposes, the passport should never be given up. As an example, in one situation, one of the authors stated that he felt uncomfortable giving up his passport to the hotel, thanked them for their time, and stated that he would find another hotel. To avoid the loss in the sale of a room, the hotel staff readily complied with his request.

- Never lay the passport down anywhere – get in the habit of immediately putting the passport away after using it.

- Keep the passport separate from other paper materials – this could prevent it from accidentally being thrown away or misplaced.

- Consider having a dedicated area on the body for the passport – that way it is always in the same place every time; the traveler will only have to access that location for their passport; and, they will not get it confused with other paper documents.

- When using the passport NEVER let it out of sight. If a person should walk away with the passport, call it to their attention and request to go along with it.

- Some travel sites also recommend that the passport be secured in the hotel safe. While this may be a good option, the traveler must ask him or herself: Is it really safe? In some cases it may not.

- Never pack the passport in checked luggage. If the luggage should become lost, the passport will also be lost. A person who has access to the luggage could also steal the passport. Valid passports are a very valuable commodity.

- Never carry the passport in a purse, backpack or fanny pack (aka a "bum bag" in England). If these items are stolen, so too is the passport.

PUBLICLY DISPLAYING THE PASSPORT

Publicly displaying a passport should be avoided at all times. For example, the passport's cover will readily serve as a means to identify a traveler's nationality. Displaying the American passport could expose the holder to a confrontation or even a criminal attack. One option that the traveler may consider is to purchase a passport cover in order to camouflage it. Many of these covers are sterile in appearance. Some points to consider when buying a passport cover include not purchasing a cover that has the name or imprint "PASSPORT" on it. This immediately tells an observer that the traveler is from an English speaking country. Another option would be to purchase a foreign passport cover. For example, one of the authors of this book has different passport covers. When traveling in Europe for example, he uses a burgundy-colored passport cover that is embossed with: "United Kingdom of Great Britain and Northern Ireland," implying that his citizenship is British. Other passport covers from other countries can be readily purchased on many on-line shopping sites.

CARRYING THE PASSPORT

As pointed out earlier, the traveler should always physically carry the passport. A traveler may never know when they will need to immediately leave a country, and they may not have time to go back to where the passport was stored to retrieve it. It is usually much safer with the owner than in another location.

The passport must be properly secured. For example, it should be kept in a secure pocket. A secure pocket is not a back pocket on a pair of pants. Instead, the traveler should consider carrying it in a shirt pocket that is secured by a button or zipper. If the traveler knows that it will not be needed for some time, then it should be kept in a concealed money belt, neck pouch, or in another concealed or secured place, such as a zippered travel sock.

Passports should not be stored in objects that are commonly removed (such as outerwear). For example, a traveler may take their jacket off, and in the process, they may leave it behind. Therefore, the best option is to carry the passport in a secured pocket (zippered or buttoned) in a permanent article of clothing.

LOST OR STOLEN PASSPORTS

According to the U.S. Department of State, if a U.S. passport is lost or stolen, the loss should be immediately reported to the nearest U.S. Embassy or Consulate and to local police authorities. For those not holding U.S. passports, meanwhile, the loss needs to be reported to the appropriate consulate or embassy. This is important in order to ensure that it is not misused in some way. For example, it could be used by someone else to gain entry into other foreign countries, including the United States.

In case of theft or loss, it is important to have a color copy of the first page of the passport to facilitate the issuance of the new passport. There are several ways to ensure quick access to the passport copy:

- Carrying a copy of it that is separate from the passport and kept in a suitcase or another secure location.

- Giving a copy of it to another co-traveler (that is properly secured).

- Keeping another copy of it at home, making sure that the person entrusted with it knows where it is.

- Scanning the first page of the passport into a .pdf file and then storing it in an e-mail account or flash drive.

- Taking a digital photo of the first page of the passport with a camera.

It is strongly encouraged not to use just one method, but to use multiple methods to ensure ready access to the copy. That way, the traveler will have immediate and ready access to it in practically any location in the world. The traveler should also consider bringing an extra set of passport photos with them. A passport photo will be required for the new passport. The U.S. Department of State also provides a Passport Services Information Card with the issuance of the Passport. This card contains relevant contact information in case of loss or theft. On the front of the card is a space where the traveler can list their passport number and expiration date. The State Department encourages travelers to carry this card with them, separate of the passport, to help facilitate the replacement of the passport, if necessary.

If the passport is lost or stolen, a traveler will need to stop by the local embassy or consulate. The traveler will be required to complete a DS-64, Statement Regarding a Lost or Stolen Passport (if the passport is U.S. issued). After the passport is reported lost or stolen, it is invalidated and it can no longer be used for travel.

If it is used for travel, anyone using the passport can be detained upon entry into the United States. Even though it can no longer be used for travel, if the traveler should later find it, its recovery must be reported to the U.S. State Department and sent to them for cancellation.

CONCLUSION

The passport is perhaps the most important item taken on a trip. In the context of pre-departure activities, the international traveler must first make sure that they have a passport. If not, it must be obtained from the U.S. Department of State. For those travelers who already have a passport, it must be valid. This chapter has also shown the importance of keeping the passport secure when traveling. Of utmost importance is the fact that the passport should be securely carried and never be entrusted with other persons. Copies of the passport, meanwhile, should also be readily accessible in those rare occasions where a passport becomes lost or stolen.

4
VISAS

While the Passport is required for entry into the majority of foreign countries, many also require a visa. A visa is an entry stamp or document that allows the holder access into the foreign country. In many cases, it is simply a stamp in the holder's passport. In other cases, it could be documentation that the traveler must carry with him. The purpose for the visa, in simple terms, is that it allows the country to effectively monitor and screen who is coming into their country and for what reasons. In essence, it is a permission slip for a non-citizen to gain entry, remain in, or move through a country.

Americans may have the least restrictive entrance requirements in comparison to citizens from other nations. Usually, most countries will grant U.S. passport holders a 30-day tourist visa upon entry into their country, which is usually just a stamp in their passport that they receive at the immigration checkpoint at the airport. To be safe, however, a traveler should always research any visa requirements that exist before traveling to that particular country. The traveler also needs to research specific requirements related to each visa. Depending upon the country (and specific requirements for the type of visa requested), a traveler may have to:

- Have a number of visas required for entry/admission and travel within the country.
- Present return tickets and evidence of funds sufficient to finance the intended stay.
- Meet compulsory currency exchange regulations on entry.
- Have proof of vaccinations, etc.

These are just a few examples of some visa requirements that exist. To be ensured of trouble-free travel, therefore, a traveler needs to understand the visa process.

TYPES OF VISAS

Depending upon the country, the nature of the travel (i.e., tourism, business, study abroad), and the length of stay, there are several different types of visas. Each type of visa has a distinct purpose and only allows a temporary stay in the country for which the visa was granted. In other cases, meanwhile, a visa may not be required. Some countries have a visa waiver program which is an agreement between two countries. This allows their citizens to visit one another's country for a period of time (usually 90 days) without a visa.

Tourist Cards

Some countries do not require a visa for a short tourist stay. Instead, a traveler may need to obtain or purchase a tourist card. In many cases, the tourist card is part of the airline ticket price; the traveler is given a form while on-board the aircraft that is presented at the immigration checkpoint. This form is then stamped, certifying that the traveler is legally admitted into the country. If entrance is not by air, this same form is completed at the border. Depending upon the country, tourist cards may not be required if the traveler is in the country for less than 72 hours.

Stopover Visas

Stopover visas allow the holder to use the country as an international travel connection. They allow the traveler access to the international part of the airport terminal (or a port) only, for a certain period of time. In some cases, these are also referred to as Airport Transit Visas.

Transit Visas

Transit visas give travelers permission to temporarily enter and travel through that country to a third country. Another way to think of a transit visa is that if or when a traveler uses one country's port of entry to get to another country (i.e., the traveler is just passing through), they may need a transit visa. To obtain a transit visa, a traveler must provide evidence of onward travel (a plane or train ticket) and possess a valid entry authorization for their final destination. For example, if a traveler is going from China to Russia and traveling through Kazakhistan, they will need a transit visa to pass through Kazakhistan. Usually transit visas do not allow a traveler to return to the country that they traveled through, unless they go to their destination first, and then purchase another transit visa for the return trip. In the above example, for instance, a traveler cannot use a transit visa to re-enter China via Kazakhistan without first going into Russia. Transit visas usually have short time periods (i.e., 72 hours or less).

Residence Visas

These types of visas allow the holder to remain in a country if the person has the intent on applying for a residency permit. These are usually longer in length (i.e., 6 months).

Study Visas

The key behind a study visa is that the holder is a student participating in a program at an educational institution; is carrying out academic research at an academic institution; or has some type of internship with an organization in that particular country. These are also referred to as student visas.

Temporary Stay Visa

Depending upon the country, these visas are given to persons seeking medical care (and their family members). They can also be issued for employment or non-employment purposes. Temporary visas can also be issued to family members visiting a relative who is in the country. These are often for longer periods of time (i.e., over 90 days).

Short Stay Visa

These are called a variety of different names, depending upon the country. In some countries they may be called tourist visas. In others, they may be called visitor or business visas. Short stay visas have limited time periods, often ranging from 30 to 90 days in length.

Work Visas

As the name implies, these types of visas are required to be legally employed in the destination country. There are several different types of work visas or permits.

Multiple Entry Visas

If a traveler is planning on moving from country to country and then returns to the original country more than once, they will need a multiple entry visa. Depending upon the country and the needs of the traveler, they can request a double or multiple entry visa. These are usually more expensive than single entry visas.

VISA REQUIREMENTS

Besides the different types of visas, visa requirements vary according to the length of stay and the country or countries that a person is traveling to. Some countries, for example, have no visa requirements for short stays related to tourism. Others, meanwhile, may have complex requirements. Therefore, it is of the utmost importance for the traveler to research the destination country for any visa requirements. Otherwise, a traveler could literally be denied permission to enter their destination country.

The U.S. State Department's "Foreign Entry Requirements" (Department of State publication M-264) reviews the entry requirements for foreign countries. It also explains where and how to apply for visas and tourist cards. This publication is updated annually. Another readily available source is the State Department's website that provides up-to-date, detailed visa requirements for all countries in the world. Besides these sources, a good travel agency or even up-to-date travel books can also provide some useful information on visas.

A quick review of visa requirements from the State Department website shows that they vary from country to country. Some countries, for example, require confirmation from a tourist organization or hotel where the traveler has reservations. Here, the tourist visa is only valid for the dates of the hotel reservation purchased in advance. In other cases, a traveler will need to be able to prove that they have sufficient funds to finance their travels within that particular country. In fact, the traveler may have to provide copies of their bank statements or provide an affidavit of support from a family member indicating that they will provide financial support during the trip.

In some cases, and depending upon the type of visa, the traveler may need to get a letter of invitation from an organization or person within that country that they want to travel to. For a business visa in Russia, for example, a Russian business must submit a letter of invitation to the Russian Ministry of Foreign Affairs (MFA). The MFA then will send a fax or an original letter to a Russian Consular office in the United States. Once the letter has arrived at the Russian Consulate, the traveler can then submit the visa application form for processing.

Applying for Visas

Each country has different application requirements, fees, and lengths of time to process applications. If the destination country requires a visa, it is recommended to get the visa first, before purchasing the plane ticket. If a plane ticket is purchased before obtaining the visa, it is important to make sure that the ticket is refundable or there is the option of changing the date of departure in case there is any problem or delay in obtaining the visa.

Some of the common components of visa application include:

- **A Passport** – A traveler will need a passport before obtaining a visa. If a traveler already has a passport, it is important to check its expiration date. Some countries will refuse issuing a visa if the passport has less than six months before it reaches its expiration date. Some countries also require that the passport be mailed to them; others simply request photocopies of the first two pages of the passport.
- **Medical Exams** – Some countries require proof of medical vaccinations for entry. Others may require an HIV test if a traveler plans on staying in the country for a long period of time (90 days or more in most cases).

- **Photographs** – In some circumstances, photographs are also required. Usually these are the standard-sized passport photos. If a traveler is unsure of the need for additional visas at their various destinations (i.e., "side trips"), it is always a good idea to carry a few extra passport photos. This could expedite the visa application process, if done overseas. Additionally, guards at border crossings (depending upon the country) may require a traveler to fill out a transit travel form that includes a photograph.

- **Processing Fees** – Processing fees vary from country to country. Usually the embassy or consulate requires that a money order be submitted with the visa application.

When applying for a visa, the applicant is usually asked if they have held previous visas. They will ask the applicant to provide details, including the type of visa, serial number, date of issue, and the place of issue. Therefore, a traveler should never destroy old passports or visas as often a consular official may ask to see them (i.e., to see if it has been stamped as revoked after issue). Of course, it is good to be able to photocopy the old visa and attach it to the application. In addition, always take the old passport and any expired visas to any consular interview when seeking additional visas.

Where to Get a Visa

There are two ways to get visas: 1) through consulates or embassies in the United States prior to travel; and, 2) obtained in foreign countries as the person travels. It is best to obtain visas before leaving the United States. That way, the traveler is assured that there will be no problems. In some cases, meanwhile, the traveler may not be able to obtain visas for some countries once they have departed.

Consulates and Embassies

In the vast majority of cases, visas can be obtained directly from that country's Embassy or Consulate in the U.S., in person or through the mail before traveling abroad. A list of embassies in Washington, D.C., can be found on Embassy.org (http://www. embassy.org/embassies/). This site provides a list of all foreign embassies in Washington, D.C. As pointed out earlier, travelers can also obtain visa information from each country's website or through the U.S. Department of State (http://www.state.gov).

In Foreign Countries

In some cases, it might actually be quicker and cheaper to get a visa in a foreign country as a person travels. As an example, if a person wants to travel to Russia from Hungary, they could visit the Russian Embassy in Budapest. By going to the foreign embassy or consulate, the visa process may be expedited. However, the traveler should keep in mind that there may be long lines (queues) and security processes that could delay meeting with a consular official, taking valuable time from the travel schedule.

- *Security Regulations at Consulates and Embassies*

  In many, if not all cases, security levels are quite high in embassies. For example, luggage and/or large parcels are usually not allowed in consulates and embassies. The U.S. Embassy in London, England, for example, has signs posted stating that if a person attempts to enter carrying a large backpack or bag, entry will be denied, and the appointment will be canceled forthwith.

  If a traveler has their luggage with them, they must leave these items at a railway or airport luggage facility (such as a locker) and then attend the embassy/consular appointment carrying only the documents that they have to present. Electronic equipment (such a laptops, iPods®, mobile phones, music players, etc.) is often prohibited on consulate property for security reasons.

  In addition, embassies and consulates are not open to the general public. In the majority of cases, unless a person is named on the letter received from the embassy/consulate, they will not be allowed to accompany the scheduled visitor, even if they are related. Therefore, a traveler should plan on attending the meeting by themselves.

- **Airports and Ports of Entry** – Depending upon the country, in many cases the traveler can obtain a visa upon entry into the country. For example, immediately after disembarking from the plane, foreign travelers may be instructed to go to immigration. At the immigration check-point, they will be required to obtain a visa. En route to this checkpoint there are often explanatory notes for the traveler to assist them in the visa process.

Assistance in Obtaining Visas

In some cases, the visa process may be complicated and time consuming. Therefore, a traveler could consider using:

- **Visa Support Companies** – There are several private companies that provide visa services for a fee. This may be a hassle-free and a timely alternative than doing all of the footwork oneself.

- **Travel Companies** – In some cases, travel companies will also provide visa services as part of their travel package.

- **Airports** – In some cases, travelers can pick up visas at airports, upon arrival or departure.

- **Borders** – In some countries, immigration authorities can grant various types of visas. A traveler will need to check in advance to see what types of visas are issued at border stops. As pointed out earlier, in some cases visas are less expensive at border stops in comparison to obtaining one at the embassy or consulate.

- **Hotels, etc**. In some countries, hotels can process visa applications. As an example, some hotels in Bahrain (and other nations) can provide a business visa for their guests for an additional cost.

How Long is a Visa Valid?

- **Visas are Temporary**. Depending upon the country and type of visa, they can range from days, weeks, or even years. In some cases, the visa may be valid until the pass-port expires. When a visa expires, a new visa is required to gain entry to the foreign country.

- **Visa Extensions** – In some cases, visas can also be extended and renewed. To extend and/or renew a visa, the traveler needs to contact that particular embassy or consulate **prior** to the expiration of the visa. Simply being ignorant of the expiration date is not a good reason for an extension! If a person is traveling on an expired visa (or has no visa at all for that country) they can be fined, imprisoned, and/or deported.

REVOCATION OF VISAS

A visa does not guarantee entry! Even if a traveler has a visa, they can still be denied entry into the country. That decision remains the right of the immigration officials in the country concerned. A country may refuse entry to visitors who do not comply with requirements regarding general appearance or clothing. Denial can also be refused based on a health problem. Once in the country, visas can also be revoked for being suspected and/or involved in criminal activities, disturbing the peace, violating conditions set forth on the visa, falsifying information on the visa, and a variety of other reasons. Visas can also be denied or cancelled for reasons beyond the traveler's control (i.e., evicting all foreigners for diplomatic reasons). Additionally, the immigration laws of most countries do not have provisions for appeal.

Revocation of the visa also means removal/deportation from the country in a swift manner. That is, the traveler may have to leave within a 24-hour period (or on the next flight) and at his or her own expense. While waiting for their flight, the traveler may also be imprisoned or detained, depending upon the actions that led to the initial revocation of the visa. Revocation of a visa from one country could also cause problems for future travel. A traveler may be banned from that country for a particular period of time. The traveler could also have problems getting a visa from other countries, too. Many visa applications have questions related to whether the applicant has ever had a visa revoked or denied in other countries.

In other cases visas can be canceled "without prejudice." In these cases, often another visa is issued although the prior visa is still valid. For example, if a traveler is "on" a student visa and then graduates from the educational institute, but wants to stay in the country to work, they may have to obtain a work visa. In this situation, the study visa would be canceled "without prejudice" and a new work visa would be issued.

CONCLUSION

A visa allows entry into a foreign country. A visa is not a substitute for the passport. The passport is the international ID document, while the visa is the document that indicates that the traveler's credentials have been reviewed, and that they have permission to be in the country for a set period of time, and for specific purposes (i.e., tourism, study, work). Each country has its own visa requirements; some are quite simple and only consist of a stamp in the traveler's passport. Other country's requirements, meanwhile, are more complex. Therefore, it is important for the traveler to understand the visa application process for each country they wish to visit in order to ensure that all requirements are met and followed.

5
HEALTHY TRAVEL

A ccording to the Canadian Ministry for Health, medical issues can fall into four main categories when traveling:

- Not being protected against diseases for which there are vaccines;
- Consuming contaminated water or food;
- Not taking preventative medications, such as malaria pills; and,
- Taking risks, such as being tattooed, having unsafe sex, and drinking excessively.

Of interest with these medical issues is the simple fact that through proper planning and engaging in safe activities while traveling, many health-related issues can be prevented. This chapter will provide the reader with an overview of some of the major issues involved in healthy travel, and how simple preparatory actions and changes in behavior while traveling will ensure a safe and healthy journey.

BEFORE LEAVING

Planning ahead is essential to safe travel in the context of health issues. One of the first pre-travel questions a person should ask is: How can I reduce my exposure to medical-related issues while traveling? A traveler should consider how their activities abroad could put them at a greater risk of injury or illness. Therefore, a traveler needs to seriously analyze what they plan on doing and perhaps consider some alternatives. Sports-related activities (climbing, hiking, etc.), other strenuous activities, and alcohol consumption, for example, could expose a person to an increased risk of injury. In fact, one of the most dangerous activities according to the U.S. Department of State is driving vehicles or motorcycles in a foreign country. Knowing the fact that renting vehicles and motorcycles account for a large

51

number of injuries for American travelers per year, a traveler may consider using public transportation instead.

Plan for Health-Related Emergencies

It may sound odd, but travelers should plan for their own medical emergency. This will naturally better prepare the traveler for any emergencies that should arise. This planning should include procedures to follow and any items that can be brought along to mitigate the health issue(s). This planning should also deal with the logistics and psychological aspects of a medical injury, ranging from the degree of dependency (i.e., psychological, emotional, knowledge of the area and travel in general) travelers have on the injured person(s). Perhaps the best way this can be achieved is to simply develop some "what if" scenarios and questions.

Research the Country

It is very important that a traveler researches the destination country for any disease and health-related issues. Some good sites to begin this research include the:

- U.S. Department of State (http://travel.state.gov/travel/tips/health/). This site provides a wealth of information ranging from general health information to insurance providers and medical evacuations.
- World Health Organization (http://www.who.int/en/). This website provides up-to-date reports on disease outbreaks and specific health conditions. Additional information about the risks of communicable diseases associated with travel is available in the WHO yearly publication "International Travel and Health."
- Center for Disease Control (http://cdc.gov/travel/). This website provides a comprehensive worldwide analysis of health information for travelers. It also provides detailed information by destination or location of travel. The Centers for Disease Control and Prevention (CDC) maintains a toll-free number for public inquiries about travel related health issues. The number is 877-394-8747.

Besides these websites, a traveler should also consider investigating each destination country's website. These websites may provide more accurate, up-to-date and detailed information on health and disease-related issues specific to that country or region of the world. Contacting the U.S. embassy or consulate in that particular country, and/or that country's embassy or consulate in the U.S. could also yield some additional information. Of course, talking to other travelers who have been to the same countries in question will also yield some additional insight into any health-related issues that may exist.

Get Checked Out

Regardless of age and health status, a traveler should make an appointment with their physician. At this appointment, the traveler should review their medical history and planned travel destination(s). The traveler should also discuss what vaccinations are needed and inquire about any preventative medicines that can be used. According to Passport Health®, a network of travel health and immunization centers in the U.S., a physician should focus on six topical areas:

- Pre-travel immunizations specific to the destination and transit route
- A briefing on health issues that cannot be prevented through vaccines
- A review of products that can make the trip safer (water, insect repellants, etc.)
- Health insurance for foreign travel
- Malaria prevention
- Prevention of traveler's diarrhea

Besides a full physical, the traveler should also have a thorough dental checkup before leaving. Dental health is oftentimes overlooked before traveling.

Immunizations

Some countries will not let a traveler in unless they can prove that they are vaccinated against various diseases (i.e., a certificate of Yellow Fever vaccination may be required for entry into certain countries in Africa). It is therefore important to check the requirements from each country, the CDC and State Department to make sure that all required and recommended vaccinations/immunizations are covered and are up-to-date.

Vaccines for travelers include: (1) those that are used routinely, (2) others that may be advised before travel; and, (3) those that, in some situations, are mandatory. Yellow Fever and Cholera are two of the most common/required vaccinations. Other immunizations include:

- Polio
- Tetanus and Diphtheria
- Measles, Mumps, Rubella
- Whooping Cough
- Hepatitis A and B
- Rabies
- Tick-Borne Encephalitis
- Japanese Encephalitis
- Meningitis

Some of these immunizations may involve a series of shots and visits to the doctor. Therefore, a traveler should start early (6-8 weeks before traveling, if not earlier) and not wait until the last minute to get them.

Of course, a vaccination record is very important when traveling. All shots and/or prescriptions should be recorded on the International Certificate of Vaccination (ICV), also known as the "Yellow Book." The ICV is approved by the World Health Organization as the official document that verifies that proper procedures were followed in administering vaccinations for foreign travel. It is used to demonstrate receipt of required vaccinations for entry into foreign countries. And, it is designed to fit into a passport. Additionally, the ICV is used to record the following information:

- Date and dose of all vaccinations received for foreign travel
- Medical exemption from receipt of required vaccinations

- Personal health history
- Drug allergies
- Current medications
- Prescriptions for eyeglasses or contact lenses

Family physicians should have blank ICV's available (check when scheduling the appointment in order to avoid making another trip to the doctor). Otherwise, a traveler can purchase their own at bookstores and through Internet sites including the WHO and CDC. The ICV must be stamped or signed by the traveler's physician. Sometimes a traveler will need to show this proof of vaccination to enter a country. Additionally, the traveler should treat the ICV form just like the passport. It must be properly secured at all times. In fact, consider carrying this with the passport at all times.

> **Travel Tip**
>
> In some cases, travelers will need to continue their immunization regime after returning home. One example is anti-malarial prescriptions that often require a course of treatment over several weeks that could actually extend beyond the travel period.

Just because a traveler has received a series of immunizations does not mean that they are fully protected. Doctors can also provide some additional medications (i.e., anti-malarial, antibiotics) that could serve to further protect against a variety of illnesses.

Research Medical Facilities in the Host Country

Part of the planning process is the traveler knowing what they are getting into if a medical emergency should arise. Inasmuch, it is important to research the existing nature, quality of, and locations of medical facilities in the host country.

Before leaving, a traveler may want to locate the nearest clinic(s) or hospital(s) at their destination(s). The traveler should also consider e-mailing or telephoning the clinic or hospital to inquire about any health issues that exist. It would also be wise to ask questions about insurance and any payment/billing related concerns. The traveler should also create a list of medical contacts for that country in case an emergency should arise while traveling. A traveler may also want to consider contacting the International Association for Medical Assistance to Travelers. This organization supplies the names of English-speaking doctors in the destination country, immunization requirements, and more (their phone number is (716) 754-4883). The information from this organization is free.

Pre-Existing Medical Conditions

Many pre-existing medical conditions do not prevent travel. These conditions, however, will require some additional planning to ensure safe travel. Some points to consider include, but are not limited to:

- Let the airlines know about any medical concerns as soon as the flight is booked.

- When boarding, notify the flight attendants of any medical condition(s).

- Inform other travelers of any medical conditions. Provide at least one of these travelers a copy or list of known medical conditions.

- Carry a Medical Emergency Card. This card should include all relevant medical-related issues and emergency contact numbers. Besides this card, a traveler should also consider carrying a flash drive with their medical history on it. This can be a normal USB drive device, properly marked "medical history." Otherwise, a traveler can also buy a USB device that is distinctly marked with the Caduceus ⚕ medical symbol.

- Wear a Medic Alert Badge. This badge/medallion/bracelet has the traveler's name, medical condition and emergency contact information stamped on it. The Medic Alert Foundation keeps a database of patient details and medical histories that can be accessed by phone worldwide.

- Check to ensure that travel insurance (if purchased) covers any pre-existing conditions.

Insurance

It is also important to review existing health insurance policies to see what, if anything, is covered. A traveler should also consider purchasing a policy designed for short-term health and emergency assistance overseas. In many cases, existing health insurance policies may not provide payment for medical care outside the United States. For example, Medicare and Medicaid do not cover health issues abroad.

Even if a traveler's health insurance does provide reimbursement for medical care abroad, in the event of a serious illness or accident, health insurance policies usually do not pay for medical evacuation from a remote area or from a country where medical facilities are inadequate. An evacuation from countries that have sub-standard medical services, to "clean" and modern facilities could virtually mean the difference between life and death. Therefore, it may be wise, in some cases, to explore purchasing medical evacuation insurance.

PRESCRIPTIONS AND MEDICATIONS

Always consider what prescriptions are needed and any other over-the-counter drugs that may be useful when traveling. Regardless if it is a prescription-based or over-the-counter drug, consider the following points:

- **Is it Legal in the Host Country?** – If there is any doubt about the legality of carrying a certain drug into a country, check with the country's embassy or consulate beforehand.

- **Make Sure There is Enough** – In fact, bring at least an extra week's worth of medication, just in case some gets lost or damaged or there is a delay in getting home. Consider splitting or dividing each prescription that is carried. For example, carry one-half in the carry-on and the other half in the checked luggage. That way, if one bag is lost, there is enough medicine until it can be replaced.

- **Bring along Duplicate Prescriptions** – Make sure the prescription is legible and the medication has its generic and brand name on the prescription. Also, consider bringing along a letter, signed by a physician that provides a detailed description of any medical condition and medications that will be used when traveling. This is especially important if the traveler has any narcotic-based prescriptions; customs officials may be interested in such drugs.

- **Corrective Lenses** – If a traveler wears corrective lenses, it is also important to take a copy of the lens prescription in case they need to be replaced. The traveler's optometrist will be able to provide a letter detailing the prescription. Travelers should also carry a spare set of lenses. A traveler should also consider wearing glasses instead of contacts while traveling. Glasses are easier to use and they will reduce the odds of contracting an illness as the result of the traveler placing their fingers in their eyes.

- **Keep Medications in Their Original, Labeled Containers** – Other containers could result in a traveler being slowed down through the screening process and customs.

- **Time Zones** – When taking medication, always consider time zone changes. Always work off of the time at home – not the time at the destination. Some web pages on the Internet provide a pill time calculator that could be helpful. Otherwise, the traveler should write down their medication schedule based on the new time zone.

- **Needles and Syringes** – If a traveler's medication requires sterile syringes/needles, it is important to have a doctor's letter (and prescription) explaining the need for these devices. In some countries where drugs are a problem, a traveler could be facing a situation with the police, customs, etc. if found in possession, without adequate explanation.

- **Pacemakers, etc.** If a traveler has a pacemaker or some other medical implant, it is also necessary to have at least a letter or card that identifies that the traveler has an implanted medical device. Information of this nature could speed up the airport screening process. If the device should fail overseas, in many instances, the issued cards (i.e., Pacemaker Identification Cards) also provide information on the type, manufacturer, etc. that would be beneficial if treatment was required.

WATER, FOOD AND INSECT-BORNE DISEASES

Some of the most dangerous elements of travel are those that cannot be readily seen. They include parasites and microbes in food and water. It also includes small, but often lethal insects that carry a wide variety of diseases.

Water and Food-Borne Diseases

One thing that travelers may take for granted is water quality. Water supplies in the United States and other industrialized countries are very safe. In other countries, however, a traveler will need to be wary of its water supply. In fact, according to the Centers for Disease Control, food- and water-borne diseases are the primary cause of illness when traveling.

- Don't use ice cubes. They are most likely made from tap water.
- Drink only bottled water – make sure the seal isn't broken – a common scam in many countries is to sell tap water (or worse) in refilled bottles.
- Drink bottled beverages instead of tap water – these are usually safer than water from a tap.
- Use purified/bottled water when brushing teeth.
- Parasites, etc. can enter the body through mucous membranes in the eyes, nose and mouth. A traveler should use facial cleaners or bottled water only when washing their face.
- Be careful when even washing one's hands with tap water. Consider bringing along alcohol-based hand wipes.
- A traveler should keep their fingers out of their mouth, nose, and eyes.
- Consider packing iodine tablets to sterilize questionable water.
- In some facilities (hotel rooms and even trains) there are faucets in bedrooms or bathrooms that provide water. However, it may not be drinking water! Be very cautious.

Traveler's Diarrhea

Every year, millions of international tourists develop diarrhea, making it the most common illness among travelers. Parasites, viruses and bacteria that contaminate both food and water can cause traveler's diarrhea. While most cases usually last less than a week, diarrhea (as well as other "bugs") could ruin a trip fast.

In many cases, diarrhea is associated with third world countries such as Mexico (i.e., "Montezuma's Revenge") and a traveler may assume that they are safe in industrialized countries. This may not be the case, based on the simple fact that different strains of bacteria may be present in these countries that the travelers' immune system has never encountered, causing diarrhea in the process. Some points to consider to reduce the odds of contracting food- and water-borne illnesses (or a more serious illness) include:

> **Travel Tip**
>
> In order to avoid issues with food and water, many travelers follow this simple tip: "BOIL IT," "PEEL IT," "COOK IT." All else, avoid.

- Avoid food and drink purchased from street vendors and/ or roadside stands.
- Avoid raw or undercooked meat and seafood and raw fruit unless it is washed or peeled by the traveler *only*.
- Avoid contact with other people to prevent the spread of germs, etc.
- Wash hands with soap and water frequently – be wary of water! Therefore, alcohol-based hand solvents or towelettes may be the way to go.
- Don't share food and drink with others.
- Eat only fully-cooked meals.
- Eat vegetables only if they are fully cooked.
- Eat only thick-skinned fruits that have been personally peeled by the traveler.
- Be wary of plates, drinking glasses, and eating utensils.

- Avoid salads, uncooked shellfish, and re-heated foods.
- Consider carrying Imodium® or another anti-diarrhea medicine.

Insect-Borne Diseases

Besides food and water-borne disease, travelers also need to keep in mind that insects carry disease. For example, Malaria and Dengue Fever is carried and spread by infected mosquitoes in many tropical countries, while Yellow Fever is also caused by mosquito bites in Central Africa and South America. With some diseases, such as Malaria, the traveler could have this particular disease the rest of their life. Therefore, specific attention should be given to this issue when traveling to tropical or subtropical areas of the world.

There are many preventative measures that can be taken to reduce exposure to insect-borne diseases. They include:

- Wearing long-sleeved shirts and long pants in areas of high mosquito concentration, if possible.
- Tucking the pants into socks or boots will prevent both mosquito bites and ticks attaching to the body.
- Using insect repellant that contains DEET (at least 30% DEET).
- Sleeping under Bed Nets/Screens – make sure no part of the body rests against the sides of the screens while sleeping.
- Using flying insect spray to kill insects in rooms, etc.
- Sleeping in air-conditioned rooms (insects don't like the cold).
- Use insect coils (while awake and sleeping) for further protection.

STAYING HEALTHY

In addition to the points already reviewed in this book and chapter, there are some other ways to stay healthy:

- **Use Preventative Medications** – Use those preventative medications recommended by doctors (and the WHO and CDC).

- **Eat Healthy When Traveling** – Follow proper nutritional practices and avoid questionable dishes that could cause health problems, ranging from allergic reactions to food and water-borne illnesses.

- **Take Vitamins** – Check to see which vitamins should be taken along to maintain a healthy immune system.

- **Get Enough Sleep** – A traveler should not allow their immune system to get weakened.

- **Wear Proper Clothing** – Clothing can protect a traveler from insect bites. It can also protect from sunburn, which can be very debilitating, especially in equatorial countries where the sun is much "hotter" than what the traveler is most likely accustomed to. Proper clothing can also protect against minor cuts and abrasions that could lead to more serious health issues.

> **Travel Tip**
>
> Natural fibers (i.e., cotton and wool) are often better than synthetics, because they breathe and thereby reduce fungal-related infections.

- **Wear Proper Footwear** – To prevent fungal and parasitic infections, the feet need to be kept clean and dry. The traveler should never go barefoot. As pointed out in the Blending In chapter, in order to prevent foot-related injuries, a traveler should never wear sandals or open-toed footwear.

- **Avoid Swimming** – Water quality can be quite questionable in many countries, not to mention parasites that exist in the water in certain parts of the world.

- **Be Aware of the Surroundings** – Many injuries are the result of being inattentive to one's surroundings to the point where a traveler may be struck by a motor vehicle. Being safer could be as simple as looking in both directions before crossing a street.

- **Sunscreen** – Bring along and wear sun block to protect against sunburn. Keep in mind that sunscreen is not just for the tropical and subtropical regions of the world. Some brands also contain insect repellant, too.

- **Avoid Engaging in Risky Behaviors** – These range from drinking too much alcohol (and the poor decisions associated with that), and exposing oneself to criminal opportunities. It may also include engaging in risky sexual activities and/or participating other activities specific to the trip, such as rock climbing, etc. As pointed out earlier, limit these risky behaviors by adjusting the travel lifestyle accordingly.

First Aid Kits

Because health care may be substandard or non-existent in many countries, consider packing and carrying a small first aid kit. This kit will provide the traveler with the essentials to take care of minor injuries. It will also ensure clean and sterile instruments if medical care is received from a clinic or hospital. In some countries, HIV and AIDS are in epidemic proportions, while other diseases (Hepatitis, for example) can be spread through medical equipment that is not properly sterilized. To avoid these issues, the traveler should bring and insist on using his or her own equipment.

Some basic items to include in these kits should include:

☐ Sutures	☐ Iodine
☐ Alcohol	☐ Antibiotic Creams
☐ Scissors	☐ Anti-diarrhea medicine
☐ Scalpel	☐ Antibacterial hand wipes
☐ Tweezers	☐ Pain Relievers
☐ Bandages and Gauze Tape	☐ Antiseptic
	☐ Hemostats

This medical kit should be readily available and small enough to be carried at all times. The kit will serve no purpose if it is at a hotel 50 miles away. A traveler can build these kits themselves, or they can be purchased from a medical supplier.

SICKNESS AND INJURIES OVERSEAS

Already, the traveler should have a list of medical facilities and clinics if they have done their homework. If a traveler should get sick or injured and if time allows, they should contact the nearest U.S. embassy or consulate for a list of local physicians and medical facilities. If the illness is serious, consular officers can help the traveler find medical assistance from this list. At their request, the consulate will also inform family or friends. If necessary, they can also assist in the transfer of money from family or friends in the United States. Listed below are some points to consider:

- **Treat every illness, no matter how trivial, as a serious situation** – Even the most trivial injury, at times, could ruin the traveler's vacation for themselves and others. Or worse, the health of the traveler could be dramatically affected. Unlike in the U.S. where medical facilities and subsequent care are readily available, quality medical assistance could be hours, if not days, away, where the trivial, minor injury or infection could now develop into a serious situation because of the lack of adequate medical care.

- **Carry a medical emergency card in a wallet and another place on the traveler's body** – In anticipation of getting sick and not having the ability to effectively communicate the illness, a traveler should always have an emergency medical card with them. In other cases, meanwhile, a traveler's wallet and subsequent medical information may be missing. If the traveler is incapacitated, they will not be able to share their medical issues with others. Therefore, it is recommended to carry another card somewhere else on the body. For example, the authors know some individuals that have a non-magnetic dog-style tag (in order to prevent problems with metal detectors at airports) that have their name, social security number and blood type stamped on it and interlaced in their footwear. A traveler could also have information written on the inside of their jacket, waistband, or on some other item, including a USB device that is attached to a zipper, etc.

- **Don't Count on the Embassy or Consulate** – The assistance they will provide may include contacting family members and assisting in translating, etc. Don't assume that they will assist in paying medical bills, etc.

- **Payment for Services** – Payment of hospital and other medical expenses is usually the responsibility of the traveler. In many cases, the traveler will be required to pay up front for medical assistance (in cash) before any medical services are provided. Personal insurance (if covered), will later reimburse the traveler for their expenses.

- **Consider Leaving the Country** – Because medical care may be below those standards that exist in industrialized nations, it might be a wise decision to get to a major capital in an industrialized nation *fast*. The Internet abounds with stories of individuals dying from common ailments in countries that have sub-standard medical care. There are also the stories of those who got out and survived. If a traveler waits too long, meanwhile, the country or the airlines may also refuse the traveler to fly for public health or liability reasons.

- **Other Assistance** – Several credit cards may offer emergency assistance "referral" services to traveling cardholders. The services may include trip insurance, lost baggage coverage, legal service referrals, and referrals for medical assistance. In most cases, these are referral activities only. To find out what specific services the credit card company offers and their limitations, the traveler should contact their credit card company and review the card's coverage before leaving.

TIPS FOR HEALTHY FLYING

Besides the physical exertion and stressors associated with planning for the trip and getting into and through the airport, travelers also need to realize some health issues associated with flying. Some of these issues are reviewed below.

Dehydration

Dehydration is an abnormal loss of water from the body. It is one of the causes of jet lag. Dehydration is accelerated during flying because the traveler is in a pressurized cabin. Alcohol consumption also accelerates the dehydration process. The effects of dehydration will cause headaches, discomfort and nausea. If traveling by air, a person will need to ensure that they have drunk plenty of liquids, preferably water, which is why flight attendants regularly offer bottled water to passengers. Hydration is especially important on long haul flights. The intake of liquids, however, should not include alcohol. Travelers also need to make sure that they stay properly hydrated throughout the trip by drinking safe water and/or other fluids.

Deep Vein Thrombosis (DVT)

Deep Vein Thrombosis (DVT), also known as "economy class syndrome" occurs when blood clots form within the deep veins of the body, especially the legs. DVT can occur in all travelers, regardless of age. It is the result of being inactive for a long period of time, such as sitting in a confined space on an airplane. These clots could break off and eventually lodge in the lung, causing serious health risks. Even if the clot(s) do not become dislodged, DVT can cause discoloration, swelling and discomfort in the legs.

Preventing DVT

Some ways to prevent DVT, according to flighthealth.org, are listed below:

- Always drink plenty of water to avoid dehydration.
- Do not drink alcohol before or during the flight, as this can compound dehydration, leading to DVT issues.
- Try to keep the thighs clear of the edge of the seat. Use footrests as much as possible.
- Take a brisk walk for 30-minutes before the flight.
- Try a few simple exercises to keep the legs moving. Try rotating the ankles, pointing the heel and toe alternately, and lifting the knees every half hour.

- Try to tense the leg muscles as regularly as possible throughout the flight.
- Wear elastic flight socks (elastic compression stockings) specially designed to reduce the risk of DVT. These are available at most drug stores.
- The day before the flight, take a low dose of aspirin. It is also recommended that aspirin be taken during the flight, and for three days following the flight.

Many airlines also have exercise-related videos during the course of the flight. A traveler should take advantage of these videos and any other physical activities that can be performed during the flight. Wearing loose clothing and removing shoes while flying to increase blood circulation will also be helpful in preventing DVT.

Jet Lag

Jet lag is a physiological condition caused by the traveler's natural body clock (their circadian rhythm) becoming disrupted by time zone changes, which results in the traveler's normal sleep cycle being disrupted in some manner. In combination with changes in the sleep cycle, changes in eating patterns and nutrition could also cause a variety of medical symptoms. These symptoms can include fatigue, insomnia, and a range of other conditions ranging from irritability to motor coordination problems that fall under the auspices of "jet lag."

To reduce the effects of jet lag, some medical experts recommend getting extra sleep before, and during the flight. They also recommend trying to synchronize mealtimes with the destination time to get on the new rhythm. Reducing alcohol intake, and drinking enough fluids, especially water, while flying is also important. Upon arrival, it is also recommended to try to relax as much as possible for the first day, establishing a routine and then slowly adjusting to the new local time, etc. Others recommend spending time outdoors. Because circadian rhythms are regulated by sunlight, being outdoors may further assist in the body transitioning to the new time period. Furthermore, some experts adopt the rule of thumb that for every time zone crossed, a day of recovery is needed.

CONCLUSION

Staying healthy is a crucial element of safe travel. In many cases, medical issues can be prevented through awareness and simple lifestyle changes while traveling. Healthy travel begins prior to departure where the traveler should plan for any foreseeable health emergencies, get checked out, and research the quality of medical facilities in the host country. A review of health insurance policies should also be conducted, and the traveler should consider what prescriptions and over-the-counter drugs will be needed for the trip. This chapter has also pointed out that water, insect, and food-borne diseases are also an issue. However, simple modifications and changes to one's lifestyle will serve to mitigate many of these issues. This chapter also pointed out several other simple precautions that can be taken to stay healthy. It also reviewed some of the major issues to consider if a sickness or injury were to occur, where it was emphasized that every injury or illness, no matter how "trivial," should be treated seriously. Last, the chapter gave tips for flying healthy. These major health issues include staying properly hydrated, dealing with issues associated with DVT, and mitigating the effects of jet lag.

6
LUGGAGE

A quick scan of an airport, train station, other public transportation facilities, and hotels readily reveals the novice traveler. They are often the ones that are battling an excessive amount of luggage! To prevent this and/or similar incidents from occurring, this chapter will review some of the main issues related to luggage, primarily in the context of air travel. The reader should keep in mind, however, that many of the same principles of traveling light also apply to other common carriers including trains and buses.

SELECTING LUGGAGE

An often-overlooked component to travel is selecting the right luggage. In this context, luggage should be considered to be a tool. Like any tool, it must be appropriate for the task at hand where issues related to function, size, quality, appearance, and operation should therefore be examined.

Function

Always consider the function of the luggage. Some individuals may prefer luggage with multiple compartments; others may not. If, for example, a person is traveling for business, they may want a garment-styled bag for business attire. If a person is using the luggage for vacations, meanwhile, traditional-styled luggage may be preferred.

Luggage can be hard- or soft-shelled. Hard-shelled luggage is usually constructed from some type of plastic. These plastics/polymers can take a lot of abuse, they are easy to clean, and are resistant to staining. They can also protect fragile items (if items are properly packed). With plastics, however, there is the possibility that the suitcase could eventually crack and break.

In the context of soft cases, most are constructed of quality ballistic nylons and polyesters. Both materials offer durability and have the ability to resist the rigors of airline travel. With soft-shelled luggage there may be the temptation to overstuff a suitcase because it provides a little more flexibility.

Size

The size of the luggage is contingent upon length of stay and the traveler's ability to carry the luggage. Often travelers forget that they will have to carry their luggage through airport terminals, hotels, etc. When selecting luggage, while it may appear to be maneuverable and easy to carry in the store, keep in mind that this same luggage will be filled (and heavy) when traveling.

Quality

Select well-constructed, high quality luggage. The last thing a traveler wants to happen is to have their carry-on or checked luggage fail. Therefore, promotional bags or luggage constructed from inexpensive materials should never be used. All too often straps will break, seams will become unstitched, or the fabric will tear, leaving the traveler in a bind.

Airlines can actually refuse to accept fragile or damaged pieces. They could also require the traveler to sign a waiver releasing the airline from responsibility of damage to the suitcase, and its contents, if the luggage looks questionable in the context of quality.

Appearance

A traveler should select plain looking luggage that is neutral in color and appearance. Colorful and/or designer-styled luggage simply draws attention to it. Luggage with logos or any other identifiers including company, patriotic or nationalistic logos and/or colors should also be avoided. Coordinated pieces are not a necessary part of travel. Too many people are concerned about looking coordinated with their luggage. Coordinated pieces could show the would-be criminal that the traveler has some degree of status or wealth. Expensive looking luggage could also serve as an indicator of the contents of the luggage.

Operation

Operation also needs to be considered. Some suitcases have extendable handles, hidden wheels, and a variety of straps to secure and add on other components to the bag. While some of these components may be beneficial for travel, it is important to make sure that they actually operate as designed. In some cases, for example, finding the levers or buttons may be difficult. Or, they may not be as easy to operate as they were when in the store. It is therefore recommended that a traveler becomes familiar and comfortable with the operation of their luggage prior to travel. That way, they will not be like many travelers seen in airports who are trying to figure out how to operate their luggage.

Perhaps one of the most important issues is, if the luggage allows for hands-free operation. A traveler will need to use their hands a lot. Therefore, luggage should be selected that at a minimum will allow for at least one hand and/or arm to be completely free to deal with travel-related issues. For example, carry-ons that have a shoulder strap allow for both hands to be free. Wheeled suitcases, meanwhile, allow for mobility and at least one arm free.

In some cases, a shoulder version may be a good option because it allows for hands-free operation and control of the bag. However, these types of bags can become quite heavy over time. With wheeled versions, meanwhile, the user can give up control of the bag, whereas a stranger could easily pick the bag up or wheel it away from the unaware traveler. Nevertheless, wheeled versions may be easier to move and may be less fatiguing.

CARRY-ON LUGGAGE

As the name implies, carry-ons are bags or cases that the traveler can carry with them onto the airplane and store under a seat or in the bulkhead storage area. Carry-ons can be wheeled, have a shoulder strap, and in some cases, they can even have a combination of wheels and a shoulder strap. Carry-ons can be a good addition to checked luggage, or in some cases, the carry-on can accommodate all of the needs of the traveler. With carry-ons the traveler can maintain control of their expensive and fragile items. A traveler can also pack essentials in these bags to ensure that the "basics" are covered, in case checked luggage should become lost.

Carry-On Standards

Just because a bag is labeled or looks like a carry-on does not mean that it meets the standards set forth by airlines for carry-ons. In fact, each airline may have their own carry-on restrictions. The standards for major U.S. carriers typically range from 9" x 13" x 22" (23 cm x 41 cm x 57 cm) to 10" x 16" x 24" (25 cm x 45 cm x 56 cm), in a normal, un-overstuffed size. To prevent carry-ons from being stowed in the cargo hold, or worse than that, placed on a different flight, it is recommended that the traveler contact their airline to check their policy regarding carry-on luggage. Each airline's homepage also provides guidelines on carry-on size restrictions.

Typically, airlines follow the International Air Transport Association (IATA) standards for carry-ons which mandate that a traveler can have one piece of luggage that does not exceed 10" x 18" x 22" (25 cm x 45 cm x 56 cm) **AND** one additional item that could be a:

- Garment bag which, when folded in half, does not exceed 9" x 22" x 22.5" or, 23 cm x 56 cm x 57 cm.
- Briefcase, or laptop style computer bag, not exceeding 4.5" or 12 cm in thickness.
- Purse not exceeding 4.5" or 12 cm in thickness.

Not all airlines may allow a second piece, depending upon the number of passengers, space availability, and the size and type of airplane. In effect, there are no guarantees. Therefore, it is again best to travel light and check the airline for any additional carry-on restrictions.

Travelers should also keep in mind that even though the luggage may be classified as a carry-on, it could still be heavy and difficult to use. A good rule of thumb is that if the traveler cannot personally carry their carry-on luggage for long distances, or they cannot lift the luggage into a bulkhead on their own, they should consider using a smaller carry-on or have the bag checked.

TSA Restrictions

The Transportation Security Administration (TSA) also has restrictions on the size and amount of items that can be carried-on. A detailed description of restricted carry-on items can be found at http://www.tsa.org. In the context of allowed carry-on items, especially fluids, the best way to remember the TSA restrictions is through their 3-1-1 System, which is:

- 3 ounce bottles or less, placed in a
- 1 Quart-Sized, clear plastic Zip Lock® Bag; and,
- 1 Quart-Sized Bag Per Passenger only

At the screening point, this bag must be taken out of the carry-on and placed in the screening bin so TSA screeners can visually inspect it. In addition, a traveler should:

- Not wrap or package gifts. They may have to be opened by TSA personnel.
- Make sure there are no prohibited items in their carry-ons.

CHECKED LUGGAGE

Checked baggage is luggage that is checked at the ticket counter or curbside, which is then stowed in the cargo holds of the aircraft. It is not accessible during the flight. Some issues to consider with checked luggage, according to American Airlines, is shown below:

- Only check luggage that is sturdy enough to withstand airline baggage handling systems.
- Never check a bag that doesn't completely close. If a luggage strap or bungee cord is needed to keep the bag closed, it probably won't survive the trip.
- Most briefcases, tote bags, plastic garment covers, and items received through retail promotions are not designed to be checked luggage.

- Don't over-pack. Over-packing puts a strain on zippers, seams, frames, and hinges.

- Clearly label all bags with the owner's name, current address and phone number.

- Luggage can be quite similar in appearance. Therefore, check all bags carefully in the luggage claims area before leaving the airport to make sure the correct luggage has been taken.

- Remove all baggage tags from previous trips to avoid any confusion by baggage handlers.

- Consider replacing old or worn luggage. Luggage that is several years old may not be able to withstand today's automated baggage handling systems.

Additionally, if the luggage is old, consider placing a reinforcement strap around it. This could prevent the luggage from opening up during the baggage handling process.

In some cases, individuals purchase very large stowable luggage. This is fine as long as the traveler follows the rule that they should be able to carry and lift their luggage on their own. A common mistake is to purchase luggage that is so bulky or large that the traveler cannot carry it on his or her own. Even though this luggage is stowed in the cargo holds of airplanes, a traveler should also keep in mind that they will have to, at a minimum: 1) carry and move this luggage to and from the airport; 2) carry it in various forms of public transportation; and, 3) haul it to and from the lodging facility. Therefore, it must be manageable.

A traveler should also adopt the attitude and practice that they are completely responsible for their luggage from start to finish, requiring them to carry the luggage in various settings, long distances and over long periods of time. To make sure that the luggage is manageable, the traveler should take it for a trial run, walking up some stairs, and over long distances. Engaging in these "dry runs" would be a good indicator if the size, weight, and load of the luggage could be managed while traveling. If, however, the traveler should have some difficulties, it is strongly encouraged that the weight and quantity of luggage be reconsidered.

Do Not Lock Checked Luggage

Luggage should be locked, until it is checked in. The TSA is required by federal law to screen 100% of all checked baggage. In some cases, TSA screeners will therefore have to open baggage as part of a random in-depth screening process, or if it alarms for some reason. If the bag is unlocked, TSA personnel will simply open and screen the baggage. If it is locked, meanwhile, and they cannot open the checked baggage through other means (they have tools to open many locks), then the locks may have to be broken. If a lock is cut, TSA personnel will leave the clipped lock in the baggage along with a Notice of Inspection. The TSA, however, is not liable for damage caused to locked bags that must be opened for security purposes. Furthermore, the TSA will not reimburse passengers for unrecognized locks broken as a result of the security screening process. A list of approved locks can be found in the http://tsa.gov website under "TSA Accepted and Recognized Locks."

Baggage Restrictions and Requirements

Each carrier has its own restrictions related to luggage. In some cases, chartered flights have more stringent restrictions than commercial airlines. These restrictions can vary from flight to flight, depending upon the aircraft. It also varies according to:

- Dimensional Size of the Suitcase
- Weight of the Luggage
- Number of Bags

In order to prevent any delays at the airport (or even having the baggage refused), travelers should always check the airline's homepage for luggage requirements and restrictions. If the ticket is purchased directly from the airline, often the inside flap of the ticket folder has some printed information regarding baggage restrictions. The traveler should also keep in mind that some common carriers will charge for excessively heavy baggage or additional bags. Therefore, it is important to check each common carrier's restrictions on the number and weight of allowed baggage.

Of course, excessive amounts of luggage and weight can hinder a person while traveling. Excessive amounts may hinder other travelers, too. On one overseas trip, for example, a student over-packed, bringing along 3 large suitcases (against the advice of the authors). He soon became fatigued while carrying his bags, where he had to rely upon others to assist. His travel companions did not think too highly of his inconsiderate actions.

PROHIBITED ITEMS

For both carry-ons and checked luggage the Transportation Security Administration prohibits certain items on-board aircraft. A list of these prohibited items can be found on the tsa.gov website. Besides the TSA site, travelers should also check their airline's homepage for any other prohibited items.

Travelers also need to be aware that customs laws in certain countries can have additional prohibitions on what can be brought into the host country. These could range from fruits, vegetables, and animals, all the way up to sexually suggestive materials (i.e., lingerie, certain magazines), alcohol (even in mouthwash) and pornography. To check for prohibited items, travelers should go to the U.S. Department of State's Website as well as the host country's website. This will ensure that the traveler has no problems going through immigration/customs.

LOST LUGGAGE AND MISSING PROPERTY

In 2005 alone, airlines lost 10,000 bags per day! While the majority of these bags were later recovered and returned to their owners, in other cases they were permanently lost or stolen. This statistic, however, does not include the amount of stolen items from luggage. Therefore, a traveler should plan, and be prepared for the loss of their luggage. In fact, a traveler should consider it a bonus when the luggage arrives with their flight!

Ways to Prevent Losing Luggage

In most cases, lost luggage turns up. It may, however, take some time. In order to prevent luggage from getting misplaced or lost, consider the following points:

- **Always Tag Luggage** – Make sure that all luggage (carry-on and checked bags) is properly tagged. Do not use personalized luggage tags that have a company logo or school name on it, as this could reveal the traveler's social status, occupation, etc. The traveler should also make sure that the luggage tag has a flap on it that conceals personal information. Always write down a work address without the name of the company, if possible. That way, if the luggage is stolen, the thieves will at least not have the traveler's home address.

- **Be sure to place contact information in the luggage** – Luggage tags can get readily torn off in the baggage handling process. Therefore, it is wise to place a duplicate tag inside the luggage so handlers can readily identify whom it belongs to. Also, be sure to include contact information related to the destination; otherwise, the luggage may end up at the traveler's permanent home address instead of the destination address.

- **Pay careful attention when the bag is tagged at check-in** – Know the airport code of the destination airport and double-check to make sure the code is correct – the airlines staff can make honest mistakes.

To Ensure Recovery/Reimbursement

To receive reimbursement for lost or stolen items, a traveler will need to provide a detailed list of items that were contained in their luggage. Below are some tips to prepare for such problems:

- Take a photograph of the contents of the suitcase so a good, detailed description can be provided. Use a digital camera, cell phone, or traditional film camera.

- Inventory the contents of the suitcase(s) and carry a copy of it, separate of the luggage (don't keep a copy of it in the suitcase!). Be sure to record name brands, etc. Better yet, have the inventory list stored in an e-mail account. That way, the list can be accessed anywhere in the world – including the claims counter at the airline. Be sure to leave a copy of it at home too. A sample luggage inventory form can be found in Appendix I.

- Put a copy of the travel itinerary in the bag. That way, the airline can identify and find the owner, even if the tags get separated from the luggage.

- Write down the name brand, color and size of the suitcase. This will aid in locating the suitcase. It will also assist in reimbursement for the value of the luggage.

- Always keep the luggage check-in receipts. Store them in a safe area, such as in a passport wallet. Do not store them in the luggage.

When Luggage is Missing or Lost

Procedures for reporting missing or lost luggage are not standardized. They vary from carrier to carrier. When it is discovered that luggage is lost or stolen, some of the standard procedures to be followed include:

- Notify a baggage service agent prior to leaving the airport. Complete all paperwork and forms out at the airport – do not wait to do it later, or on-line. Request copies of all of the forms that have been filled out. Also, get the name of the employee(s) that provided assistance, a local phone number, and a 1-800 number. The traveler should not settle for the 1-800 alone. Instead, they should insist upon another number and a name of a person who can be contacted locally.

- The traveler will then be given a Property Questionnaire. This can be issued in person or it can be mailed to the traveler's permanent address. If the luggage is not found within a given time period (i.e., 5 days), this form should be completed with a detailed description of the contents of the suitcase(s) within the deadline established by the airline. This detailed questionnaire on the contents will assist the airline in finding the luggage. After a certain time period (i.e., 30 or 45 days), if the luggage is not found, the airline will then negotiate a financial settlement.

- Ask for (or in some cases demand) reimbursement-related expenses. Depending upon the carrier, the traveler may be eligible for reimbursement for expenses related to the lost luggage. Northwest Airlines, for example, will pay for clothing and toiletries. They will reimburse up to $50 for the first 24 hours and $25 per each additional day of delay, up to $150 per ticketed passenger. Receipts for expenses are usually turned in at the airlines Luggage Service Office located at the airport. The traveler should also keep in mind that the airlines readily do not tell individuals that they may be eligible for reimbursements related to the loss. Furthermore, many (if not all) airlines will not pay for consequential damages (expenses) for car rentals, phone calls, hotel stays or meals related to the lost luggage.

- Travelers who have lost/stolen/delayed luggage may also request a complimentary kit. This kit usually contains a comb, deodorant, razor, shaving cream, toothbrush, and toothpaste. It can be obtained from the Luggage Service Office.

- NEVER leave without filling all appropriate paperwork and getting copies of all of the forms that have been completed.

- Airlines will deliver the recovered luggage once it is found. Therefore, the traveler will need to provide them with an address where the luggage should be delivered.

While airlines will reimburse for costs related to the loss of the luggage, the period before a traveler will receive financial compensation for their loss can be quite long. The traveler will also need to provide the airline receipts for expenses related to the lost luggage (be sure to make copies of all receipts before sending them to the airline) in order to be reimbursed. Travelers should also save all receipts, just in case the airline demands proof for the cost of any replaced items at a later time.

The amount of reimbursement for the loss is limited. Some airlines limit their liability for the loss to the fair market value of the luggage and contents, not to exceed $3,000. The owner is responsible for anything over this amount. In many instances, however, credit card companies will often pay the difference between what the airline has paid for and the actual loss, as long as the traveler used their credit card to purchase the ticket. Like the airlines, the credit card company should be contacted as soon as possible after the event. Depending upon the credit card company, the traveler may have other benefits related to the loss of their luggage.

Missing Property from Checked Luggage

Besides lost luggage, in some situations, objects can be stolen from checked luggage. Therefore, it is important for the traveler to check the contents of their luggage as soon as possible after arrival. The key to missing property (and damage) is to report it immediately by phone or in person.

All of the airlines have different policies regarding missing property. For example, Northwest Airlines requires that domestic claims be filed within 24 hours at the airport where the travel was completed. For international flights, meanwhile, the traveler has a period of 7 days from arrival at the airport where the travel was completed. This information is then sent to Central Luggage Service Department where it is reviewed. Customers are then contacted in writing by the Central Luggage Service staff approximately 20 days from the date the initial report was filed, regarding the status of the claim. As is the case for lost property, the traveler should record the name of the person who assisted them, and obtain a local phone number in case follow-up calls are required.

The procedures for missing luggage are very similar to the procedures for lost luggage. In order to be eligible for recovery, the traveler will need proof that the object was stolen. Therefore, written and photographic documentation is very important in order to be successful. As was the case with lost luggage, the traveler will need to be persistent with the airline in order to be reimbursed.

Lost Luggage and Theft Insurance

Additional loss and theft-related insurance can be purchased from airlines at the check-in area or from private insurance companies, prior to the trip. As pointed out earlier, in many cases, credit card companies provide insurance against loss and theft, simply on the basis that the traveler used their credit card to purchase the ticket. Benefits vary according to the credit card company. Therefore, the traveler should contact their specific company to see what benefits they provide. In some cases, home-owners' insurance may cover the loss of personal possessions, too.

PROTECTING LUGGAGE AND ITS CONTENTS

The loss of luggage or the theft of certain goods can cause serious problems for the traveler. Listed below are some tips to avoid this situation from occurring.

- **Have some type of distinct identifier on the luggage** – This way it can be readily identified. It could be as simple as bright stickers on the luggage or a multi-colored reinforcement strap.

- **Watch the person physically load the luggage into vehicles** – When leaving and returning to the airport and other locations, mistakes can be made, where a traveler's luggage could be purposefully or mistakenly left behind.

- **Immediately go to the baggage claim area** – A travel-er should be at the baggage claim area when the luggage arrives and begins to unload onto the carousel. In many airports, the baggage claim area is in close proximity to exits. Combined with the fact that many airports never have personnel match claims tickets with luggage, it is quite easy for someone to steal bags and immediately flee the airport.

- **Don't leave luggage curbside** – Luggage could easily be taken in the confusion of loading and unloading.

- **Don't let porters carry any luggage until they have been verified as legitimate employees** – In some coun-tries it is quite common for non-airport employees to take a traveler's bags under the false pretenses that they are a legitimate employee, and then literally hold the bag(s) hostage until they are paid for their "services."

- **Don't leave luggage unattended** – When using rest-rooms or in other areas of the terminal, as well as outside the terminal, a traveler should watch their luggage or have a trusted person watch it for them.

- **Keep luggage in sight (and feel) at all times** – Luggage must also be constantly watched. When sitting, for example, a traveler should consider placing their luggage in front of them, and drape their legs over the luggage to prevent it from being stolen. If the luggage has a strap, meanwhile, a traveler should consider placing their foot or even the leg of a chair through the strap to prevent it from being easily carried away. All of these techniques are important, especially if the traveler should accidentally fall asleep.

PACKING FOR THE TRIP

The underlying theme when packing for a trip is to pack light! The most common mistake made by travelers is that they over-pack. Lugging excessive luggage is fatiguing and at times very frustrating to maneuver, especially on some types of public transportation. Excessive luggage also makes a person stand out, increasing their odds of being a victim of crime.

Tips to Prevent Over-Packing

Listed below are some tips to prevent over-packing:

- *Make a List* – Make a list of everything that is needed for the trip. Let the list sit for a day and reduce it by 25%. The following day, do the same thing, further reducing the list by another 25%.

- *Have a Friend be the Devil's Advocate* – Have a friend critically review all of the items that will be taken on the trip. This friend should ask some hard questions related to the necessity of all of the items under consideration.

- *Pack Neutral Colors Only* – Neutral colors will ensure that all of the packed clothing will match one another. A traveler should choose a color scheme so everything goes with everything else. This will reduce the number of clothes needed for the trip. If a traveler needs some color, meanwhile, a colorful scarf or tie that takes up very little space can be packed.

- ***Research the Climate and Weather*** – Research the climate and weather conditions at the destination. A quick review of the Internet and even viewing the Weather Channel® will provide up-to-date and detailed information about weather conditions and the subsequent clothing and outerwear that may be required for the trip.

- ***Downsize Toiletries*** – The size and quantity of liquids are limited for carry-ons. There are, however, no liquids restrictions for stowed luggage. Nevertheless, a traveler should consider purchasing travel-size versions in order to save space. If additional products are needed, they can usually be purchased in the host country.

- ***Bring Clothes That Can Be Thrown Away*** – Consider bringing along old undergarments, T-shirts, and shoes and throw them away when they become soiled or are no longer needed. This will free up space and lighten the load on the return trip when the traveler is most likely going to be tired from the trip. It will also make room for souvenirs. Travelers can also purchase disposable clothing, such as paper underwear, that are available at many drug stores.

- ***Plan Travel Days/Create an Itinerary*** – Creating a general itinerary of daily clothing needs prior to packing will allow a traveler to better plan for and limit the types and amount of clothing that will be needed. A traveler should also keep in mind that they can wear the same outer clothing day after day, if necessary.

- ***Pack Washable Clothes*** – Consider packing clothing that is washable. A traveler can take advantage of hotel services, host families, coin-operated laundries, and even the sink and shower to do laundry while abroad.

- ***Pack Outside The Luggage*** – Travelers will often pack to the capacity of their luggage, regardless of whether they need an item or not. In order to avoid this issue, a traveler should lay items to be packed next to their suitcase(s). Then, these items should be packed. This will provide a good overview of all of the items that intend to be packed, compared and checked against the itinerary that has already been created. It will also prevent a traveler from adding unneeded or unnecessary items just because there is room for them.

- *Buy Items Over There* – Toiletries and other fluids could leak and ruin clothing, etc. Therefore, limit the amount of fluids and other potentially damaging items that are packed. Instead, buy toiletries, etc. in the host country. When departing, leave them behind to reduce the risk of spills.

- *Do Some Homework* – A traveler should check to see what resources are available at the destination in order to avoid bringing unnecessary items (i.e., towels, hair dryers). A traveler should also check with co-travelers to see what items can be shared with one another to further reduce the number of items needed for the trip.

- *Consider Shipping* – Consider shipping some items or luggage to the destination. A traveler can often arrange in advance with their destination to receive packages. Upon departure, a traveler should also consider shipping home some items. Not only will this lighten the load, but it can also shorten a traveler's time at customs.

- *Limit Footwear* – Footwear takes up a lot of space and it is often heavy. To limit "shoe weight," wear the heaviest shoes, and pack only one more pair of shoes for the trip.

- *Rolling Your Clothes* – Rolling rather than folding clothes will help prevent wrinkling at times. It will also allow the traveler to pack more into a smaller space.

- *A Trial Run* – After packing, a traveler should take the packed luggage on a trial run. It should be carried upstairs and for long distances. If the luggage is found to be too heavy or unmanageable, the traveler should assess what could be eliminated, and re-pack.

TSA Packing Tips

The Transportation Security Administration also has some helpful hints on packing carry-ons and checked baggage that is reviewed below. The TSA *DOES NOT* recommend packing the following items in the checked baggage:

- Jewelry
- Cash
- Laptop computers
- Electronics
- Fragile items (no matter how they are protected)

Some other TSA travel tips also include:

- Don't put film in checked baggage because screening equipment could damage it.
- Pack shoes, boots, sneakers, and other footwear on top of other contents in the luggage.
- Avoid over-packing bags so screeners can easily reseal the bag if it is opened for inspection. If possible, spread the contents over several bags.
- Avoid packing food and beverages in checked baggage in order to prevent leaks, etc.
- Don't stack piles of books or documents on top of each other; spread them out within the baggage.
- Put all undeveloped film and cameras with film in carry-on baggage. If a bag passes through an X-ray machine more than five (5) times, ask for a hand inspection to prevent damage.
- Label laptop computers. Tape a business card or other identifying information on the bottom of the laptop to avoid the loss or accidental exchange by other passengers.
- Check ahead of time with the airline or travel agent to determine the airline's baggage policy, including the number of pieces that can be brought, as well as size and weight limitations.
- Think carefully about personal items packed in carry-on baggage. Screeners may have to open the bag and examine its contents.
- Place personal belongings in clear plastic bags to reduce the chance that a TSA screener will have to handle them.
- Do NOT pack or bring prohibited items to the airport.

CONCLUSION

Traveling light is an important component of safe travel. Too much luggage will limit a person's mobility, increase their level of fatigue, and perhaps make them a target of crime, relative to other travelers who are not over-burdened with baggage. This chapter has identified that the first thing a traveler needs to do is to select the proper luggage for their travels in the context of function, size, quality, appearance and operation. Travelers need to be aware of size restrictions related to their carry-on luggage. They also need to make sure that the checked luggage is suitable for travel and meets all guidelines set forth by the airlines and the TSA. Lost luggage and missing property can also be part of the travel adventure. There are, however, some ways to reduce the risk of loss and theft. And, if an incident does occur, it is important to have a complete inventory of the contents of the luggage. It is also important that the traveler follows all lost luggage procedures set by the airline, in addition to being persistent to ensure recovery. This chapter has also provided ideas to protect luggage from theft or loss. The key is to never leave it out of sight while to and from the host country. Besides loss or theft, perhaps the most common mistake made by travelers is over-packing. As this chapter has shown, some simple pre-packing procedures will serve to reduce the amount of clothing, etc. for the trip without impacting the journey in any way.

THE AIRPORT

A irports and their surrounding areas can often be high-crime locales. In many instances travelers are too absorbed with their schedules and trying to find their gates, and they can soon forget about their personal safety and security while at the airport. However, in order to prevent oneself from becoming a victim of theft (as well as other crimes), the traveler needs to use common sense and practice good judgment at the airport.

BEFORE LEAVING FOR THE AIRPORT

Prior to leaving for the airport, a traveler should begin planning for safety and security issues which might affect the trip.

Consider the following:

- Always monitor world events. An emergency situation in one country, for example, can adversely affect the travel schedule.

- Always try to book flights early in the day. Early flights are less likely to be delayed. The ripple effects of other flight-related problems throughout the country and/or world are less in the mornings.

- Always try to book non-stop flights. This will eliminate layovers and transfers. And, it will naturally reduce the odds of becoming a victim of a crime.

- Check the status of the flight (by calling the airlines or checking online) before leaving for the airport.

- If a traveler can choose between airports, they should always check the State Department and other web pages for safety-related information in airports. The level of safety among airports varies throughout the world. Some may be designated as dangerous.

- Travelers should familiarize themselves with the layout of the airport to gain an understanding of the distance and the time it will take to get to their gate. This should be done prior to arriving at the airport. All major airports have their own website that provides information of this nature.

- A traveler should also become familiar with the security procedures at the airport(s) they are using. A great deal of information can be obtained from the www.tsa.gov website, from airport websites, and from talking to others who have used those particular airports.

- A traveler should also be mentally and physically prepared for large crowds and the stressors associated with these situations.

- Make sure that all necessary and/or vital documents are taken on the trip. At a minimum a traveler should have their ticket (or e-ticket), passport, and another official form of identification.

- Let others know the travel schedule. Also, let them know what airports and airlines are being used, and the flight numbers, in case of emergency.

- Know the existing threat levels. The higher the threat level, the longer the delays. The TSA threat level system is shown in Box 7-1.

Box 7-1
TSA Advisory System

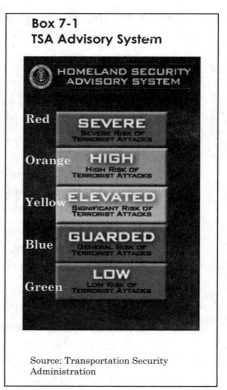

Source: Transportation Security Administration

AT THE AIRPORT

In addition to the pre-departure activities, travelers also need to be safety-conscious when on or around the airport property. In fact, it could be argued that in many cases, parking lots and surrounding areas could be far more dangerous than activities in the airport terminal itself.

Using Personal Transportation

It is recommended that a traveler should avoid taking his or her own vehicle to the airport. Instead, the traveler should use a shuttle, public transportation, or have friends take them. Not only will this save on expenses related to parking, but it would also eliminate the risk of a vehicle break-in at the airport while away. Getting a ride to the airport will speed the process up, too. The traveler can most likely be dropped off at the terminal, reducing the travel time (and dangers) related to parking and walking or riding to the terminal.

If a traveler should decide to take their own vehicle to the airport, listed below are some issues to consider:

- Consider paying a little more for concierge parking. Usually this parking is closer to the terminal, in comparison to the long-term or economy lots that are often quite a distance from the terminal.
- When selecting and parking the vehicle:
  - ▶ Lock all doors.
  - ▶ Park in well-lit and well-traveled areas.
  - ▶ Park as close to shuttle stops as possible.
  - ▶ Clean the car out – eliminate all tempting objects – CDs, charger cords, loose change, electronic devices, etc.
  - ▶ Secure larger objects in the vehicle's trunk.
  - ▶ Remember where the vehicle is parked, in order to prevent wandering a parking lot when returning. Write down the parking zone on a piece of paper. Usually all airports have zone signs posted on streetlights, etc.

▶ If a traveler should feel unsafe in the parking area, they should call the airport and have a shuttle bus pick them up at their vehicle instead of at the shuttle stop.

▶ Check the area for any odd or dangerous activities and/or persons before leaving the vehicle.

▶ A traveler should take their parking pass/receipt with them. Without a ticket, a thief will have problems getting the vehicle out of the parking area.

If or When a Shuttle is Used

- Public transportation and shuttles should drop a traveler off as close to the ticketing airline as possible. Shortening the travel distance may decrease the odds of becoming a victim.

- A traveler should stay with their luggage. Instead of placing it in the back of the shuttle, for example, they should hold onto it. If it is placed in the back, a criminal could steal it when the shuttle is stopped, and the tailgate is unlocked or opened. Other riders on the shuttle could also take the bags (on purpose or by accident). In most cases, a shuttle driver has no idea who is the rightful owner of the stowed luggage, and they may allow persons access to all of the luggage.

- If the parking area and shuttle service is off airport property, a traveler should make sure that there is 24-hour pick up. A traveler should check in advance to see what time periods exist between shuttle runs.

- When dropped off at the vehicle on the return trip, the traveler should also ask the shuttle driver to wait until they are in their vehicle and the vehicle is started.

- When waiting for a shuttle on the return trip, a traveler should wait inside the terminal for the shuttle, whenever possible.

- Many airports have several private "Park N' Rides." Remember which one was used.

- As is the case with on-site parking, do not keep the parking receipt in the vehicle. Store it in a safe location.

Also, write the phone number of the shuttle service on the receipt (if it isn't on it already).

- Many shuttle services require that the traveler call them for pick-up at the airport. In order to avoid standing and waiting for the shuttle, call them well in advance.

Pedestrian Safety

- Traffic is usually quite heavy at airports. Be especially careful when crossing streets, etc.

- Look out for public transportation, taxis, and baggage handlers at the airport. There is a lot of vehicular traffic that could lead to accidents and injuries.

- Parking ramps are very dangerous to use. They often have a lot of blind spots; police or security may not frequently patrol them; and, oftentimes lighting is poor. Therefore, a traveler needs to be particularly careful about motor vehicle accidents and criminal activities in these locales.

IN THE TERMINAL

Once within the terminal, the traveler still needs to be diligent in the context of safety. Within the terminal there are a variety of threats that could cause personal injury. There are also some criminal threats that a traveler needs to be aware of.

- A traveler should keep in mind that the general public is still allowed in the common areas of the airport. Ticketed passengers only, are allowed beyond the screening check-points and gates. Therefore, the risk of crime still exists in airports.

- Allow enough time. Running through an airport draws attention. A traveler also faces the risk of physical injury from a trip and fall-related accident.

- Avoid executive and airline membership lounges. Using these types of amenities makes a person stand out as an executive or upscale traveler, making them a better target for criminals.

- Stay away from unattended bags, trash cans and other receptacles that could contain explosives.

- Guard bags and other valuables. Thieves are well aware that travelers often have large amounts of cash and other items of value with them.

- Depending upon the country, a traveler should not be surprised or alarmed to see military personnel and/or police armed with rifles and machine pistols in airports.

- Be aware of the surroundings at all times. Look for safe areas to move to if there is trouble.

While in the terminals, travelers should also:

- Look for people paying too much attention to them.

- Remain alert and focused: Walk with confidence and determination.

- Familiarize themselves with emergency exits.

- Never leave bags unattended or carry any article given to them by a stranger.

- Never sit or wait by windows. Flying glass debris as the result of explosions, etc. is often the primary cause of injury and death.

- Be especially careful in large crowds for pickpockets and thieves. Large crowds provide anonymity for criminals. They also provide the opportunity for criminals to accidentally bump into the traveler, a tactic of the pickpocket. They also allow a thief a better opportunity to take luggage, purses, jackets, etc.

- Only allow authorized personnel to handle their bags.

- Never give luggage or the ticket to anyone unless at an official security checkpoint or ticket counter. A legitimate airport employee will never ask a traveler to surrender these things anywhere else in the airport.

- Be wary of people asking questions. They could be diverting the traveler's attention, while an accomplice grabs the property. This advice applies to tourist attractions and public transportation as well.

Airport Check-In

Once in the airport terminal, a traveler will most likely need to check some luggage and obtain their boarding pass. Listed below are some issues to consider that are related to check in:

- Check in early. If a flight is overbooked, the last persons to check in are usually the first ones bumped.

- If bags are checked curbside, don't assume the luggage is safe just because it is on a cart and adjacent to airline personnel. A traveler needs to make sure that their luggage is loaded on the conveyer belt and it is going into the terminal.

- A government-issued form of photo identification (federal, state or local) will be required at check-in. A passport is required at check-in for international travel.

- E-ticket Travelers. E-tickets are often a faster and safer way to make it through initial check-in because a traveler can limit their exposure to crowds and criminals.

  With E-tickets, travelers can check in up to 24-hours before the flight by printing the boarding pass from their home computer. Travelers can also change seats on-line and even e-mail friends with the details of the flight when using the E-ticket option. Travelers can also print their tickets at one of the automated check-in kiosks at the airport, which is similar to using an ATM. If there is no luggage to check, the traveler will not have to stand in line at the ticket counter.

- The traveler should also be sure that their name on the ticket and boarding pass is spelled correctly, and it matches their identification. Otherwise, they might have a problem at the screening stages.

Security Checkpoints/Screening

Following checking in, a traveler should go through the screening process as soon as possible. It is much safer on the "gate side" than on the public side of the terminal. The nature and extent of security at this stage varies with the existing threat level, what airlines the traveler is flying with, and the country they are flying from. A traveler should also be prepared for the fact that increased threat levels will mean more in-depth security, and perhaps longer waiting periods.

There are usually two stages in the screening process. At stage one, a screener will verify the identification of the flyer and inspect the boarding pass. The next stage is for the traveler to physically go through the metal detectors and pass any carry-on, shoes, etc. through the x-ray machine. Depending upon the country, however, there may be additional layers of screening including a physical pat down, and in some cases, a complete search of carry-on luggage. Some additional points to consider include:

- *Be Prepared* – To speed the process up, the passport, boarding pass and another official form of identification should be ready for the screener. The name on two forms of identification must be an identical match to the name on the pass.

- *Cooperate with Security* – A traveler's rights and civil liberties are different in other countries. Therefore, security, police, and military personnel may have greater powers than they do in the United States. For example, a person may be physically searched and patted down by military personnel in some countries. Regardless of the process, the key is to cooperate with security personnel, remembering the simple fact that the traveler's rights as a U.S. citizen do not apply in foreign airports. A traveler should also be patient and avoid making any comments about security measures that could be misinterpreted and cause problems for them.

- *Don't Change Places in Line* – Changing places in line will disrupt the order of the bags going through the x-ray machine. It could also lead to flyers picking up the wrong property or bag at the end of the conveyor. It also allows the opportunistic criminal a chance to steal property. One well-known ploy that can occur is when a person cuts in front of a traveler and then sets off the metal detector, subsequently delaying the traveler's passage through the detector. By this time, however, the traveler's items have been scanned through the x-ray machine, and the criminal's partner, who is on the other side of the detector, has taken the property and disappeared.

- *Don't Forget Items* – The authors have personally observed flyers walk away without their bags, purses, jackets, and even their laptop computers after going through screening checkpoints. Therefore, it is always important to be diligent and alert when going through security checkpoints, remembering all items that were fed through the conveyor.

- *Wear Shoes that can be Easily Removed* – In the U.S. and the majority of foreign countries, a traveler will be required to remove their shoes, which will then be sent through the X-ray machine. This is perhaps one of the largest hold-ups in the screening process – taking off and putting on shoes. To speed the process up, a traveler should wear shoes that can be easily taken on and off. For example, slip-on shoes will be easier to deal with, in comparison to lace-up footwear.

- *Wear no Metal Items* – Metallic items will activate the alarms on airport magnetometers. A traveler should not wear or carry any metal objects (i.e., belt buckles, jewelry, change) in order to avoid a more detailed search and delays. If any metal items are carried, the traveler should always be sure to place them in the container provided by the screeners prior to going through the metal detector.

- *Electronic Items* – Laptop computers will need to be removed from their case and then sent through the X-ray scanner. The traveler may also be required to turn it on for security personnel. Therefore, a traveler should make sure the battery is charged for this purpose. Security personnel may also perform additional checks on other electronic devices, too.

- *No Prohibited Items* – In the U.S., the possession of prohibited items is illegal. Prohibited items including over-sized fluids and gels (or too much of them) will lead to delays and perhaps an in-depth search of the traveler's luggage. As pointed out in the Luggage Chapter, it is important to know and comply with all TSA requirements (and any other requirements) that exist.

Once in the Gates/Through Security

As pointed out earlier in this chapter, one of the safer places to be in an airport is in the terminal beyond the screening checkpoints. Only ticketed passengers and airport employees are allowed beyond the screening checkpoints and into the gate part of the terminal. Nevertheless, a traveler must recognize that they can still be victimized after passing through the screening stage. Therefore, the traveler should:

- Know where emergency exits are and sit near them.
- Make sure that there are unobstructed sight lines when seated.
- Stay in public view, whenever possible.
- Be aware of their surroundings at all times.
- Never leave bags unattended. In fact, in many airports security personnel will readily confront a person leaving an unattended bag.
- Avoid sleeping. Sleeping in airports is not recommended. If a traveler has to sleep and if they are with others, they should have a least one of the traveling companions awake, keeping watch.
- Look for safe areas to move to if some type of trouble should arise.
- Know where the closest security or police checkpoint is.
- Report anything unusual immediately to the police, security personnel, or airport staff.
- Do not sit near major walkways or aisles. A traveler should sit close to an exit, with their back towards a wall with no seating behind them. That way, a traveler can see everything and be alert to their surroundings. Another option (if traveling with others) is to sit back-to-back so the travelers have a full 360-degree field of view.
- When using restrooms, etc. do not set bags down or leave them unattended. In these situations, have a travel companion watch any belongings. If this is not an option, the traveler should carry their luggage in the stall with them, drape it over their shoulder, or come up with some other

way where the bag(s) can be physically prevented from being taken. A traveler should also be wary of hanging items on hooks or over the top of restroom stalls. It is very easy for a thief to take bags that are stowed this way.

- Be cautious when engaging in conversations with strangers. Seemingly innocuous conversations could jeopardize a traveler's safety.

- Review the Blending In chapter in the context of demeanor when in the airport.

- When using restaurants, etc., sit in an inconspicuous area. Be mindful of pickpockets and thieves.

- Immediately report any unattended items to the nearest airline or security personnel.

- Be cautious when dialing phones with credit or phone cards – someone may be watching to steal the access numbers. The same issue applies to computer and ATM passwords.

- Be aware that security personnel can search travelers at any time. They can be random in nature, or in some cases, an agency canine (i.e., a customs dog) could alert to something in the traveler's bag (such as fruit, candy, etc.).

- The quality of security and law enforcement personnel in foreign countries may not be as good as what is typically found in the United States. Therefore, a traveler should be prepared for varying degrees of professionalism and courtesy when traveling overseas.

At the Gate/Boarding the Aircraft

Perhaps the last stage in the airport security screening process will be at the departure gate. In order to be prepared for any security-related activities, the traveler should have their passport and other official forms of identification ready for review by airline or security personnel.

Security checks at the gate vary. In some cases, airline personnel will want to verify the identity of the traveler against their boarding pass. In other instances, TSA personnel (and other authorities) have been known to conduct random spot checks at the gates, where they will ask for identification and perhaps conduct a pat-down search and inspection of any carry-on bags. Gate security in other countries, meanwhile, could also be much more thorough at the time of boarding the plane, depending upon the country and the current threat level that exists.

ARRIVAL IN FOREIGN COUNTRIES

Part of the airport security experience is also going through immigration and customs control. The immigration/customs process actually begins on the airplane where flight attendants pass out required forms to passengers. Usually these forms include a landing card and a customs declaration card.

The key at each of these stages is to be prepared by having all required forms readily available for review. At any one of these stages a traveler may be required to submit to a more thorough interview or inspection of their luggage and even themselves. In some cases, it is because the traveler has piqued the inspector's suspicion. In other cases, however, it is purely random in nature. There is nothing that a traveler can do in these situations, but to comply. The worst thing a traveler can do is to question or challenge the authority of these individuals. The authors have seen this occur, and it usually leads to further delays and a more in-depth search and/or interview.

Passport/Immigration Control

After de-boarding the plane, travelers (and their carry-on luggage) will be directed to the passport/immigration control area. This is a secure area and the use of all electronic devices is prohibited. Usually, there are separate lanes for citizens and non-citizens. There may also be lines, based on language, where for example, an American tourist should seek out the English language line where an English-speaking inspector will be present. Usually, this process is quite fast. The inspector will ask for the passport and any other forms required (such as visas), and verify the information on the entry/landing form. Information on this card usually includes general background information, questions related to the nature of travel, contact information on where the traveler is staying, and questions on how long the traveler will be in the country. On the back of the card there may also be some spaces that will be completed by immigration officials. An example of a Landing Card for the United Kingdom is shown in Box 7-2.

Box 7-2
UK Landing Card

Customs Declaration

The next stop is the customs hall. If a traveler has checked luggage, it can be found on the designated carousel in this area. Once the luggage is collected, the traveler then moves on to the declaration area. Here, the customs official(s) will ask for the customs declaration form. Officials may also ask to see any items that have been declared. To ensure that the customs process goes well, a traveler should make sure that the form is legible and accurately filled out. A traveler should also have receipts for all their purchases readily available if a customs official should have any questions regarding the value of some items.

The customs declaration process may vary from country to country. For example, European Union citizens who have nothing to declare when returning back to an EU country can take the "Green Lane," which is considered an express lane. However, in this area, there will be Customs Officers who may conduct spot inspections, which may be verbal or a complete review of all items being brought into the country. Non-EU citizens will go through the "Red Lane," where they will be required to submit their declaration form to customs officials and be subjected to a verbal and/or complete inspection of their luggage.

Of utmost importance regarding customs is that the traveler needs to know what they can and cannot bring into the country. For example, in one country certain agricultural products may be banned. In another country, certain amounts of money (i.e., carrying financial instruments with values over $10,000) must be declared, or the total value of merchandise brought in (items that will remain in the country – not the clothing in luggage, etc.) must be declared. If the goods should exceed a certain value, the traveler will then have to pay a tax or duty on these items. A quick review of the country's custom's web page is advised, so a traveler knows what (as well as the quantities) items can be brought into the country.

A traveler should also be aware of the fact that prohibited items can be seized and not returned. Any misrepresentation of the value or the contents of items brought into the country could also lead to arrest and/or a denial to enter the country.

FLIGHT CANCELLATIONS

Flight cancellations are unfortunately part of the travel experience. Cancellations can occur for a variety of reasons including "Acts of God," and Managerial/Administrative issues on the part of the airlines itself. Regardless of the reason why the flight is cancelled, there are some things a traveler can do to ensure their safety in such situations.

Preliminary Issues

As pointed out earlier in this chapter, always check the flight status prior to leaving for the airport. This can be readily accomplished by checking the airline's web page, calling the airline, or even checking with the airport itself to see if there are any issues that could lead to cancellations, such as poor weather. A traveler should also monitor the weather forecast and conditions for the day before travel as well as the day of departure. In some instances, where severe weather is quite certain, airlines may begin canceling flights or even divert flights to other locations.

Know the Options that Exist

It is also important for the traveler to know in advance what options the traveler has with their airline tickets in the context of a flight cancellation. For example, some airlines have policies that offer a traveler: 1) a full or partial refund; 2) the option to change tickets without penalties; 3) flexible changes up to a certain period of time prior to travel; and 4) the ability to change tickets completely, purchasing a ticket even for a different destination. In order to see what options exist, check the airlines "contract of carriage," travel agents, and airlines representatives prior to booking.

Other Tips

- A traveler should also consider looking up the perform-ance reports for delays and cancellations based on the air-line and the airport in order to get a better understanding of the probability of delay or cancellation.
- Travelers can also sign up with airlines for automated voice or text message. That is, when a flight is cancelled or delayed, an automated voice or text message will alert the flyer of the situation.

If a Cancellation is Suspect

There are several "clues" to indicate that a flight may be delayed or cancelled. They include the following:

- No aircraft at the assigned gate 30 minutes prior to departure
- No airline booking agents at the gate
- There is poor weather at the specific airport or even at other airports
- There are other flights delayed or cancelled. Be sure to check both the departure and arrival screens at the airport. If flights are not operating on time, this may be a clue that there is poor weather, etc. somewhere else that will disrupt air traffic. Checking the arrival board will also provide some idea if there will be enough aircraft available for everyone to fly to their destination.
- Check to see if there are large numbers of flyers stranded at the airport. If other flights are delayed or cancelled, most likely your flight will be delayed or cancelled, too.

A traveler should also be prepared for cancellations. For example, they should move to the vicinity of the ticket counter so they can be the first in line (or at least toward the front). Once an announcement is made, travelers will immediately flock to the ticket counter line.

If a Cancellation Occurs

If a cancellation occurs, speed is essential. The first thing a traveler should do is to get in line at the ticket counter at the airport to seek the assistance of airline personnel. While this is most likely the worst thing to do because it is the slowest way to re-book, etc., do it anyway; airline personnel can provide some assistance. While in line, however, a traveler should engage in the following activities (or assign a companion to do the following who is not in line):

- Consider booking another flight. Do this using the 1-800 reservation number or do it on-line. This will most likely be a lot faster than waiting in line at the airport. Be sure to have the 1-800 reservation number for the airline(s) for situations of this nature. Even if a flyer is successful in booking the flight online or over the phone, still stay in line. That way, the airline's personnel will be able to print the boarding pass and ticket.

> **Travel Tip**
>
> If a cell phone is brought along on the trip, have 1-800 and local numbers for hotels, etc. pre-programmed into it – Speed is the key in these cases.

- Reserve a hotel room. If a cancellation is suspected, reserve a hotel room immediately in order to prevent from being stranded and sleeping in the airport terminal. Be sure to have the local and 1-800 numbers readily available so a call can be made fast – local hotels will fill up fast. Use the direct local number first because in many cases hotels have "set aside" rooms that are already reserved for walk-up customers (the 1-800 center may report the hotel as full even though it really isn't). Of course, booking the hotel through the internet is another option. Also, keep in mind that airlines are not responsible for providing hotel accommodations or compensating travelers for weather-related events. Even if the reservation is made and it is later determined that the room is not needed, most hotel chains allow for cancellations before a certain time without any penalty (be sure to check cancellation policies when booking).

- Consider renting a vehicle, if it is appropriate. As is the case with flights and hotels, have the 1-800 and local numbers for car rental agencies readily available for such occasions. Otherwise, try booking a vehicle on-line.

The Airline's Response to Cancellations

If the above recommendations are followed, the impact of the flight cancellation will be mitigated in the context of safety and security. How an airline will deal with a cancellation depends upon the situation. Generally, they can be divided into "Acts of God" and Management issues.

"Acts of God"

"Acts of God" are those issues that are beyond the scope or control of the airlines. Usually weather is the best example, followed by aviation system delays. In these situations, airlines are limited in their responsibilities to the traveler. They are exempt from being required to compensate passengers for expenses related to lodging, food, and transportation. In rare occasions, however, an airline may make some accommodations for the stranded traveler. However, do not expect anything for the airline in these situations except an apology from them for the inconvenience.

Administrative/Managerial Issues (i.e., Within our Control)

In the case of administrative or managerial issues, the airline has a greater responsibility to the traveler.

- **Overbooking** – in the case of overbooking, U.S. law requires that the airline compensate the flyer who is involuntarily bumped. Usually, this is in the form of a voucher for use in a future flight. Airlines may also offer accommodations, free phone use, and reimbursement for transport and food if the re-booked flight will not leave on the same day. In a lot of cases, the airline announces in advance that the flight is overbooked, where they ask for volunteers who will be reimbursed for "the bump."

- **Cancellation in the Control of the Airlines** – These issues include mechanical delays, no aircraft, no flight crew, etc. In these situations when the airline cannot get the traveler to the destination on the expected arrival day, they will usually provide overnight accommodations, vouchers for food and transport and a voucher for future travel.

Travelers should also keep in mind that with "Within our Control" cancellations, a traveler can usually ask for a refund. Depending upon the airline's policy and contract, a traveler may also request that the airline transfer the flyer to another airline that can get them there in a timely manner. This is known as "Rule 240" in the airline industry.

A flyer may have to be a bit forceful, but polite, to receive various types of compensation (i.e., lodging, vouchers). Airlines at times have been found to be not too generous in giving away such perks for cancellations. In those cases where a traveler feels that they are not receiving the appropriate level of service or compensation for the cancellation/delay, ask the airline attendant for a "Corporate Number." Contacting the corporate headquarters (or the threat thereof at times) could yield some positive results for the traveler.

CONCLUSION

A traveler can be exposed to a variety of dangers and security issues once within the confines of the airport. To reduce the risk, the traveler must first prepare for their airport experience before leaving for the airport. Next, the traveler must recognize that there are some safety and security-related issues outside the airport terminal, especially in parking areas, when walking, and when using shuttles. Once inside the terminal, meanwhile, the traveler needs to be aware of their surroundings at all times, and proceed through the airline check-in in a timely manner and then on to the security checkpoints. In order to expedite the screening process, the traveler needs to be prepared to verify their identity with their boarding pass. They also need to be prepared for a search of themselves and their property. Once through the security screening and at the "gate side," safety cannot be discounted. Travelers still need to be diligent and be on the lookout for any suspicious activities. The last airport experience will include the customs and immigration checkpoints. Here, the traveler will be required to submit to a series of questions, where, upon completion, they can begin their overseas journey. One of the last issues reviewed in this chapter addressed flight delays and cancellations. As pointed out, a traveler should be prepared for such events where speed in response to the situation is paramount.

8
AIRCRAFT SAFETY

Already, this book covered some of the major issues related to airport safety and security. The next logical step is safety on-board the aircraft. While this chapter deals primarily with aircraft security, many of the safety and security principles reviewed in this chapter can also be applied to other forms of transportation, including buses, trains, and cruise ships.

There are certain things a traveler can do to ensure that their flight is as safe as possible. One of the key points to remember on an airplane is the simple fact that it is a public place. An airplane is simply a "bus with wings," where the traveler has rented a small space that is accessible to all of the passengers, to some degree. Airplane passengers, meanwhile, are a microcosm of society where there may be some individuals who may be motivated to commit a variety of activities ranging from theft to sexual harassment. If the reader should question the validity of these concerns, consider the point that some airlines have toyed with the idea of installing video surveillance cameras in their aircraft cabins to observe the behaviors of their passengers!

PLANNING AHEAD FOR ISSUES

Like all other aspects of safe travel, the traveler must plan ahead for safety-related issues while on an aircraft. Some points to consider include:

- When booking the flight, always reserve a seat near emergency exits. This will allow a faster exit from the aircraft if an emergency should arise. Usually, these rows have more leg room too. If emergency exit row seats are already taken, the next best option is to request aisle seats near the emergency exits.

- Center seats should be avoided. Center seats are very difficult to get out of in times of emergency. Consider for example, any de-boarding procedure. Immediately after

107

the "fasten seat belt" sign turns off, everyone jumps up, blocking those in the non-aisle seats from getting up and out.

- Planning also means wearing the appropriate footwear and clothing. Consider, for example, footwear. It would be very difficult to rapidly evacuate a plane wearing high heels or sandals. The same applies to clothing. Clothing must be suitable for evacuation (i.e., using the evacuation slide). For example, some experts recommend not wearing any synthetic materials because they could melt under high temperatures.

- As pointed out in the Getting Ready Chapter, make sure that dependable/responsible friends and/or family members have been entrusted with the flight itinerary, if an emergency should arise.

The Boarding Stage

Issues related to pre-boarding have already been covered in the chapter on Airport Security. In the boarding stage, some of these same principles must be observed because the traveler could become a victim of pickpocketing or theft. The traveler must also be concerned about their own safety in the context of trip-and-fall related accidents while boarding. In the majority of situations, sky bridges often have a relatively steep incline to the aircraft, which could cause the traveler to stumble and perhaps fall. If not a sky bridge, the traveler will have to board the aircraft by using a steep stairway.

Once on the Aircraft

Once on the aircraft, a traveler must still continue to be diligent on protecting themselves and their property against theft. A traveler must also be wary of trip-and-fall related incidents. All too often the authors have seen passengers trip over the feet or baggage in the aisle, causing them to fall against a seat or another person. While these injuries may be considered to be minor, they could easily impact the trip's outcome.

The traveler also needs to mentally and physically prepare themselves for emergency situations. For example, the traveler needs to visually scan and review the entire cabin areas and consider the following points:

- Locate and count the rows to the nearest emergency exits and create an escape plan.

  One method that works well is to physically count how many rows there are to the emergency exit and mentally repeat this number until it is memorized. This is a very important activity. If a cabin should fill with smoke, it will be very difficult to see the exits. The traveler will most likely have to feel their way out. Planning on how to get to the exits is important. For example, the traveler may consider using the aisle or crawling over the seats to get out. Having a "Plan B" evacuation plan – because the original escape route is blocked – is also important. That is, make sure there is a secondary escape plan.

- Where is the closest emergency exit? Without planning, passengers may head for the exit that was used to board the plane, usually in the front of the first class cabin, which may not be the first emergency exit on the plane. Instead, the closest emergency exit may be behind the traveler. Therefore, it is important to be familiar with ALL exits.

- Mentally plan the escape. Ask: How am I going to get out of here in an emergency? When mentally planning the escape, also consider what passengers will be a barrier to the evacuation. It is also important to identify any physical barriers that exist. They could include luggage.

Carry-On Items

Carry-on items are also a safety and security concern when on-board aircraft.

- Avoid placing heavy objects in the overhead bins. These storage areas should be for jackets, soft bags, etc. There have been incidents of these bins popping open during an emergency and/or turbulence, where passengers have been injured because of heavy items falling on them. Heavy carry-ons should be stowed under the seat.

- If a traveler is sitting in an aisle seat, they should be aware that people stowing or retrieving items from an overhead bin could accidentally drop these items on them. In almost every flight that the authors have been on, passengers have been seen getting struck by heavy objects.

- Use the overhead stowage across the aisle, from the assigned seat, so property is in view at all times.

- Consider using a plastic tie strap to secure zippers on carry-on luggage, especially if it is stowed in an overhead bin. This will prevent the unauthorized access of the bag.

- Always remember that aircraft are public places and that anyone can be a victim of theft!

Once Seated

There are also safety and security issues once the traveler is seated and the flight is preparing for departure.

- Travelers should immediately belt themselves in as soon as they are seated. The traveler should also fasten and unfasten the seat belt a couple of times and watch to see how it works. There are several kinds of belts, and in an emergency, the traveler does not have the time to waste fumbling with a buckle.

- A traveler should make sure that the belt buckle can be operated through touch/feel alone.

- Review the safety information card. Even if a person has traveled many times beforehand, emergency exits are often in different locations in the plane, depending upon the type of aircraft.

- Pay close attention to the safety briefing provided by the flight personnel. Their primary responsibility is the safety of passengers – not passing out peanuts and beverages. In some cases, flight attendants may appear to be complacent on these safety briefings because they have done them so many times. Regardless of the cavalier attitude of flight personnel, treat these as serious briefings.

- Know how the emergency exits work. This is particularly important if the traveler is positioned at an emergency exit: others are depending upon them to get the emergency exits open.

- Know how each emergency device works and where they are located (life preservers, oxygen masks, fire extinguishers).

- When sitting in an emergency exit, the traveler must be physically capable, aware of their responsibilities, and willing to perform all emergency functions. If not, the traveler should request another seat.

- If there's anything that a traveler does not understand about safety, they should ask the flight attendants for help.

Keep the seat belt fastened at all times

A traveler should consider the airplane to be their vehicle and ask him or herself: would I take the seat belt off in my car while it was operating?

As is the case in an automobile, the seat belt should be on throughout the flight. The belt should be snug and placed across the hips. Having the seat belt on at all times will protect a flyer from the consequences of turbulence and other maneuvers made by the aircraft.

One of the primary reasons for keeping the seatbelt on is turbulence. Turbulence happens quite often and it is not predictable. In fact, in-flight turbulence is the leading cause of injuries to airline passengers and flight attendants. According to the FAA, approximately 58 passengers per year in the United States are injured from turbulence.

The best protection from a turbulence-based incident is to stay in the seat, be belted in, and limit moving around the cabin. For example, on one flight that one of the authors was on, the aircraft had to engage in an evasive maneuver. This occurred on the final approach where a lot of passengers disregarded the "fasten seat belt sign" and were busy getting their items from the overhead bins. When the aircraft engaged in an evasive maneuver (it was too close to another approaching aircraft) some of the passengers were literally thrown off their feet and collided with others.

Guarding Valuables While on the Aircraft

Just like in the airport, the protection of one's property is also important while on the aircraft. Some points to consider include the following:

- Do not stow valuables in the seat pocket. All too often passengers stow their wallets, passports, and other valuables in the seat pocket in front of them. These items or their contents can be stolen if the traveler should fall asleep or leave their seat. In addition, the traveler may forget these items when disembarking. If a traveler needs to empty their pockets for comfort, they should always transfer these items to another secure pocket, such as a buttoned shirt pocket.

- When getting up to walk around or to use the restroom, do not leave any valuables unattended.

- Avoid engaging in conversations that reveal social status, destination, etc. Information of this nature may serve to target the flyer to be a victim of a crime later on. Instead, a traveler should sit down, open a book and avoid casual conversations. If someone should try to engage the passenger in conversation, it is important to be vague on certain details.

- Avoid using English – this also lets other individuals know the traveler's nationality.

- Be sure not to leave any valuables in the restroom. There are many cases of passengers leaving their watches, rings, wallets, purses, and passports in airplane restrooms.

De-Boarding

Some of the same issues related to safely boarding the plane also apply in the de-boarding stage. There are however, additional concerns. One of the most important de-boarding safety issues is to remain seated until the plane comes to a complete stop and the flight crew states that it is safe to remove the seat belt. Aircraft often make sudden stops when they are taxiing to the airport gate, which is why it's important to stay seated with the seat belt fastened. Most likely, flyers will have to wait and stand for a long period of time anyway, until the door is opened and passengers begin to file out. So, it makes no sense to be hasty.

Safety on the Tarmac

In some situations and in some countries, travelers will not de-board the aircraft using the sky bridge. Instead, they will leave the plane by walking down a stairway and then walk across the runway tarmac. The traveler, for example, may have to walk across a tarmac to get to a bus that takes them to the terminal. Or, in other situations, they may have to walk a short distance to the terminal. When disembarking an aircraft by way of the tarmac be aware of:

- Jet blasts from aircraft turning or moving on the tarmac. Flying debris could cause eye injuries.

- Propellers – know where they are in relation to the door. Even though engines should not be running, always exercise caution. Propellers can also rotate unexpectedly.

- Rungs on the stairway can be slippery. They are often steep, too. Be wary of slip-and-fall related accidents and other passengers who may lose their balance. Therefore, always use the handrail as an added protection to prevent a fall.

- Service vehicles on the tarmac – they may not be attentive to passengers.

Emergency Evacuations

Flying is perhaps the safest mode of transportation for travelers. Nevertheless, there have been some aircraft accidents, requiring the evacuation of the passengers and crew. According to information from the FAA, after an air accident the National Transportation Safety Board (NTSB) always talks to survivors to try to learn how or why they were able to make it through safely. They've discovered that, as a rule, it does help to be prepared. Therefore, avoiding serious injury or surviving an air accident isn't just a matter of luck: it's also a matter of being informed and thinking ahead.

In any emergency evacuation, the key word to remember is **speed**. The traveler needs to get out of and away from the airplane as fast as possible. Other points to consider include:

- Remember the "10-minute rule." For 10 minutes after take-off and 10 minutes before landing, be alert. The majority of aircraft emergencies occur during takeoffs and landings.

- Brace for the impact based on the information given in the safety briefing.

- Stay calm. Panic is often the #1 problem in an emergency situation.

- Keep others calm. Your life may depend upon the assistance and cooperation of others.

- Leave all possessions behind. Adopt the rule that whatever is taken on the journey is disposable – no possession is worth a human life. Attempting to take any possessions along could slow down an evacuation and block aisles and emergency exits.

- Listen to the crew members and do what they say. The cabin crew's most important job is to help passengers leave safely.

- Before opening any emergency exit and leaving the aircraft, look outside. If flames are present, don't open it, or the flames may spread into the cabin. Instead, resort to "Plan B" – the alternate escape route.

- Travelers should always keep their shoes on.
- Stay low and breathe slowly, smoke and fumes rise.
- Place a cloth over the nose and mouth – people generally do not burn to death. They die from the inhalation of smoke, heat and fumes.
- Follow the floor lighting to the emergency exits and be prepared to "feel one's way out."
- If the aisle becomes clogged with people, consider crawling over the seats to get to the emergency exit.
- Jump feet first onto the evacuation slide (if one is available). Don't sit down to slide: it will slow down the evacuation of others. A traveler should also place their arms across their chest, elbows in, legs and feet together, and jump, preparing for the impact of the slide.
- If no slide or escape ladder exists, do not hesitate to jump out of the aircraft.
- Exit the aircraft and clear the area fast. Spilled fuel and other flammable items could ignite.
- Remain alert for emergency vehicles.
- NEVER RETURN TO THE AIRCRAFT.

SURVIVING A HIJACKING

Even rarer than an emergency evacuation are hijackings. Even though they are a rare event, this issue nevertheless needs to be addressed. Below are a few pointers to consider:[12]

- Travel with an airline that does not have a lot of political enemies. Many airlines are owned, controlled, or subsidized by countries that are targeted by terrorist organizations. Historically, these airlines have been a target for terrorists and the aircraft and the hijacking has been used to demonstrate the weakness of that particular country.

---

[12] Kingshott, B.F. (2005). Understanding and surviving an aircraft highjack. *Journal of police crisis negotiation, 5*(1), 57-68.

- Don't wear military-styled clothing. A traveler wearing this style of clothing could be mistaken for military personnel, which could increase the risk of injury, etc.

- If the plane is hijacked, do not draw attention to oneself. Be quiet, avoid eye contact with the assailants, and follow their instructions. The best way to survive a situation is to not draw attention to oneself.

- Consider sitting in or moving to a non-aisle seat. Aisle seats may draw the attention of hijackers, simply because the passenger is easier to see and extract from their seat, if necessary. This point, however, must be balanced with the need for emergency evacuations.

- Book the flight in tourist/economy class. Tourist/economy class is considered "neutral seating." If terrorists want to target individuals, they may target those in first class because of their perceived increased wealth, importance, and social status.

- Don't wear religious and political slogans when flying. The terrorist may not share the same beliefs, and target the wearer for those reasons.

- Travel in loose, comfortable clothing. A traveler may be there for a while.

- Don't try to reason or negotiate with a hijacker. They may consider this to be a provocation and strike back.

- Be aware that the aircraft may have an Air Marshal aboard who may not act immediately. If and when they do act, stay out of this person's way and don't make the Marshal think that you are a hijacker.

- Be alert for rescue operations.

- If the plane is boarded by rescue personnel, stay seated in order to prevent being injured, impeding the rescue, and/or being mistaken as a hijacker.

- If it looks like death is imminent, fight back.

AIR RAGE

Air rage is the term commonly used to describe a variety of disruptive behaviors committed by passengers. These behaviors may include physical assaults against passengers and flight attendants, vandalism, defecating on trays (believe it or not) and other forms of "passenger rebellion" ranging from verbal abuse, threats, and intimidation. Estimates of the nature and extent of these incidents vary. However, they are relatively common (about 5,000 per year) and they have caused some flights to turn around and/or conduct emergency landings. Air rage is not a new issue. It has always existed, but now airlines have taken steps to protect employees and passengers from this problem.

How to Avoid Air Rage

The research points out that anyone is susceptible to air rage. It is caused by a variety of environmental and personal conditions. Some factors that could lead to air rage include the lack of sleep, lost luggage, the lack of adequate levels of oxygen in the aircraft cabin, nicotine withdrawal, excessive use of alcohol, delayed flights, the fear of flying, and cramped conditions. Combining these conditions with a preexisting psychological issue, an air rage incident could easily occur while flying. In order to avoid feelings of helplessness, anxiety, and even rage, some ways a traveler could avoid becoming an "air rager" are listed below:

- Accept the fact that delays, cramped conditions and rude airline employees are part of the adventure.
- Have a realistic understanding of air travel. If a seat is booked in economy class, the traveler should have a realistic understanding on what will be encountered (i.e., cramped conditions, loud people, crying babies, mediocre service).
- Get enough sleep the night before departure.
- Avoid drinking alcohol before boarding and while flying (a large portion of air rage incidents are alcohol-related).
- If a traveler suffers from anxiety, prescription medications from a physician may be a wise choice.

- Make sure that the travel itinerary is devoid of as many stressors as possible (i.e., allow enough time between connecting flights).

There are some ways to control and perhaps prevent an air rage incident:

- If someone is drinking too much or acting in an abnormal manner, bring it to the attention of the flight crew immediately.
- Avoid engaging in any provocative discussions with others that may make them aggressive.
- If a friend or family member is displaying signs of stress or anxiety, engage in some calming activities. Try to get their mind off the stressor(s).
- Do not verbally or physically engage a stranger who is in a state of air rage. This rage may be displaced against the innocent traveler who is trying to calm the situation.
- If an air rage incident occurs on the airplane, a traveler should try to place as much distance between themselves and the aggressor in order to avoid any physical injuries.
- Be polite and courteous towards others. In some cases, air rage is contagious and a traveler's actions could add fuel to the fire.

CONCLUSION

Airline passengers often take safety and security for granted when they board an airplane. For example, they may ignore the crew's pre-flight announcements by reaching for a magazine instead of the safety card, and not physically and mentally plan for an evacuation. They may also leave personal property unattended or exposed to theft. As this chapter has pointed out, aircraft safety is the responsibility of the traveler, where a variety of issues need to be considered at the pre-boarding, boarding, in-flight, and de-boarding processes. Some of these issues include guarding valuables, staying belted at all times, and being prepared for emergency evacuations. While uncommon, the traveler should also be aware and be prepared for hijackings and air rage incidents.

BLENDING IN

This chapter will review some of the basics to "blend in" so a person can be an inconspicuous traveler. Perhaps the best way to look at this topic is to consider the fact that a traveler should look as sterile or as neutral as possible in a crowd, based on their dress and demeanor. In fact, a traveler should be sterile in appearance to the point where the would-be offender has difficulty in determining if the traveler is a native to that region or country. In order to achieve this goal, a traveler must be as invisible as possible in the crowd, keeping as low a profile as possible, based on their clothing/appearance, personal accessories, and demeanor.

BEGINNING THOUGHTS ON BLENDING IN

Before getting into the specific components of this chapter, it is important to reflect upon those attributes that could make a traveler stand out in a crowd. Listed below are some points for consideration:

- *Height* – Is the traveler taller or shorter than the majority of individuals in the host country?

- *Weight* – Is the traveler heavier or lighter than the general population? In some nations, weight signifies wealth (only the rich have the ability to buy enough food).

- *Body Piercings* – May be a trend for those from western nations.

- *Earrings* – Signify wealth, and may be prohibited for religious reasons in some countries or regions of the world.

- *Hair Style* – Is the traveler's hair long or short, shaved, conservative, or contemporary? This may make a difference if it is significantly contradictory from the existing styles in the host country.

- *Hair Color* – Is it a natural color or is it dyed? Even if it is natural, a traveler may draw some attention. For example, one of the author's hair color is blonde. In southern Germany and Austria many individuals asked him if he was Norwegian. In the Caribbean, meanwhile, that has predominately dark-haired individuals, he has also been asked about his nationality.

- *Tattoos* – May be a trend for those individuals from western nations.

- *Nail Polish* – Can reveal socio-economic status/wealth. Nail polish and manicured fingernails may also denote individuals who do not perform manual labor.

- *Makeup* – In some countries only the wealthy can afford cosmetics.

- *Complexion* – Being fair-skinned (or the opposite thereof) in some countries may make a traveler stand out.

- *Degree of Attractiveness* – Is the traveler so attractive (or the opposite) that they stand out in the crowd?

- *Facial Hair* – (or lack thereof) – Some cultures require facial hair; in others, it may not be a current style or trend.

- *Personal Grooming* – Looking too neat or unkempt may make the traveler stand out.

- *Age* – May be relative in the context of the setting a traveler is in.

- *Race* – If a traveler's race is not the dominant one in the host country, this may draw some attention to them.

- *Gender* – Some countries may be more restrictive on the activities of women, for example.

- *Physical Handicaps* – Some physical handicaps, by their vary nature, may draw unwanted attention.

While some of these points may appear to be trivial in nature, they may all serve to notify the would-be offender that the traveler is a foreigner and perhaps has some degree of wealth (comparable to theirs). In some cases, travelers cannot readily control some of these variables (i.e., natural hair color, height, age, and weight). In other cases, meanwhile, subtle changes in how the traveler dresses and behaves (which will be covered later) could serve to make them less of a target.

CLOTHING AND APPEARANCE

Contemporary society is quite fashion-conscious at times. The type and quality of clothing often reveals a person's social status, nationality, and profession. In the context of traveling, however, fashion should not be a primary issue. Selecting clothing for travel should be considered to be an exercise in function and utility first, followed then by *some* fashion. Therefore, it is the traveler's responsibility to look as inconspicuous as possible. The traveler needs to find that balance in their clothing, making sure that they are not over- or under-dressed for the occasion. Listed below are some issues to consider when selecting the proper clothing in order to blend in.

Wear Clothing the Locals Wear

In order to make sure that a traveler does not stand out, it is important to always consider the question: "What do the locals wear?" Determining what the locals wear can be quite easy in today's world. A traveler can simply go on the Internet to see what some of the fashions are for that particular country or region of the world. A traveler can also talk to individuals that have journeyed to those areas to get some tips on what type of clothing is appropriate to blend in, balanced with the environment.

While it is recommended to wear the same type of dress that the locals wear, it is also advised not to go completely native. In some cases, a traveler may go overboard where they may actually wear the wrong clothes, which would draw more attention to them. For example, one of the authors' co-workers recalled an incident on a trip to Africa where some of the men on the trip bought native clothing to wear. It turned out that the men purchased and subsequently wore female clothes! This, of course, drew a lot of laughter and unwanted attention from the local population. In another instance, an acquaintance of the authors, while

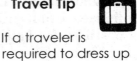

Travel Tip

If a traveler is required to dress up for an occasion, consider changing clothes at that specific location where the event will be. Wear normal clothing to and from the event to remain anonymous.

traveling to Pakistan (under armed security), wore a floral colored shirt, based on the photos that he showed the authors. He was a colorful, visible target relative to the security personnel dressed in khaki –there was no issue at all in identifying him as an outsider!

A traveler should also keep in mind that in some situations, native dress is now reserved for the poor and elderly who cannot afford western styles, or choose to adhere to traditional forms of dress. Everyone else may be dressed in western-styled clothing. Some cultures (or individuals within those cultures) could also be offended if a westerner was wearing their native clothing. Consider, for example, a male westerner in a Middle Eastern country wearing a headdress. This may have both religious and social ramifications that could lead to a confrontation. For example, the color of one's headdress in the Middle East is often affiliated with a tribal association. The same issue applies to wearing a turban in the Indian subcontinent. Turbans are worn by Sikhs as part of their religion. Wearing a turban, therefore, could be considered offensive, based on religious principles. If an ethnic headdress is deemed to be appropriate clothing, it is therefore best to seek the advice of a trusted, local associate.

When selecting the appropriate clothing, that country or region's religion should also be considered; dress and religion are often intertwined. Therefore, the traveler needs to be sensitive to cultural norms and expectations. As an example, the Islamic faith promotes modesty and has a conservative dress code for both males and females. The wisdom behind this dress code is that it minimizes sexual enticement and degradation in society as much as possible (for both men and women). Islam forbids any sex appeal and physical allurement outside of marriage. Islam also encourages sex appeal and physical attraction for both men and women within the privacy of the home, between married couples. Obeying this dress code is a form of obedience to Allah. In fact, in some Muslim countries a tank top and shorts would be considered offensive to the point that individuals could be refused admission to some tourist sites and other establishments.

Another example of the importance of clothing can be seen in the dress requirements for Muslim women. According to some

Fiqh Schools, when leaving the home, female clothing must cover the entire body from neck to toe; only the hands and face may remain visible. Other Muslim societies, meanwhile, may be less strict, requiring the female to only cover her hair and follow other requirements that may include:

- Clothing material must not be so thin that a person can see through it.
- Clothing must hang loose so that the shape / form of the body is not apparent.
- It must not resemble a man's clothing (i.e., pants, shirts).
- The design of the clothing must not resemble the clothing of the non-believing women (i.e., western styles).
- The design must not consist of bold patterns, colors, etc. which attracts attention.
- Clothing should not be worn for the sole purpose of improving one's reputation or status in society.

The dress code for men, meanwhile, calls for loose fitting clothes that are modest in appearance that do not have any resemblance to a woman's form of dress. A man must also always wear clothing from the navel to his knee. This is the absolute minimum covering required. He must never, for example, go out in public wearing a short bathing suit.

Of interest is the fact that these requirements are almost the ideal style of dress for travel. Exclusive of its religious under-pinnings, this style of dress (with the exception of head coverings and perhaps "neck to toe" coverage) is based on simplicity and not drawing attention to oneself – the key to safe travel.

In order to find and wear appropriate clothing, travelers may want to consider purchasing clothing from within the destination country. Not only could this save on the amount of luggage needed for the trip, but it could also ensure that there may be a better "fit" in the context of appearance. In fact, to save money, a traveler could shop at a thrift store in the host country. These clothes would also look used or worn and not new in appearance. When done traveling and before leaving the country, meanwhile, the traveler could be a good world citizen and simply donate the clothing to a charity, or give them away.

Another perspective on wearing the appropriate clothing is to try to dress as generic as possible. That is, a traveler should try to find a style of dress that could be worn anywhere in the world, without "standing out." While it may not be possible to dress exactly like the locals, some generic issues to consider are shown below:

Avoid Being "American"

American and western cultures at times can be readily identified. Some of the features of American culture include:

- T-shirts, especially those that have University or sports logos on them.
- Tennis or running shoes.
- Hats, especially baseball-styled hats.
- Patriotic Clothing (i.e., USA logo, American flag). Keep in mind that some clothing manufacturers may integrate the colors of the American flag into their logos.
- Buttons, pins, etc.

In other situations, a traveler needs to consider what aspects of their clothing, combined with habit or American practices, could reveal their nationality. For example, an English acquaintance of one of the authors pointed out that she could tell that the author was an American as far away as she could see him. The author asked her if it was his body language or clothing, which it was not. It was simply the wear mark of the author's wallet on the back pocket of his blue jeans. She explained that Englishmen do not carry their wallets in their back pocket. Because pickpocketing is such a problem in the United Kingdom, men carry their wallets in their front pockets. This wear mark, though trivial, was an indicator of the author's nationality.

Travelers should also avoid using brands and/or frequenting locations that are associated with the United States. People are creatures of habit and will use American products ranging from soft drinks, alcoholic beverages, and cigarettes to name just a few items. If available, a traveler may also patronize American-based restaurants, clubs, etc. These products and locations, however, may increase the probability of being identified as an American and thereby increase the traveler's exposure to a variety of threats.

Cover as Much of the Body as Possible

As pointed out earlier, some cultures (i.e., Muslim nations) do not look favorably on exposed arms, legs and hair. This means that in some countries, females may need to wear a head scarf, while males may need to wear long pants. Even if a traveler does not completely fit the cultural norms, efforts to conform to cultural expectations can go a long way with the local population.

In addition, a traveler should also keep in mind that the functional aspects of clothing are to protect the wearer from the climate and other environmental hazards. In this context, covering as much of the body as possible will protect a traveler from the effects of the sun and wind. It will also protect against disease-carrying insects and other objects that could cause small injuries and abrasions to the skin.

Don't Wear Souvenir-Related Clothing

Souvenir-related clothing and accessories readily make a person stand out as a tourist: simply go to Orlando, Florida, or Las Vegas, Nevada, and take a look at tourists on the street wearing Disney and Vegas-related hats and shirts. They are readily identifiable. College students, meanwhile can be commonly seen wearing university clothing and hats that naturally identify them as students, and when overseas, as a foreigner. In combination with other identifiers previously covered in this chapter, these items will naturally increase the traveler's exposure to risk.

Don't Advertise

As pointed out earlier in the book, the goal for safe travel is not to stand out in a crowd. In order to achieve this goal, a traveler should also avoid wearing bright colors. Neutral colors that blend in with the surrounding areas would be a better choice. In fact, a traveler should consider clothing to be a form of urban camouflage and select that clothing whose colors make them blend in and not contrast with the environment.

Do Not Dress Provocatively

In some countries, clothing is related to the sexual availability of the person. That is, the more revealing the clothing, perhaps the more sexually available this person is perceived to be. Wearing provocative clothing can therefore lead to unwanted advances and perhaps the danger of a sexually-motivated attack.

Do Not Wear Military-Styled Clothing

Military-styled clothing (hats, pants, jackets, luggage, footwear) at times may have some utility or function when traveling in the context of comfort, durability and function (i.e., lots of pockets). Military clothing, however, may make a traveler stand out and make others think that this person is a member of the armed forces. In combination with the fact that some countries may not be too receptive of U.S. foreign policy, certain individuals could be confrontational toward travelers wearing such clothing.

Wear Safety-Related Clothing

Besides color and style, a traveler should always select safety-conscious clothing. Clothes that have pockets that secure with buttons, Velcro®, or zippers will provide increased levels of protection against theft from pickpockets and/or thieves. They will also better secure the traveler's belongings from accidental loss.

Other clothes may also have hidden compartments. For example, several manufacturers market shirts and pants, and even socks that have hidden chambers. When considering the fact that the average criminal will most likely not want to spend a great deal of time searching their victim, they will go for the common areas only – pockets and the waistband for the money belt, for example, and hopefully overlook other areas of concealment.

PERSONAL ACCESSORIES

Besides clothing-related issues, in other situations, a traveler can often be readily identified through their accessories. Therefore, the traveler should always limit the amount of personal accessories that are carried. Some of these accessories are listed below:

- *Sunglasses* – While sunglasses are common, avoid expensive name brand styles.

- *Backpacks* – Backpacks signify a lifestyle (i.e., backpacker, college student). Criminals can also easily access a traveler's backpack. In some cases, for example, a traveler may not be able to feel and see their pack being unzipped if it is on their back. If a traveler should decide to travel with a backpack, they should avoid using bright colored, new, and/or expensive-looking backpacks. Those backpacks that are made in the U.S.A., and have logos that readily identify them as such, should also be avoided.

- *Fanny Packs* – While fanny packs (also referred to as waist packs in Europe) may offer a means to carry personal items and offer a degree of concealment, they may also signify that the owner is a tourist. Additionally, these may not be the safest and most secure method to carry personal items and valuables, since they could be easily taken away from a traveler.

- *Cameras* – Cameras send a huge signal that a tourist is present! In fact, one could argue that the camera is an icon of the tourist. Therefore, cameras and other photographic items must be carried and used inconspicuously. A traveler should always keep their camera concealed when it is not in use, and not leave it hanging around their neck, for example. Besides the increased probability of theft, placing the strap around the neck could cause neck-related injuries if it were forcefully taken away. Carrying the camera in a case secured to the belt, or if small enough, in a pocket, would be a safer alternative.

- *Electronics* – These devices (such as I Pods®) are often a hot commodity for criminals. To avoid any issues with items of this nature being stolen, a traveler may consider changing their lifestyle while traveling and simply not carry these items. If these items are carried, meanwhile, they should only be used in private locales. Using them in public places should be avoided at all times. Travelers should also keep in mind that the use of such devices also prevents them from hearing approaching threats, including motor vehicles.

- *Purses (aka: Handbags and/or Shoulder bags)* – Purses can also suggest a person's socio-economic status and nationality. Therefore, it is recommended that travelers avoid carrying expensive purses. In fact, if a traveler can avoid carrying a purse at all, this would be the best option. In those cases where a purse is carried, it should be kept concealed, under the arm, between the carrier and a trusted friend (to serve as a protective barrier). As was the case with cameras, the traveler should never have the strap over or around their neck. Also, when carrying the purse, it should be kept away from the street side. Carrying the purse on the street side makes it more accessible to thieves – some of which have been known to approach unsuspecting tourists from scooters and stripping them of their property.

- *Maps/Brochures, etc.* – A visible map or brochure in a traveler's back pocket or standing on a street corner reading a map readily advertises to all observers that a tourist is present. In order to avoid these situations, a traveler needs to keep all tourist-related materials concealed. A traveler should plan their day in advance, and study the map in the privacy of their room. If the traveler needs to write down directions, etc., this should be done on a plain piece of paper or in a notebook – not on a map. In those cases where a map does need to be referenced, the traveler should always find a private location, such as a restroom, where it can be studied. This point will be further reviewed in the Street Smarts Chapter.

- *Avoid Wearing Jewelry* – While traveling, jewelry should be considered to be like fishing lures. Just like a fish that will strike at bright shiny objects, the common street criminal will be attracted to the traveler's jewelry (earrings, piercings, watches, etc.). A traveler should consider leaving all of their jewelry at home. If the decision is made to bring jewelry, it should be properly secured in carry-on luggage (not stowed luggage that is prone to theft), in a safe, or in another secure position where the traveler is staying. This jewelry should only be worn for special occasions. Even though some safe travel experts recommend wearing less expensive costume jewelry when traveling, wearing any type of jewelry increases risk: a would-be criminal will most likely be unable to differentiate real from imitation precious metals and gems. All they see is jewelry that they may interpret as valuable. In the context of watches, meanwhile, a traveler should consider purchasing an inexpensive watch when arriving at the host country.

FOOTWEAR

Consider the following example about footwear: In the 1950s one of the authors' mother traveled to Europe. While traveling she wore saddle shoes – a hot American trend at that time. Because of her shoes, people identified her as an American and approached her to see her shoes. While this example is over 50 years old, the same issue applies today. Shoes are often a sign of wealth or social status. If not a sign of wealth or social status, they could easily be a sign of one's nationality. Therefore, the following points should be considered when selecting footwear for a trip.

- Make sure the shoes are not trendy or readily identifiable as American. Consider purchasing comfortable walking shoes that have no logos on them, that are also neutral in appearance (i.e., don't wear orange running shoes).
- Do not wear military styled boots – this may make individuals think that the traveler is a militant or a member of the military.

- Never wear high heels – this type footwear is not designed for long periods of wear. They may be difficult to run in, too.

- Avoid wearing sandals, etc. – Always consider foot-related injuries. There are many dangers (i.e., uneven walkways, broken glass, metal shards) that could lead to a trip-ruining foot injury. Sanitation may be also an issue. Many sidewalks and streets in foreign nations can be covered with litter, sewage, and even human waste.

CONDUCT IN PUBLIC

The traveler must also consider how their demeanor and conduct in public can make them stand out in a crowd. In the context of travel, demeanor, like clothing, should be neutral in nature. Some specific points to consider include:

- *Personality* – If the traveler is naturally a gregarious and talkative person, they may need to adjust their personality while traveling and be less forthcoming in their actions.

- *Be Aware of One's Actions/Behaviors* – In some cases, inadvertent or normal behaviors in the United States could be quite offensive in other countries and draw unwanted attention (specific examples can be found in the Culture Chapter).

- *Loud Talkers* – Talking loudly draws attention, where those individuals within earshot will also find out that the traveler is speaking English or has a dialect when speaking the host country's native tongue.

- *Laughter* – At a minimum, it could also draw unwanted attention. It may be contrary to social norms in that country, too.

- *Body Language* – The majority of the way that people communicate is through non-verbal forms of communi-cation. This is known as body language. In the context of safe travel, a person must be cognizant that their subtle actions could be provocative in nature. To prevent these non-verbal cues from revealing one's status, always "study the crowd" and gain an understanding of how gestures, posture, and body positioning all come into play. The traveler should gain an understanding of these practices, compare them to their own, and adjust accordingly.

The traveler must always consider the fact that others may interpret or judge individuals through the actions of others. If others in the travel group are loud, etc., it is important to correct their actions or behaviors and let them know they are making themselves and others stand out in the crowd. At the same time, the old adage that there is safety in numbers is relatively true. A traveler should keep in mind, however, that the larger the group, perhaps the more attention that group is drawing to itself. Consider one's own experiences where large groups have been observed. Often these groups are readily identifiable as tourists or outsiders. To deal with this issue, consider traveling in smaller groups to be less conspicuous.

LANGUAGE

The use of the host country's native language is also very important in order to blend in. In this context, there is often the temptation to try to blend in better by using the local vernacular and jargon. This should be used with some caution. In some cases, a person may use the wrong vernacular, causing confusion. In other cases, local citizens could actually consider it to be intrusive upon their culture and thereby offensive in nature. Therefore, caution should be exercised, and it would most likely be better suited for the traveler to use his or her own vocabulary skill sets when communicating. The traveler should also avoid using slang (informal usage of vocabulary – "Hit the Road," 'Walk in my Shoes") as this could cause confusion. Jargon or words peculiar to a particular profession or trade (such as medical jargon) may also cause confusion and should therefore be avoided when at all possible.

Electronic Language Translators

Handheld electronic dictionaries and translators have recently emerged as a modern and perhaps fashionable solution to language barriers. The cost of these items range from under $50 to over $500. Many of the more advanced, and expensive devices are based on advanced text-to-speech and speech recognition technologies and have the added functions of a business organizer. Many also include a personal travel organizer, an address book, currency converters and time zone information.

There are some disadvantages to these handheld electronic translators. First, they clearly indicate to all within sight (and perhaps sound) that a non-native speaker is present. These items are also valuable. Therefore, a traveler could be more vulnerable to becoming a victim of a crime by using one of these items in public. In addition, these items require batteries or a charging device, increasing the number of items that need to be brought along for the trip.

CONCLUSION

It is crucial that a traveler "blends into" the existing cultural environment of the host country. The blending in process first begins with a self-assessment on what personal attributes the traveler may possess that makes them significantly different from attributes in the host country. Blending in also involves clothing. In this context the traveler should try to "dress neutral," avoiding American forms of dress, while covering as much of the body as possible. Clothing that has logos or that may appear to be provocative or military in nature should also be avoided. Next, the traveler needs to reflect on some issues related to personal accessories. In many instances, personal accessories will identify a person as a tourist, and their socio-economic status. Therefore, tourist-identifiers including cameras, other electronics, as well as other items need to be concealed when traveling. Last, the traveler and their companions' conduct in public needs to be considered in the context that actions and demeanor at times can draw some unwanted attention.

LODGING SECURITY

F inding appropriate and safe lodging facilities is important when traveling. Depending upon their location, some are safe, while others are simply too dangerous to stay in. For example, some establishments have been the targets of terrorist attacks to the point where hotels in high-risk cities (e.g., Jerusalem) have strong perimeter security measures and blast-resistant barriers to protect the hotel and its occupants.

Of course, lodging establishments in the U.S. and abroad have always been the target of criminals who seek out the inexperienced and perhaps unsuspecting tourist. In some cases, criminals have actually been staff members. In other cases, guests, visitors of guests, and unauthorized persons have committed both personal and property-related offenses against patrons. Whatever the type of lodging facility, the traveler should not assume that they are completely safe. And, a traveler should not waive the responsibility for their security to others. In fact, a traveler should always consider this simple point: the lodging facility is not home. Instead, it is a public-access facility that offers the user some limited privacy and safety. Therefore, some planning is required.

SELECTING LODGING FACILITIES

The first step is selecting the type of lodging facility to stay at. There are many different types of lodging facilities throughout the world. Listed below are some of the more common types that will be encountered in foreign countries.

Hotels

Hotels are usually located in cities. They offer lodgers a wide variety of services and amenities that may include restaurants, swimming pools, health and wellness centers, conference rooms, and business centers. The rooms in hotels also vary in quality and size. And, depending upon quality, they can be quite luxurious.

One common denominator with hotels is that the guest rooms are usually accessed from the interior of the establishment.

Motels

The term "motel" is derived from the term "motor hotel," (circa 1950's) which originally meant that the hotel provided parking and was located along highways and on the outskirts of cities. The term motel today is generally used to define a "limited service" property (i.e., a facility that provides a limited number of amenities and does not have restaurants). Some motels are also referred to as budget hotels because they are usually less expensive than hotels. Motels are usually smaller than hotels. Another feature of the majority of motels (and some hotels, too) is that rooms can be accessed from the exterior of the building.

Hostels

Hostels are dormitory-styled lodging facilities that are often inexpensive. Rooms can hold six or more people and are usually segregated by gender (some may have a family room, however). More than half of the youth hostels in the world are in Europe, with the greatest concentration located in Germany, Scandinavia, the United Kingdom, and Eastern Europe. Most hostels around the world are open to everyone. However, some hostels still give preference to people under the age of 26 (as is the case of Hostel International member hostels in Bavaria that have an upper age limit of 26).

Pensions

A pension or pension house is like a bed and breakfast and motel. It is usually more affordable than hotels, and it is more intimate, like a bed and breakfast. Usually, pensions are small in size and they can be operated and owned by a family who rent out rooms. Or, they can be similar in appearance to hotels.

Gated Resorts

Gated resorts, as the name implies, are hotel/resort establishments that have physical security measures around their perimeter. Gated resorts provide complete amenities – all within the confines of the hotel/resort. For example, Mexico has many gated resorts containing the hotel, private beach access, bars, and restaurants – all without leaving the comfort and safety of the resort property. In some countries that have high crime rates, these might be the best lodging option.

Other Types of Lodging Establishments

There are many other types of lodging facilities available for travelers in the world. Consider for example, the different types of lodging establishments in the United Kingdom (England, Scotland, Wales and Northern Ireland).

- **Hotel** – Formal accommodation with full service.
- **Small Hotel** – A personal touch, but limited service.
- **Town House Hotel** – High quality and located in a city/town center.
- **Metro Hotel** – Full service, no dinner, but close to town center restaurants.
- **B and B** – Rooms in a private house with up to six paying guests.
- **Guest House** – Owner and staff give more services (e.g. dinner), with over six paying guests.
- **Farmhouse** – Guest accommodations, but on a working farm.
- **Inn** – Rooms in a pub, where the bar is open to non-residents, and food can be obtained in the evening.
- **Restaurant with Rooms** – Restaurant with overnight rooms.

Each one of these lodging accommodations (and even others such as cruise ships) has their own strengths and weaknesses in the context of safe travel. In order to determine the strengths and weaknesses of each type of establishment, it is thereby important to do some pre-travel research.

SELECTING THE ESTABLISHMENT

After determining what type of lodging facility meets the traveler's personal needs, wants, and interests, the next stage is to find out as much as possible about the facility. To determine the quality of the establishment and to identify any issues related to its location, overall safety, crime in the area, etc., a traveler may consider:

- Having a basic understanding of the lodging rating system for the destination country.
- Checking guest reviews on various websites.
- Visiting the establishment's website.
- E-mailing questions to the establishment.
- Contacting the establishment by phone.
- Using various mapping websites to locate the hotel and its surroundings.
- Talking with trusted and savvy travelers.
- Contacting the local U.S. Embassy/Consulate for advice.
- Contacting the local police and chamber of commerce.

Box 10-1
Hotel Rating Systems

THE HOTEL STAR RATING SYSTEM	
*	A no frills economy or budget hotel/motel. Simple, accommodations, small rooms.
* *	Affordable basic accommodations, some business services, bellhop, recreation facilities; small to medium-sized property.
* * *	A first-class quality facility that has personalized service. Some amenities (valet parking, fitness center, restaurant) and larger, spacious rooms).
* * * *	A higher quality deluxe/upscale facility that has bars, lounges and restaurants. Provides a variety of amenities (i.e., concierge, fitness center, valet). Quality linens, bedding, etc., pools, large business centers and meeting facilities. Excellent landscaping and grounds.
* * * * *	The finest luxury hotels that have flawless guest services, state of the art facilities, and the highest comfort standards. Excellent architecture, high quality rooms, linens, lobbies and grounds. 24-hour service, excellent business centers and meeting rooms.

Using as many of these information sources will provide a good understanding of the establishment and its surroundings. In order to determine its overall safety, some safety/security points to consider, regardless of the type of establishment, include:

- How close is it to police and fire services?
- How close is it to the U.S. Embassy/Consulate?
- Does the establishment have full or part-time security?
- Have there been criminal incidents at the establishment?
- Does the establishment conduct background investigations and criminal history checks of its staff?
- What is crime like around the facility?
- What is their reputation?
- How close is it to medical facilities/hospitals?
- Who does the lodging facility cater to (i.e., youth, businesses, foreigners)?
- Its proximity to the majority of the planned destinations.
- Its proximity to restaurants and other facilities.
- Its proximity to airports and mass transportation.

Other issues to consider include the following:

- **Age and Construction**

A traveler should always consider the age and construction of the establishment. Many European hotels, for example, are quite old and are built of wood. In other areas of the world, fire and other safety codes may be substandard in comparison to those that exist in the United States. For example, halls and stairways may be narrow, and emergency lighting may be nonexistent. While perhaps quaint and/or unique, they may be a firetrap and very difficult to evacuate from if an emergency should arise.

- **U.S. or Foreign Owned?**

There are two schools of thought when selecting the hotel based on ownership or its affiliation with a particular nation (or even a western democracy). First, a person may consider selecting a U.S. hotel chain. These hotel chains will most likely have standards similar to those found in the United States. These large chains may also be more concerned about their reputation and will therefore make sure that their health standards, security, etc. are superior to other non-U.S. owned facilities. On the other hand, U.S. businesses and organizations could be a greater target for terrorism and criminal activities. As pointed out earlier in this chapter, some hotels have been bombed in the Middle East, simply because they were frequented by individuals from western nations. Additionally, criminals may target these establishments because they know that wealthy westerners use them.

Quality

Besides crime and security-related issues, travelers are also concerned about quality. In an effort to rank the quality of hotels, various countries and vendors have created rating systems. The United States and the United Kingdom, for example, use the Star System that is shown in Box 10-1. These rating systems range from a diamond or star system in some countries to the French system, which is based on 22 different criteria. To confuse the issue even more, websites may have their own criteria that they use when ranking lodging facilities. Therefore, some travel sites and experts warn that hotel ratings are at best general indicators or broad guidelines only.

Booking/Reservations

In comparison to the U.S., lodging establishments may be limited in number and availability in some countries. In other cases, some establishments close early (such as hostels) and may not admit the late night traveler or even answer their doors after hours. Therefore, it may be prudent to make lodging reservations in advance.

A room guarantee or reservation will at least ensure that the traveler has a place to stay that night. Perhaps the best way to make reservations is through the Internet where the traveler has a printout of their reservation number, etc., if an issue should arise upon arrival. If reservations are made over the phone, the traveler should also make sure that the date of transaction, the name of the employee, and the room reservation number is recorded, in case an issue should arise.

SELECTING THE APPROPRIATE ROOM

The next step after selecting the establishment is to find the appropriate room. First and foremost, if a traveler is unsure about a room (and even the facility), they should ask the hotel staff to take them to the room for inspection. The traveler should also pay special attention to whom the hotel caters to and what the other visible hotel guests look like, and any observable activities that are going on. Last, if a traveler should feel unsure about the hotel, they should trust their instincts and select another establishment.

Room Location

- When making reservations, try to reserve a room that is no higher than 7 stories. Most fire and rescue equipment will not reach any higher. Also, avoid rooms on the 1st and 2nd floors (keep in mind that the 1st floor in Europe is actually the 2nd; the main floor is referred to as the ground floor). Rooms on the ground floor can be easily accessed and exited through the window. They are also more vulnerable to forced entry, blast damage, and motor vehicle accidents. Rooms on the second floor can also be accessed from the ground and are of particular concern if they have a balcony that could be readily accessed by short ladders, standing on someone's shoulders, or even from the roof of a car or truck.

- Always select establishments where there is no access to rooms from the exterior. Making individuals access through lobbies and locked doors (perhaps) serves as one more physical barrier to the room.

- Consider selecting a room that is not near an exit. Rooms near exits (such as doors and stairwells) may allow for easier access, less visibility, and a fast escape route for criminals, in comparison to a room that is more centrally located. Centrally located rooms may be quieter, too. This thought, however, must also be balanced with the need to evacuate if there is an emergency.

Rooms with Balconies or Terraces

- Always select a room that does not have a balcony or terrace, if possible. As previously pointed out, balconies provide another means of access to the room.

- Avoid rooms that have adjoining balconies and/or terraces. Adjoining balconies/terraces provide easy access to a room from adjacent room(s).

- If a traveler cannot select a room without a balcony or terrace, they should always make sure that the balcony/terrace door is locked at all times. Even if the room is located on higher floors, the traveler must keep in mind that a threat could move from balcony to balcony at times – both vertically and horizontally – to gain access to the balcony/terrace and room. Also, a traveler should never sleep with the balcony door open and/or unlocked.

- If the balcony/terrace door has a sliding-styled door, it is also important to make sure that something is wedged into the track of the door to prevent it from being opened. A traveler should consider setting a chair in the track to prevent it from being opened. Otherwise, books or other objects can also be placed in the track to serve as a means to block the door from sliding.

Rooms with Adjoining Doors

Adjoining doors link two or more hotel rooms together. While convenient for families, etc. a traveler also needs to consider that these doors are also another access point to the room. Therefore, some points to consider are listed below:

- If a traveler should choose a room with an adjoining door because their traveling companions are using the adjacent room, it is still important to always secure this door when sleeping and going out. A traveler should never entrust

their personal security and the protection of their valuables to others who may accidentally leave their main door
open, allowing access to the traveler's room by the means
of the adjoining door.

- A single traveler should ask for a room that doesn't have
an adjoining door. If the room does have an adjoining door,
meanwhile, it is important to make sure it is locked at all
times. A traveler should also consider placing a heavy
barrier against the door for additional protection against
unlawful entry.

Concierge Rooms/Floors

For added safety, security, and increased privacy, a traveler
may consider a club level or concierge room. Concierge rooms are
usually located on a private floor or wing of the hotel. They
generally have keyed access to the floor, where only registered
guests of that floor have access to it and any services provided
therein. Because of the limited access, these floors may be more
secure than others. Usually these rooms will have an upgrade
charge. In some situations, however, a traveler can request a
concierge room for their personal safety and a hotel may oblige
with no upgrade charge. One of the drawbacks to a concierge
room is that the guest may inadvertently be advertising their
wealth or that they are an out-of-the-ordinary traveler, which
could actually bring unwanted attention to them.

Toilet and Bathing Facilities

A traveler should check to see if there are bathing facilities
and toilets in the room. Some European lodging facilities may not
have bathing facilities and toilets in the room (if they do, there
may be an upgrade charge for these amenities). In lieu of
personal toilets and baths, many facilities have communal or
shared toilets and showers. Although there are usually locks on
these doors for privacy, these communal facilities may expose a
traveler to greater risk because they are now outside the security
of their locked room.

If the traveler should use one of these establishments, they should never go to the toilet or bathing facilities alone. Instead, a "buddy system" where one person serves as a lookout for the other, should be used, if possible. Also, the traveler should never use these facilities during the late evening or early morning hours. During these times there may be fewer staff and guests present who may act as a visible deterrent and/or may intervene if a situation should arise.

WHEN CHECKING IN

It is best to be as inconspicuous as possible when checking in. A traveler should not loiter out in front of the establishment, or in its parking lot or valet area. Instead, the traveler should check in as soon as possible and avoid public areas.

When checking in, the traveler should also limit the amount of personal information provided to the staff. For example:

- Avoid using titles when filling out the guest registry. Titles such as Dr. or Mrs. will reveal the social status of the traveler.

- Never list the name of the organization or company the traveler is affiliated with on the registry. Affiliation with an organization could serve to reveal the traveler's occupation and perhaps their social status (i.e., student or business executive). In addition, certain companies may also be unpopular in some nations.

- Consider using a company or school address (without using the name of the company) or some other address other than a home address. A traveler's home could become the target of a crime, based on the information provided at check-in. It could also protect a traveler from later forms of harassment, and even identity theft.

- Avoid filling out public guest registries. Many guest registries are actually on display on the front counter, available for all guests to review. If optional, the traveler should avoid filling out these registries, and request that their name not be included on any computerized printouts that are publicly displayed (cruises are notorious for printing public listings of all guests for all to see). If a traveler is required to complete a form, write in an illegible manner. Furthermore, if the registry calls for addresses, nationality, etc., travelers should avoid filling out these sections if at all possible, or simply provide false information on them.

- Avoid small talk. In some cases a clerk or other staff will engage in small talk asking the traveler, for example, if they are "here for business or pleasure." Other individuals near the check-in area may do the same thing. It is best to avoid these situations for safety reasons. If pressed to respond, it is best to be vague about personal issues.

- Use work phone numbers when registering, instead of a home or personal cell phone number.

- As pointed out in the Passport Chapter, a traveler should never leave their passport with hotel staff. If the passport is required for registration purposes, request that the staff make a copy of it. When checking out, meanwhile, the traveler should also request that the hotel staff return the copy, or shred it.

- Do not openly display cash and credit cards in the lobby for all to see.

- Don't show where valuables are kept (i.e., digging in a money pouch).

- Briefcases and/or handbags should be placed in front of the traveler. If there is other luggage, it should be pinned between the traveler's legs, or positioned between the traveler and the front desk to prevent it from being stolen.

- Don't provide an e-mail address. If requested, provide a work or school e-mail address.

Never Give the Impression of Traveling Alone

A traveler should always give the impression that they are traveling with others. When traveling alone and checking in, a traveler should consider stating that another person will also be staying in the room with them: simply tell the clerk that the co-traveler is expected to arrive soon, and provide the staff with a name if they require it. If the traveler is a female, meanwhile, it is important to state that the travel companion is a male who is on his way or that "he" will be arriving soon. And, ask for two keys. A hotel, in most cases will charge for the extra guest. Even though it may be a little more expensive in some cases, it will serve as a great deterrent. Now, the hotel staff and others think that there are two people in the room.

A traveler should also keep this impression up while in their room. For example, a traveler could pretend to be talking to their co-traveler in the room while picking up the phone receiver. When leaving the room, a traveler could also give the impression that there is someone else in the room with them. For example, a simple "see you later" when leaving the empty room could possibly deter someone from trying to gain entry into the room. The traveler should also make the room look as if it is occupied by two individuals (i.e., make another bed look slept in, use twice as many towels).

Keep Control of Luggage

- A traveler also needs to make sure that they maintain physical control of their luggage. In many situations, check-in (and checkout) at a hotel is chaotic. There could be several individuals checking in and out with luggage lying around everywhere. The traveler should not set their luggage down and walk away from it. Crowds, chaos, and confusion are great places for criminals to operate in an inconspicuous manner. Consider for example, a well-dressed "normal" looking person picking up some luggage in a crowded hotel lobby – would anyone think twice that this individual was not the rightful owner if they operated in a normal or inconspicuous manner, walking right out the door, perhaps in some cases with other guests or hotel staff holding the floor for them? Besides theft, in these times of political turmoil, the last thing a traveler wants is to have somebody put something into their luggage.

- Do not leave luggage unattended in front of the establishment. In some cases, the establishment will have bellmen and carts available. Do not stack /place luggage on these carts. They may be unattended, unsupervised, and vulnerable to theft.

- Do not hand luggage to a person without first verifying their identity as a staff member. In some countries, it is commonplace for individuals who are not employed by the hotel to take a traveler's baggage and carry it for them, and then demand payment for their services before returning it to them.

AFTER CHECKING IN

The need to be safety-conscious in a lodging establishment does not stop once the traveler is checked into their room. Instead, there are a variety of safety concerns that need to be considered, as this section will review.

Be Aware of Fraudulent Activities

If the traveler should receive a phone call from someone claiming to be a staff member asking for verification of a credit card number (or other financial matter), other personal information, and/or travel plans, no information should be divulged without verifying who the caller is and why they need the information. The traveler should ask for that person's name, position, and hotel extension and then return the call. The caller's identity and position should be verified through the front desk, security, or management. The need for this information should also be verified, as in some cases a hotel employee may be involved in a criminal activity. If not an employee, the traveler should also consider that in some situations, a threat might be calling from within the hotel.

Inspect the Room

After checking in, the traveler should have a bellhop or security enter the room with them to make sure that it is safe. All locking hardware, doors and windows should also be inspected. If any are defective, the traveler should request to be immediately moved to another room. When returning to the room, a traveler should also check to make sure that the room was not entered while away. If so, they should immediately leave the room and request the assistance of the front desk or security. Keeping the room tidy with all personal items in order will also make it easier to notice if someone has been in the room.

Plan for an Emergency Evacuation

It is also very important to plan for an emergency evacuation. One of the first things that should be done is to gain an understanding of the layout of the establishment and where the emergency evacuation routes are. Emergency escape routes are usually posted on the back of the room's door. This plan should be reviewed. Also, the traveler should walk and review the escape route. In some cases, it might be a good idea to feel for and count the number of doors to the exit. In the case of fires, for example, hallways could fill fast with smoke, thereby limiting the ability to see. Also, the traveler should look for a secondary escape/evacuation route, just in case the first one is blocked. The escape route should always be down, toward the ground, and not up to the rooftop. Rooftop doors could be locked and emergency equipment may not be able to reach to the roof. And, in the case with fire, evacuating in the same direction of the flow of heat, smoke, and fumes could be deadly.

Fire Safety

One of the greatest dangers that exists in any lodging establishment is the risk of fire. Fire will also require an evacuation – no matter how small it is! In many disasters, fires have started out small. In some cases these fires were so small that the lodging staff felt that it wasn't important to fully warn lodgers, or lodgers disregarded the danger. When considering the fact that a fire exponentially increases in size every minute, and a person may be delayed in detecting the fire, it is critical that the response time and evacuation time be as short as possible. That is, when alerted to a fire, leave as fast as possible, using the shortest evacuation route to safety. While speed is always essential in evacuations, there are some issues to consider when dealing with a fire-related situation.

Fire Evacuation

One of the first issues is for the traveler to decide if it is safe to leave the room. When considering this issue, a traveler should:

- Always feel the door (and door knob) before opening it. If it feels hot, do not open it. Instead, try to seal the room from smoke by placing wet towels, etc., under the crack of the door.

- If the door is cool to the touch, slowly open the door. When opening the door, open it just a couple of inches and *then* peer out into the hallway. Do not open the door and immediately look to see the situation; hot gasses rushing through the gap could cause injuries. Be prepared to shut the door if smoke pours in.

- Inspect the hallway and stairwell. If the decision is made to evacuate, make sure the room key is taken along. A traveler may have to retreat back to the safety of their room if the heat and smoke should become too intense.

- Stay low, crouching or crawling on the way out. Heat and smoke rise.

In other cases, the traveler may be stranded in their room. In these situations, consider the following points:

- Do not panic.
- Immediately call emergency police and fire to alert them to the situation and the room location. Also call the front desk to let them know a guest is trapped in their room.
- Check for an alternative way out than the door. If the room has a balcony and it is safe to go out on it, signal for help. A common signal is to hang a sheet off the guardrail.
- If no smoke and flame are present, consider waiting it out on the balcony to get the attention of rescue personnel.
- Prevent as much smoke and fumes from getting into the room. Fill any cracks of gaps in the doorway with wet linens. The same may have to be done with windows and balcony doors.

- If there is smoke in the room, turn on the bathroom vents, if there is still electricity.

- Fill the bathtub and sinks with water. The water supply could fail during a fire, and additional water may be needed to keep linens wet, or in a worst case scenario, to fight a fire.

- Breaking out windows should be a last resort. Oftentimes, windows will prevent more smoke from entering the room.

Always Know the Identity of Persons at the Door

A traveler should not open their door to a stranger. Rooms should have a "peep hole"/viewer, so people on the other side of the door can be seen before opening it. Many lodging crimes can be categorized as pretext crimes. That is, a person may knock on the door, representing themselves as hotel staff. Knowing what the hotel staff uniforms look like (and don't simply open a door if a person is wearing a staff uniform) is therefore very important. If in doubt, a traveler should always ask to see the employee identification card through the door viewer, or contact the front desk to verify their identity.

Always Create the Appearance that the Room is Occupied

Criminals will more likely seek out an unoccupied room over an occupied one. To make a room look occupied, a traveler should consider the following:

- Leave the television or radio on (if there is one) when out of the room. This will give the impression that the room is occupied. Tune the television or radio to a channel that has the same language as the host country. This will give the impression that the occupant is a native of that country.

- Keep a light on in the room when out.

- Do not leave or post signs such as "housekeeping needed," "please clean," These signs are also indicators that the room is most likely unoccupied.

Always Keep the Door Locked

Always keep the door locked. When in the room, always use the chain or privacy latch and deadbolt the door, if a deadbolt is present. Using the chain or privacy latch and the deadbolt will prevent somebody from purposefully or accidentally entering the room. While most hotels now rely upon magnetic key cards, these can be readily reproduced at the front desk. Mistakes could occur where additional card access keys are issued to the wrong room. For example, one of the authors, who has years of hotel security experience, has dealt with many situations where the front desk mistakenly entered the wrong room number on the magnetic key, resulting in a guest walking into an occupied room because the door was not secured by the occupants with a deadbolt or chain.

The traveler must also remember that locks are classified as delay devices only. That is, locks, chains and other latches can be defeated if there is enough time and/or force exerted against the mechanism(s). To bolster existing security hardware, some travelers have even been known to carry with them rubber door wedges as an added security precaution against a forced intrusion. Other items may also include a portable motion-detector or intrusion door alarm that sounds an audible alarm if the door is opened.

Keep Window Coverings Drawn or Closed

Depending upon the hotel layout and adjacent buildings, offenders could easily look into a guest room. Not only is this an invasion of privacy, but a motivated offender could see when the guest leaves, any habits that developed if observed for a long enough period of time (when the traveler is in and out, for example), not to mention the fact they now know if the traveler is alone or with someone else and/or possesses certain items of value, including laptop computers, clothing, and jewelry.

Never Leave Expensive or Personal Information in the Room

A traveler must also be aware that the room is accessible by hotel staff (i.e., housekeeping, maintenance). Staff members can be directly and indirectly responsible for both personal and property-related offenses. Indirectly, for example, housekeeping may have several rooms open at one time to expedite their cleaning responsibilities. Opportunistic criminals could take advantage of this practice and easily take items that are left out in the open in rooms.

Hotel staff can and will talk with other staff members and acquaintances about guests and valuable objects in their rooms. Therefore, a traveler needs to reveal as little information about themselves and their occupation. This can be easily accomplished by keeping personal information out of the immediate view of those who have access to the room. Travelers can best protect themselves from this issue by putting away personal objects from the plain view of the hotel staff.

A traveler should always consider using the hotel safe or safety deposit box to secure their valuables. Room safes are another option. Like the hotel safe, staff could access them, especially if the safe is key operated. More advanced room safes have electronic locks whose combination is set by the user. While the property may still be vulnerable to theft, safes are better options at times than simply attempting to hide valuables in the room, and perhaps later forgetting them.

Limit Entry into the Room

In order to prevent hotel staff from having access to personal information, deny or limit entry into the room. One simple way to accomplish this goal is to post the "do not disturb" sign on the door or notify the front desk that housekeeping services will not be needed, unless the traveler notifies the hotel staff. The housekeeping service will then avoid the room, reducing the traveler's risk of becoming a victim in the process.

Consistent with limiting who comes into the room, room service could also be a threat. Therefore, a traveler should always verify room service. In order to prevent them from coming into their room, the traveler should also consider telling room service to leave the tray out in the hall, retrieving the tray once the staff member has left. Perhaps the most dangerous activity is bringing strangers (and in some cases acquaintances) back to the room. Now, a traveler could be vulnerable to a variety of personal and property-related offenses and be virtually trapped in their own room.

Securing Valuables in the Room

Not all valuables can be locked in the room safe or at the front desk at all times (the passport and wallet, for example). With these and other valuables, a traveler should consider keeping them in close proximity at all times. For example, while showering, valuables could be moved into the bathroom. Hotel staff or even criminals may enter the room while the guest is using the bathroom. With other items, meanwhile, including laptops, there are cable locks on the market that can be used to secure the laptop to a fixed item in the room.

Luggage should also be secured when in the room. A traveler may consider purchasing plastic zip ties to secure the zippers on their luggage (many existing luggage locks can be easily tampered with). These are one-use nylon ties that prevent a person from opening and rifling through the traveler's luggage. Although they can easily be cut, at a minimum, they will deter opportunistic criminals. It will also serve to alert the traveler that their luggage was tampered with.

Clothing may also be a target. To protect expensive clothing, consider placing them on hangers under other less-expensive garments. If a criminal is in a hurry, they may miss them. A traveler may also consider storing expensive clothes in pillowcases, laying them out flat under the sheets and covers of a spare bed, or even under the mattress.

Key Control

Keeping control of the room key (either the traditional mechanical or electronic key) is critical. Listed below are some points to consider regarding key control.

- The room key should be in the guest's possession at all times. A traveler should never give the key to others.

- Be sure to carry the key in a secure pocket. That way, the traveler is always assured that they will have access to their room.

- Do not publicly display the room key. This is a subtle announcement that the holder is a tourist. Furthermore, many key cards have the hotel name printed on them. If the key card was left in plain view for all to see (i.e., on a bar or table top), for example, now a threat would know where the traveler is staying. This could lead to problems ranging from unwanted advances, harassment, and even criminal activities.

- Do not turn the key into the front desk when coming and going. In many European hotels, there is the expectation that guests turn in their room key to the front desk when coming and going. In many instances, however, the keyboard or mail slot is easily visible to everyone passing the front desk. This readily tells criminals (both external and internal threats) that the room is unoccupied.

- Lost or misplaced keys should be reported immediately. Most keys are now generic and have no room numbers printed on them. However, many keys have the name of the hotel or a logo on them. If this key were lost, for example, it would allow the would-be criminal access into the hotel. After gaining access, a motivated criminal could literally try each door until the correct one was found. If it is magnetic card access, the card can be readily cancelled and the room's lock can be easily reprogrammed with a new code. If it is a traditional key, ask (and perhaps insist) to be immediately moved to another room. In addition, the traveler should never enter their room without hotel security or staff present when a key is lost. Someone could be waiting. A good hotel will accommodate this request.

- The traveler also needs to treat the hotel as if it was their house. For example, they should never let strangers in the establishment, or hold doors open for others – make them use their own key. Using another's key to access a building is called tailgating, where the traveler may inadvertently allow a criminal free access into the building.

- A traveler should not write their room number on their magnetic key card. If it becomes lost or even seen by the criminal, they know exactly what room to go to.

- If the electronic key card is issued with a folder or envelope, in most cases, the hotel staff will write the room number on it. A traveler should make sure that they throw this away when they get to their room. It should not be thrown away in a public area (i.e., lobby or hallway). If thrown away in a public trash bin, for example, it could provide criminals with a room number.

- Be wary of establishments that use traditional keys. Many establishments do not have sound policies to re-key rooms after a key is lost. In fact, some key replacement policies do not require the immediate re-keying of rooms. Instead, the establishment may have a policy that calls for the re-keying of rooms after a certain number of keys are lost for that room, which is accomplished by exchanging lock cores with other rooms. This may mean that there are extra keys floating around that can be used to gain entrance to some other room in the establishment.

Staying in Common and High Visibility Areas of the Hotel

Staying in high visibility areas is often a safe alternative. High visibility/high traffic areas allow for the increased surveillance of areas by guests, etc. that could serve to deter some criminal activities. However, the traveler still needs to be safe in these semi-public areas and consider the following points:

- When coming and going, always use the main entrance. There is usually more traffic at the main entrances and staff on duty at the front desk. Other entrances may not be staffed after hours. Even if other entrances have secure access and even cameras, always consider the fact that a human being may not be continuously watching the monitor. Instead, it may simply be recording, if that.

- When leaving the room, hallways should be checked for any suspicious behaviors or people. If a traveler should feel uncomfortable for any reason, they should get out of that situation immediately.

- When waiting for and riding in an elevator, be aware of other occupants. If unsure of the occupants, wait for the next elevator. A traveler should always stand at the front of the elevator, next to the control panel with their back to the wall. This will allow for an easier retreat, if necessary, in comparison to being trapped in the rear of the car. In a threatening situation, the traveler can also push all of the buttons (including the alarm) and get out of the elevator as fast as possible. Having a back to the wall will also prevent being surprised by the actions of others.

- Be cautious of stairwells. In many lodging facilities, stairwells are often unsupervised and are considered to be emergency exits only – not a means to travel from floor to floor. Stairwells usually open to the exterior of a building at the ground floor level. If left unlocked or unattended, or the exit door on the ground floor is propped open, they offer easy access to the building. Moreover, in some situations, a floor can only be accessed from the stairwell by a key or magnetic key card programmed specifically to that floor. Or, they provide limited access to certain floors. Therefore, a person could become literally trapped or have a limited escape route when in a stairwell.

Revealing a Room Number

A traveler should also be cautious to whom they give their room number out to. A traveler always needs to be reserved and cautious on what information is revealed to strangers, staff, and guests. Just because a person is a guest, for example, does not mean that they are not a threat. Besides casual conversations where a room number could be revealed, travelers need to be cautious when placing their room number on bar and meal tabs that can be seen by staff members and patrons. Therefore, it might be safer at times to pay with cash to avoid this security issue.

Safety in Common Areas

In many establishments, there are common areas ranging from lobbies and swimming pools to workout areas. When using these areas, a traveler should always remember that there is increased safety in numbers. When outside of the room, for example, a traveler should always have a companion, if at all possible, even if they are on a quick trip to the front desk.

Travelers should also avoid using workout facilities and pool areas alone. Using a buddy system and making sure that their partner is never out of sight is crucial. Attacks can occur in pool areas, workout rooms, saunas, and especially locker rooms. If, for example, there is a need to exercise, a traveler should always do it with someone they trust, during normal business hours. Early mornings and late evenings should be avoided; there are fewer individuals using these facilities, and less hotel staff on duty.

CHECKING OUT

Checking out of the establishment is at times just as chaotic as checking in. In order to avoid the chaos and dangers associated with checking out, the morning or the night before check out, a traveler should request that their bill be brought to their room. Many reputable hotels will deliver the bill under the door in the early morning hours. This will allow the traveler to avoid the front desk to check out. Furthermore, a traveler should:

- Keep copies of the hotel bills and verify them after getting home to make sure that they are correct. A traveler should always consider paying by credit card so they have the support of the card company if there is a dispute over the bill.

- Never leave any financial or personal information in the room. Leaving credit card slips in the trash, for example, could result in an identity theft issue later on.

- Be cautious when leaving the establishment. Criminals and panhandlers could be present outside of the hotel, looking for an easy target.

- Avoid loitering outside of the hotel. These areas are often ripe for crime. Have the destination planned out prior to leaving the facility.

- If transportation is needed, this should be arranged in advance. The traveler should have transportation waiting for them when exiting the hotel. This will also limit the exposure to any threats.

STAYING IN YOUTH HOSTELS

Perhaps one of the most exciting and relatively unique experiences when abroad is to stay in a youth hostel. Hostels usually provide "bare bones" accommodations – a bed and a shower. While hostels can provide an interesting cultural experience for travelers, some caution must be exercised when staying at these facilities. Because hostels are dormitory style, by the very nature of their design, there are some increased security issues with them. Besides the points already outlined in this chapter:

- The age group that is most likely to be victimized or be involved in criminal activities is 18-24. This is the age group that hostels cater to.

- Staying at a hostel is not restricted to college students. They are open to anyone, including criminals.

- A traveler needs to pay particular attention to their belongings. Most hostels will either issue a locker or will secure personal belongings in a separate room or safe upon request. In other cases, the traveler may have to provide their own lock.

- Never leave personal items alone in the shared room.

- If the traveler should decide to keep some of their personal belongings in the room, it is important to make sure that it is secure while sleeping. For example, a traveler may consider securing their luggage to their bed frame with plastic zip ties to ensure that it cannot be physically taken or opened. Depending upon its size, a traveler may also consider sleeping with it, using it as a pillow, for example.

- Be careful when displaying items of wealth. I Pods® and other electronic devices, and even clothing and shoes, could be a target for theft.

- If a traveler should feel uncomfortable with some of their roommates, they should ask to be placed into another room.

CONCLUSION

A traveler often has a variety of lodging establishments to choose from when venturing overseas. All of these establishments have their own strengths and weaknesses in the context of safety that need to be considered prior to booking a room. Once a safe lodging facility has been found, issues including the selection of "safe" rooms, and procedures for safely checking-in need to be followed. Naturally, there are also some safety and security issues that need to be considered when staying in the facility. Some of these issues include: being aware of fraudulent activities, reviewing escape routes, knowing who is at the door, and creating the appearance that the traveler is not in the room by themselves. Other issues include keeping the door locked at all times, keeping window treatments closed, securing and limiting the amount of valuables in the room, key control, and limiting activities to the most visible parts of the establishment only. This chapter has also reviewed youth hostels. While these can be a unique lodging experience, some additional safety and security issues exist when using these facilities for a variety of reasons, including the clientele and room layout.

MONEY MATTERS

M oney is the last issue that a traveler should be concerned about on their trip. Deciding what to use (i.e., cards, currency), understanding the country's currency, having access to additional funds, and making sure that all of these financial instruments are safe and secure are, of course, very important when traveling.

BEGINNING THOUGHTS ON MONEY MATTERS

For the purpose of this chapter, "money" will be used to describe all forms of financial instruments – primarily cash, debit/credit cards and traveler's checks. Money matters, like many other components of the trip, begin with some pre-departure research, a traveler knowing their financial limitations, and making sure that there is a mix of money for the trip.

Pre-Departure Research

On many occasions the authors have also seen travelers struggling over currency. They can be seen in public settings literally handing a "wad" of currency to a vender, relying upon this person's honesty and good will to complete the transaction. They can also draw attention to themselves in other ways by having other's help them in counting money or delaying lines, etc., in their attempt to learn the currency system.

There are many things the traveler can do to avoid the above situations. First, the type of currency should be researched. For example, Western Europe uses the Euro as its currency. Switzerland and the United Kingdom, meanwhile, use their own currency systems – the Swiss Franc and the British Pound. Information of this nature needs to be known before travel. Next, the traveler should also know the value of the currency relative to the U.S. dollar (which will be covered in greater detail in this chapter) or other currencies that will be used. In addition, the traveler also needs to understand how color and size is often related to the denomination in many countries. Last, the traveler should research what financial instruments (i.e., credit cards, debit cards) can be used at their destination.

Financial Limitations

Financial planning for the trip has already been reviewed in the Getting Ready Chapter, where it was encouraged that the traveler create a budget and then multiply it by another 25%. It must always be remembered that traveling short on money (or being broke) can expose the traveler to a myriad of safety and security issues. With limited funds a traveler will most likely base their decisions on finances and not safety, choosing, for example, lodging establishments, food, transport and recreational activities that are sub-par and thereby expose the tourist to a variety of potential dangers.

Prior to departure, a traveler should therefore know the limits of each financial instrument they plan on using and taking with them. Issues including bank account balances, credit card limits and available "pocket money" should be considered. The traveler should also check the expiration dates on all of their debit and credit cards to make sure that they will not expire while traveling.

Having a Mix of Money

The traveler should always carry a mix of money (i.e., cash, credit cards, traveler's checks) when traveling. A mix of money is important because in some locations, certain financial instruments may not be accepted or work. For example, some merchants may refuse or not be able to accept credit cards, where they will require cash only. Some of the essential financial instruments to bring along include:

- Debit/ATM Cards
- Credit card(s)
- Local currency
- U.S. dollars
- Travelers checks

SAFEGUARDING MONEY

Regardless of what type of financial instrument the traveler carries, they must be safeguarded. Listed below are some ways to ensure financial solvency and to prevent and/or mitigate any problems if the loss or theft of financial instruments were to occur while traveling.

Record all Financial Information

In case of emergency, it will be important that the traveler has a list of bank accounts and credit card numbers. Any other numbers, including the serial numbers from traveler's checks, if used, should also be recorded. The traveler should also have the phone numbers of their bank(s) and credit card companies in order to transfer funds or cancel cards. This list (or even photocopies of each credit card [front and back]) should be carried (hard copy, stored on a flash drive, etc.) in a secure location. Another copy should be left with a trusted person at home in case a financial-based emergency should occur.

Divide the Money Up – Spread the Risk

A traveler should not carry any more money than that which they are willing to lose. Therefore, it is important to spread the risk. For example, a traveler could store large denomination bills and unneeded credit cards in the hotel safe, and carry only that amount of money that is needed for the day's activities with them.

A traveler should also be sure to divide that money up that is needed for the day. For example, instead of accessing a wallet (or digging in a purse) every time there is a need for money, the traveler could place a small amount of cash in a money clip or in a small wallet in their front pocket. When necessary, the traveler can then replenish this money source from their "deep storage" area. Like the passport pocket, there should also be a dedicated pocket just for money (and nothing else) to ensure that nothing can be lost when retrieving the money.

This small amount of money should be the "drop money" that the traveler is willing to sacrifice, if necessary. In the case of robbery, for example, most likely a criminal will not want to spend a lot time with their victim(s). The attack will be sudden, and the criminal will most likely not thoroughly search a person for additional monies. They will take the "drop money" and run.

Only Carry the Essentials

The traveler should also avoid carrying unnecessary financial instruments and personal information when traveling. Check-books, merchant cards, and social security cards, etc., will most likely serve no purpose when traveling overseas. In fact, they will most not likely work or have no purpose. In order to prevent identity theft, and the inconvenience of reporting and replacing these items if lost or stolen, wallets or purses should be purged of these items.

Carry Money in the Front Pocket

As pointed out earlier in this book, in many countries, pick-pocketing is a serious problem. The risk of the loss of a wallet can be mitigated by not carrying it in the back pocket of your pants.

Avoid Carrying Handbags/Shoulder Bags

Handbags/shoulder bags can also make the traveler a target for theft. If at all possible, they should not be carried. If a traveler does decide to carry one, it should be small and inconspicuous. It should also be carried under a jacket, when possible. If not concealed, it should be carried under the armpit and have short straps, fitting tight against the body. A friend of one of the authors, for example, lost her purse in the London subways. In the midst of a large crowd, a thief actually cut the straps off her purse. She got off the crowded subway and soon realized that all she had was the strap still over her shoulder. Perhaps if the straps were short, and it was carried under her armpit, this crime would not have happened.

In those cases where a purse is carried, it must always be in the immediate control and observation of the owner. For example, purses should not be placed on floors, under chairs, over the arms of chairs, etc. Besides making the purse a target for theft, it could also be accidentally left behind.

Never Carry Money in Removable Clothing

As is the case with passports, a traveler should never stow a purse or wallet or other financial instruments in clothing that can be removed (i.e., jackets, pockets). Always carry money in a secure pants or shirt pocket, for example.

Be Inconspicuous

During their travels, the authors have actually seen tourists access their waist money belts and/or other areas of concealment in public to retrieve their money. In other situations, travelers have also been seen standing in lines holding onto their credit cards or money, literally begging to be a victim! A traveler should be aware that criminals often target their victims and actions of this nature will simply make a traveler a target for crime. Therefore, it is important to be inconspicuous. To avoid becoming a victim, consider the following points:

Using Concealment Devices

Consistent with the previous points reviewed in this book, a traveler should consider using different types of concealment devices for their money. This book has already reviewed the importance of using money belts, socks and other concealed compartments. When using these types of concealment devices, the traveler should access them only in the privacy of the hotel room or even in a restroom stall. They should never be accessed in public.

Be Prepared for Financial Transactions

How often have you seen people fumbling in their wallets or purses for their money or credit/debit cards? In fact, the next time the reader is in a public setting, watch to see how many persons in public fumble for or are confused in normal financial transactions. Worse than that, oftentimes people will count their money in public.

Being unprepared for financial transactions may draw a lot of unnecessary attention. In order to avoid drawing attention to one-self, a traveler should always be prepared for financial trans-actions. The traveler should know where their money is, and know what type of instrument will be used. They should pull it out inconspicuously, use it, and return it immediately to its safe location without drawing any attention to their actions. Of course, the traveler should always be aware of their surroundings at all times.

PAPER MONEY

While some travel consultants may state that a person can travel "paperless," it is recommended that travelers still carry paper currency. Paper money provides convenience and flexibility in comparison to other financial instruments. It is also important for the following reasons:

- Having foreign currency in advance will ensure that the traveler has "pocket money" for immediate expenses upon arrival.

- Having and using paper money often speeds up trans-actions.

- Some merchants (i.e., street vendors) will not have the ability to accept credit cards. Or, they may refuse them.

- Credits cards may not work in all areas of the world.

Exchanging Currency

There are two options when exchanging currency: exchange currency before departure, or while traveling. A benefit of exchanging currency before leaving is the simple fact that the traveler will not have to spend their travel time exchanging currency. If the traveler is from a larger metropolitan area, there are usually banks that have foreign currencies readily available. If a traveler is from a smaller town or city, in most cases, a local bank can order foreign currency.

On the other hand, a traveler can exchange currency as they go. If the decision is made to exchange currency while traveling, consider the following points:

- Plan ahead for the need to exchange currency. In large cities, exchanging currency is usually no problem. In smaller towns or rural areas, it may be more difficult.

- Try to use banks to exchange foreign currency. In many cities, there are businesses that will exchange money. Usually, their fees associated with the exchange are higher than banks. In some cases, they may not be legitimate, whereas the traveler could be given counterfeit currency.

- While airports and other public transportation facilities have vendors that offer foreign currency exchange, often the processing or administrative fees associated with the exchange are higher. If not higher fees, the exchange rate may be less than what banks or other institutions may offer. People who use these establishments may also make themselves more of a target – tourists and foreigners use these facilities – not the locals.

- Only use legitimate currency exchange resources. Avoid the black market when exchanging money. The money could be counterfeit, and in many countries, it is illegal to use these resources. One common method of exchange in some foreign countries is by street vendors offering to exchange currency, often at a higher exchange rate than legitimate currency exchangers. These individuals are dangerous to deal with: they know the traveler is a foreigner and that they have money.

- Banks can refuse the exchange of foreign currency. On one travel experience, for instance, one of the authors had problems exchanging the newly designed U.S. currency for Euros. The bank he was at had never seen the new currency and would not exchange them.

- A traveler should always be aware of their surroundings when exchanging money. Criminals may frequent these areas knowing that there is easy money to be found.

- After the journey, a traveler may have to exchange currency back to their home currency. Banks will usually accept paper currency only. Therefore, coin currency should be exchanged to paper denominations when possible before leaving the host country.

Understanding the Conversion Process

In some cases, currency conversion can be confusing for the traveler. Therefore, it is strongly encouraged that the traveler understands the currency conversion process prior to their travels. Understanding the value or purchasing power of the U.S. dollar relative to other currencies will help the traveler better budget their trip. Pre-planning will also serve to reduce any misunderstandings and the frustrations associated with currency conversion. And, it will also protect the traveler from being defrauded and/or over-charged for any trip-related expenses.

Currency conversion charts are readily available on the Internet. Some sites include:

- http://www.oanda.com/convert/classic
- http://www. Currencyconverter.uk.com.
- http://www.xe.com/ucc

Many other sites can also be found on the Internet by typing in the key words: "currency converter charts." All of these sites work the same way. The user compares the value of their currency, relative to the value of the other nation's currency for that particular day. A sample currency conversion chart is shown in Box 11-1. A blank currency conversion chart to assist in budgeting, etc., is also provided in Appendix H.

Box 11-1
Sample Currency Conversion Chart

	U.S. Dollars (USD or $)	Euros (EUR or €)	British Pounds (GBP or £)
U.S. Dollars (USD or $)	1.0	0.7407	0.5044
Euros (EUR or €)	1.35	1.0	0.681

In the chart, the value of the U.S. Dollar (USD), relative to the Euro (EUR) is approximately 0.74 cents for the particular day under review (values are constantly changing). That is, for every $100 USD exchanged for the Euro, the traveler will receive 74.07 Euros in return. If a traveler needs to purchase Pounds, meanwhile, the value of the Pound (GBP or £), relative to the USD is $1.98. Therefore, if a traveler needs to purchase Pounds for their trip, for every $100 USD exchanged, they will receive £50.44 (Pounds). The traveler should also keep in mind that as they travel, they might need to exchange their foreign currency for other foreign currencies. As an example, if a traveler goes from Germany to England, they will need to convert their Euros to Pounds. Based on the above chart, each Euro is equivalent to £0.681 (€ = £68.1).

Credit Cards

Credit cards are another option. In fact, they should be considered essential due to the fact that a credit card can give the traveler access to a large amount of money for emergency situations. Additionally, credit cards offer a true exchange rate, since the transaction has gone through a bank that has used that day's currency exchange value to calculate the purchase. Credit card companies also offer a variety of protections (i.e., theft, fraud, rapid card replacement). And, they are widely accepted throughout the world.

To be safe when using credit cards, some points to consider are in the following list.

- Before leaving, the traveler should contact the credit card company and: 1) find out if the card will work in the destination country or region; and, 2) let the company know that the credit card will be used overseas. Credit card companies have "spending profiles" on each customer. Using a credit card overseas will most likely alert the company's fraud unit of suspicious activities, whereas the credit card company will call the traveler and perhaps deactivate the use of the card until verification of legitimate use is made.

- Credit cards have a maximum cash liability for the holder (expenses the owner is responsible for if the card is used without permission) if the card is stolen, etc.

- Consider taking out a new credit card that has a low maximum spending limit. Even though the holder will most likely not be fully liable for its fraudulent use (as long as loss or theft is reported immediately), the monetary loss will be minimized in such instances.

- Many cards offer some measure of protection should the item purchased with the card be lost, damaged, or stolen. The traveler should check with their card issuer regarding protection programs.

- Credit cards also offer cash advances. These cash advances can be conducted at banks and even ATM machines. While convenient, the traveler should be aware that the resulting fees and interest rate makes this an expensive option. Nevertheless, in times of emergency this may be a good option.

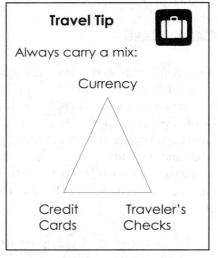

Travel Tip

Always carry a mix:

Currency

Credit Cards   Traveler's Checks

- Know the Personal Identification Number (PIN) for credits cards (and do not write the number down!). These may be needed for cash advances from ATM's.

DEBIT CARDS

With a debit card, the travelers are using money drawn from their own bank account. The advantage of using a bank debit card to withdraw money overseas is that debit cards (like credit cards) generally offer the best exchange rate available. When using a debit card, however, there are some issues to consider:

- Before departure, contact the bank that has issued the credit card to verify that it will work in the destination country or region. As is the case with credit cards, notifying the issuing bank that the card will be used overseas will also ensure that the card will not be deactivated if the bank should detect any suspicious activities. The traveler should also ask about any fees, withdrawal limits (per transaction or day) and if the PIN will work without a problem overseas.

- Look for the debit card's network affiliations to make sure the card(s) will work in the host country. For a list of ATM's throughout the world go to http://visa.com or http://www.mastercard.com. Most debit cards are "backed" by Visa® or MasterCard®.

- Get the international phone numbers for the bank that issued the card (not the 1-800 numbers – they may not work overseas), if the bank has one. A traveler will need this number if their card is lost or stolen. Carry these numbers separate of the card and leave a copy of the numbers at home with a trusted person.

- Consider opening up a new debit card account for the trip. Place a limited amount of money in that account. That way, if the debit card is stolen, the loss will be limited. If not a new account, keep the balance low and transfer funds into the account as needed to further protect against large losses.

Drawbacks to Debit Cards

There are some drawbacks to using debit cards. They generally do not offer the same level of protection as credit cards do. For example, if there is a dispute regarding a purchase, the holder is usually in a weaker position to get their money back because the merchant already has the money, which is not the case with a credit card. Even if the holder does get their money back, it will take a while to get the money back into their account.

Debit cards usually do not offer as much protection against fraudulent use as credit cards do, especially if a debit card has been taken and it has not been reported as stolen in a timely manner. Therefore, it is important to contact the issuing bank to find out exactly what protections exist and any liabilities that may be incurred if fraud would occur. The spending limits on the debit card are, of course, limited to the amount of money in the account. Debit cards also do not offer lines of credit, which is the case with credit cards.

CREDIT AND DEBIT CARD SAFETY

Of course, there are some safety and security issues associated with the use of credit and debit cards. Some of the major concerns are listed below:

- Always maintain visual contact of the cards. When giving the card to waiters, etc., make sure that it is not taken out of sight. If it is, follow the card. One method of credit/debit card fraud is when a merchant swipes the card through a magnetic reader that records the information from the magnetic strip on the back of the card. This information is then copied onto another credit card. A simpler method is when an extra imprint is made of the card, or the numbers and code on the back is simply written down by the thief.

- Keep a list of the names and account numbers of all cards in a safe place. These will be needed if the card is lost or stolen.

- Don't have the PIN number written down anywhere. Also, make sure the PIN is not a common number (i.e., date of birth, address, last 4 digits of social security number) that could be easily solved.

- Consider withdrawing smaller amounts of money to minimize the risk of losing large amounts of cash.

- Consider placing daily spending limits on the card. That way, if it is stolen, the loss will be limited.

- Never release the credit card number to someone who is not trusted.

- Save all receipts and verify these receipts by checking the account on-line or when the monthly statement is received. Original receipts will be required if there is a dispute.

- Keep all receipts in a secure place to prevent them from being stolen and the information on them used for nefarious purposes.

- Keep receipts in a secure place to protect the account number (that is still often printed on them).

- Don't carry the cards loose in pockets – they may accidentally fall out.

- Never leave the cards unattended.

- If the card is lost or stolen, immediately contact the financial institution that issued it. Local banks may be helpful in reporting the loss, too.

ATM SECURITY

Automated Teller Machines (ATMs) can be dangerous settings due to the simple fact that any criminal knows that ATM users will have money with them. Some points to consider are listed here:

- Be aware of the ATM's surroundings.

- Only use ATMs that are located at legitimate banks. Other ATMs (such as at retail settings) owned by private companies may be more prone to ATM fraud-related activities.

- Avoid using cash machines at night or those located in isolated places.

- Only use well-illuminated machines that can be seen by the public.

- Select those ATMs that require the ATM card to open a glass door to access the machine. The traveler should never let a stranger in with them. If something suspicious is seen outside the ATM booth, don't leave. If necessary, activate the panic alarm that is found in these facilities.

- Conceal the keypad when entering the PIN number, so others cannot see the code.

- Be prepared to use the card. Don't be slow. Get the transaction completed as quickly as possible.

- Immediately stow the cash away – do not count it in public.

- If using a drive-up ATM, scan the surroundings and be sure to keep the car doors locked. Place the vehicle as close to the machine as possible to prevent a person from getting between the machine and the vehicle.

- Have a buddy system when using ATMs. Never use an ATM alone.

Traveler's Checks and Cards

Traditional paper-based traveler's checks are offered by a variety of companies. With a traveler's check, the purchaser signs the checks (immediately upon purchasing them at a bank, etc.) and then signs the additional blank signature line on the check in the presence of the merchant. Traveler's checks are readily accepted throughout the world, and they can be easily replaced if lost or stolen, often in periods of 24 hours or less. Traveler's checks can also be purchased in Euros and other currencies.

There are some drawbacks. In some cases, there are fees associated with the purchase of them, ranging from 1 to 4% of the value of the purchase. In some cases, merchants may not accept them. And, if they are not in the same currency as the host country, the traveler may still have to use these checks to exchange them for that country's currency.

Traveler's checks can be obtained from banks or currency exchange companies. When purchasing the checks, a mix of denominations (i.e., 20s, 50s and 100s) should be requested. Since one of the primary benefits of the traveler's checks is replacement, the traveler should be sure to make at least two copies of the check numbers, leaving one with a responsible person at home and the other with them, separate from the actual checks. If the checks are lost or stolen, these numbers will be needed in order to obtain replacements. The international phone number and e-mail address of the credit card company should also be carried in order to ensure timely reporting of the loss/theft of the checks.

Traveler's Debit Cards

There are also traveler's debit cards available from some companies. These prepaid cards work just like a debit card, allowing the user to draw money out of their account. In some cases, the traveler can then reload their card with more money, if necessary, and access their accounts on-line. Some companies also offer emergency assistance and 24-hour replacement policies, just like the traditional paper-styled traveler's check. The traveler can also carry multiple debit cards, spreading the risk in case of theft or loss.

OTHER FINANCIAL INSTRUMENTS

There are many other financial instruments available for travelers. They include wire transfers, money orders, and bank accounts.

Wire Transfers

A wire money transfer is simply an electronic payment or transfer of funds. It is the transfer of money from one account to another. In the case of private parties, it is the transfer of money from one person to another, whereas the receiver simply stops by a local office, shows some identification and the wire transfer number, and then receives the money that was sent.

Money wires can be executed through any U.S. bank that has a corresponding or affiliate bank in the city where the traveler is staying. Depending upon the bank, money can be almost immediately available, or it could take up to 10 business days from the time the wire was processed. Wiring fees are generally paid on the U.S. side. However, fees could be incurred on both sides of the transfer. This method of payment is usually expensive.

In addition to bank wires, money can also be sent through other private financial companies including Western Union®, Money Gram®, and American Express®. As is the case with bank transfers, usually the fees associated with these services are relatively high.

Money Orders and Personal Checks

Money orders and personal checks are another means to obtain funds. These sources, however, may take a lot of time to get to the traveler. They may also be very difficult to cash. And, if cashed, there may be some very expensive fees associated with the transaction. There are some exceptions. American Express® cardholders, for example, can often cash personal checks for sums up to $1000 at American Express® offices for free.

Bank Accounts

In some long-term travel situations, a person could open a bank account in their host country. This would allow ready access to money. For example, a friend of one of the authors maintains an interest bearing bank account in Switzerland that he uses when traveling in Europe. This option, however, may not be available in all countries.

CONCLUSION

The information in this chapter has provided the reader with a variety of ideas and methods to ensure that the financial side of the trip is safe and secure. Of utmost importance in any trip in the context of money matters is that a traveler should:

- Research the currency system in the destination country.
- Know the currency conversion process.
- Identify any and all financial limitations that exist.
- Record financial-related information in case of theft or loss.
- Carry a mix of money – cash, cards, etc.
- Always properly safeguard all money.

If all of the advice in this chapter is followed, combined with the development of a "money-safe" mindset, the traveler can be assured that their financial safety and security will be maximized during the journey.

12
STREET SMARTS

The previous chapters in this book have already provided the traveler with a wealth of information on how to be safe while traveling. This chapter will further expand upon these concepts by examining safety and security in specific locations, such as while out sightseeing, and when going to clubs and restaurants. Besides specific locales, this chapter will also review issues related to drug and alcohol use. It will also explore the problem of kidnappings and abductions and how to deal with the local authorities.

WHILE OUT SIGHTSEEING

Several issues need to be considered when out sightseeing in a foreign country. First and foremost, the traveler needs to follow some general safety procedures while out walking, regardless of where they are and what they are doing. The traveler also needs to be aware of issues related to camera use in public and knowing where the danger areas are. Last, travelers also need to be aware of the dangers of pickpockets and con artists, and know what to do if threatened. The importance of having and knowing how to read a map will also be reviewed.

General Safety Tips

Some general points to consider when walking about include:

- Plan Ahead: The traveler must know where they are going.
- Know where police and fire departments are located as well as any other locations where the traveler can seek safety, if necessary.
- Be sure to research the hours of businesses and other locations that are part of the travel plans. In many European countries, shops, etc., close relatively early in the evening or they may close in the afternoon (siestas) and then re-open in the evening.

- Carry a phone card and/or spare change and know how the phone systems work and what the emergency numbers are. In England, for example, 911 is not the emergency number – 999 is.
- Eliminate all tourist identifiers, as identified in the Blending In chapter.

When out Walking

When out walking a traveler needs to be aware of dangers from both vehicles and criminals. Some points to consider include, but are not limited to the following:

- Never hitchhike.
- Whenever possible, never walk alone – day and/or night.
- Wear lighter-colored clothes when out walking to be more visible to motorists.
- Wear clothes and shoes that provide freedom of movement.
- In non-English speaking countries, limit speaking in public.
- Carry a whistle or some other personal safety device (note: chemical devices may be illegal in other countries).
- Avoid wearing headphones, etc. – the traveler's ability to hear threats approaching will be reduced when using these items. Electronics are also a hot target for criminals.
- Walk with a purpose and look confident and alert. The traveler should act as if they are a native to the area.
- Don't be overloaded with packages and bags. Packages, etc., provide an opportunity for theft. It also makes the traveler look defenseless and therefore, a good target.
- Be alert and aware of the surroundings in a 360-degree perspective. A traveler should know what is in front, behind, above, and even below them.
- Use the side mirrors on parked cars and the reflections from shop windows as mirrors to check to see if anyone is following.

- Walk closer to the street side of the sidewalk rather than the building side – doing so gives the traveler a split second longer to react in the event of an emergency.

- Don't jay walk. Cross at intersections for increased safety.

- Walk against the flow of traffic, so any approaching vehicles can be seen coming.

- Always use sidewalks. In Europe the road is where vehicles drive. The pavement, meanwhile, is the sidewalk.

- Look both ways when crossing a street. Remember that cars drive in the left lane in Britain and other countries. In fact, in many countries including the UK, "LOOK RIGHT" or "LOOK LEFT" is written on the road indicating from what direction the vehicle is coming. Americans, however, have the habit of looking left and then right when crossing a street. In England and other left-lane countries, however, the traveler needs to LOOK RIGHT and then LEFT before stepping off a curb in order to avoid being struck.

Camera Use and Photography

While photography is a component of traveling, there are some things the traveler can do to balance safety with camera use.

- Be aware of photography restrictions. In some countries, it may be illegal to photograph government buildings, military installations, police stations, airports and other critical infrastructure items. If photos are taken at these locations, the camera can be confiscated, and the traveler could be subsequently arrested.

- Keep the camera concealed – don't wear it around the neck, for example.

- Be as discreet as possible when taking photos. Pull the camera out from concealment, take the photo, and immediately re-conceal it.

- Do not photograph women, children, and/or other individuals without obtaining their permission first.

- Be VERY CAUTIOUS of a person willing to take a photograph of the traveler with his or her own camera. A thief could run away with it.

- Be sensitive to local customs regarding the taking of interior and exterior photographs of religious shrines and institutions.

Danger Areas

Listed below are just some of the danger areas that a traveler needs to consider when out sightseeing.

- Avoid high-risk places. These may include nightclubs, adult entertainment facilities, and high crime areas.
- The traveler should not assume that all areas are safe. Crimes can happen in all locations, especially around hotels and tourist areas that local criminals know are frequented by tourists.
- Avoid U.S. businesses, fast food chains, and related establishments. These are tourist magnets and therefore, high risk areas.
- Avoid isolated areas. A traveler should stay in well-traveled areas only.
- Do not stand too close to a vehicle if asked by its driver or occupant(s) for directions. In fact, avoid these situations.
- Always be wary of blind corners, alleyways, bushes, fences, etc. Give these areas a wide berth.
- Avoid dark, vacant, or deserted areas. Use well-lit, frequently traveled routes. Avoid using shortcuts through alleys, parks, etc., especially at night.
- Stay away from public demonstrations. Even though they may appear to be non-violent, they could readily escalate. In many countries, the freedom of assembly is often regulated or curtailed to the point where the local police or the military could arrest a person for simply being present at such events.
- Be wary of arenas and other areas that have large crowds. Unfortunately, there have been many cases of tourists injured as the result of hooliganism (rowdy crowds). Some have even been trampled or crushed to death.

Street Crimes

The traveler can also be exposed to a variety of street crimes when out sightseeing. A traveler is at risk for any type of violent or property-related crime. However, some of the more common tourist-related crimes include pickpocketing, con artists, and social engineering.

Pickpocketing

Some experts argue that pickpocketing has reached epidemic proportions in some countries, especially in tourist-related and/or mass transit areas. For example, in the United Kingdom large cities are filled full of pickpockets; they are often women and children.

Pickpockets work alone and in teams through misdirection and distraction. The procedures followed by pickpockets according to vonHentig[13] include:

> **Box 12-1**
> **Pickpocketing Techniques**
>
> **The Spill:** A person may accidentally spill something on the traveler. As they are apologizing, they will start rubbing/cleaning the affected area, making it difficult for the traveler to feel the pickpocket's other hand (or their partner's) as the item is being stolen.
> **The Razor Blade –** In other cases, the thief may take a razor blade and slash the pocket containing the traveler's wallet. Or, they may simply cut through the straps on a purse.
> **The Distraction –** The poor mother holding the [drugged] sleeping baby, etc., are often distracters for the pickpocket.

a) Finding the Target;

b) Closing the Gap;

c) Overcoming the victim's mental preparation;

d) Overcoming the victim's physical or mechanical protections used; and,

e) Securing the booty, often by "floating" it to another hidden accomplice.

---

[13] vonHentig, H. (May-June, 1943). *The Pickpocket: Psychology, Tactics and Technique.* Journal of Criminal Law and Criminology, 34(1), 11-15.

Diligence is the key to prevent pickpocketing. The traveler needs to be very wary when getting on a bus or train, riding escalators, and mingling in large crowds – that's when pickpockets strike. Oftentimes these pickpockets are young children and teenagers, working in collusion with adults.

Con Artists and Other Street Scams

Con artists exist in every locale and they can usually spot a tourist quite easily, who are their major targets. They come in all shapes and sizes, and their scams or cons are diverse, making it difficult to profile the "typical" con artist and their limitless scams. With all of these scams or cons, however, there is one common denominator: the gullible traveler.

Usually, the beginning of the "con" is to engage the traveler in a conversation or stop them on the street, so they and their accomplices can set the traveler up for some type of crime. To avoid these situations, the traveler should simply not stop to talk to anyone – even if they are requesting medical assistance. It is best to simply keep walking and then call for medical assistance later, if this was the case.

The traveler should also keep in mind that children are also taught in some countries from early childhood on how to con, fake, pretend, or trick in order to get money and other goods from tourists. For example, a child could ask for help while family members or others wait in hiding for the right moment to commit a robbery.

Travelers also need to be wary of the following issues:

- The traveler should not rely upon strangers for directions. It could be a setup for a crime.
- Never allow strangers to accompany a traveler to their hotel, nightclubs, or other attractions. A traveler should not allow strangers to show them "where the action is." It is common in large cities for criminals to lure tourists off the beaten path and then victimize them.

- Avoid being benevolent and giving out money to pan-handlers, beggars, etc. By giving out money, the traveler first reveals that they have money. It also shows these con artists and their accomplices where the money is kept.

- Beggars may not be as they appear. Many "beggars" are very rich. In fact, begging is their full-time career!

Social Engineering

Throughout this book, the authors have discussed the importance of the traveler not revealing a great deal of information about themselves, inadvertently through the process of social engineering.

Social engineering is a term used to describe the techniques that criminals use to collect seemingly innocent information from their victims. This information, when combined with other information, can often cause serious problems for the victim. What makes social engineering even more dangerous is at times, the criminal will collect information without even talking directly to the traveler. The next time the reader is traveling, for example, simply listen to the variety of conversations that can be overheard in public. They may include the "loud talker" telling an individual their travel plans, where they are from, what they do, where they are staying, etc.

Social engineering techniques vary, but the common denominator is the simple fact that the criminal uses everyday interactions and trickery to obtain information that can physically and/or financially injure a traveler. This information, combined with other information gathered from what appears to be a series of innocent questions, could cause a lot of harm. For example, a simple conversation that identifies a traveler's profession, where they are staying, and if they are traveling alone could lead to problems.

It is, therefore, important for the traveler to be wary of un-solicited conversations, especially those from strangers. In any conversation, meanwhile, the traveler must also be cautious on whom they talk to and what type of information is divulged. Some key points to consider include, but are not limited to:

- Do not discuss or reveal personal information in public. The traveler should keep the volume of their voice low when talking in public and be aware that at all times, there is someone listening.

- Do not reveal information about socio-economic status, occupation, etc. If pressed, the traveler should make their profession boring and from a lower socio-economic status (i.e., "I drive a plow truck for the city.").

- Be cautious about giving out information regarding family travel plans or security measures and procedures.

If Threatened

How to respond to a threat or confrontation is often mixed, depending upon the situation. If the traveler is confronted and/or threatened, the key is to get out of and disengage from the potentially dangerous situation as fast as possible, regardless, even if the traveler knows or feels that they are in the right. Some other points to consider include, but are not limited to:

- If the traveler feels that someone is following them, they should turn around and check.

- A traveler must learn to trust their instincts. If something feels wrong, most likely it is.

- If a traveler feels that they are in danger, they should not hesitate to scream and/or run. A traveler should draw as much attention to the situation as possible.

- A traveler should show their suspicions. Without being aggressive toward the threat, a traveler, for example, could turn to look at the threat in a

> **Travel Tip**
>
> If threatened, consider breaking glass. Oftentimes, people ignore arguments (or even calls for help). The sound of broken glass, meanwhile, will draw the attention of others. Shouting "FIRE!" is also effective in getting the attention of others.

non-aggressive manner. This could send a clear message that the traveler will not be taken by surprise.

- If accosted by someone from a vehicle, run in the direction opposite of the way the car is headed. That way, the criminal(s) will have problems chasing after the traveler while in their vehicle.

- Change directions. If someone is following on foot, the traveler should cross the street and vary his or her pace. If the person following the traveler is in a car, the traveler should turn and walk in the opposite direction.

- If threatened, go into the nearest store or public place. If the threat should follow, ask to use (or find) a phone and call for help. If there isn't a store or public area nearby, keep moving.

- If followed, create distance and get away from the threat.

- If abducted, a traveler should always try to escape. If a traveler cannot escape, they should fight back and never allow the threat to take them anywhere. The traveler should fight where they stand.

Map Reading and Land Navigation

Knowing how to read a map (and using it) is also critical when traveling. Box 12-2 provides some basic points on how to read a map. Besides knowing how to read a map:

- First, the traveler should buy a map. There are many compact, inexpensive maps that are available and easy to carry. In fact, some maps are the size of small notebooks.

- Be sure to pick up maps that are provided free of charge by many hotels, local authorities and tourist information centers.

- The best time to read the map is before the trip. This will help the traveler find suitable accommodations, etc. It will also assist in designing the trip agenda.

- The map should also be studied upon arrival. A traveler must get a feel for the area, marking significant land-marks, and where they are staying.

Box 12-2
Basics of Map Reading

♦ Mapmakers usually orient their maps to show north at the top. The four cardinal directions (north, south, east and west) are often on the map in the form of a compass or wind rose symbol.

♦ When reading a map, orient it to the north. A traveler should position their body in the same direction in order to get their bearings (i.e., west is left; east is right; south is behind).

♦ Always look at the scale to get a good idea of the distance between the two points.

♦ A good map will have a legend or key that will show the user what the different symbols and colors on the map mean. This is usually located on the side or bottom of the map.

♦ Many street maps have letters along the top and numbers along the side (or the opposite). These will help the traveler find the approximate location of sites or streets that are listed in the map index.

♦ Many cities are designed on the Cartesian coordinate system, where the city is laid out in a grid fashion. In many cases, cities are divided into NW, NE, SW and SE sectors with avenues running east-west and roads running north-south (or the opposite) while addresses increase in number as they radiate from the central axis. As an example, if the traveler is looking for 5045 SW 63rd Ave, they should know that it is in the SW quadrant, 63 blocks south and 50 blocks west of the central dividing point or axis. Therefore, it is very important to find the central axis of the city for that particular city, if one exists.

♦ In many European cities, streets are not organized on a grid design. Nevertheless, there are always major streets or thoroughfares that the traveler can use to orient themselves.

• Every traveler should have his or her own map. That way, if a traveler should get separated from the group, they can navigate on their own.

- Have the concierge or other trusted persons mark areas/ locations on the map that should be avoided.

- Before going out, mark the destination areas on the map, memorize the major streets; and, rehearse how to get around.

- Know the major landmarks. In most areas, there are geographical features (i.e., rivers) or buildings that can serve to orient the traveler. The traveler should find these on the map and know where they are in relation to them. Knowing the major landmarks will also help the traveler determine (i.e., through triangulation) their position through the use of these landmarks, if they should become disoriented.

- If a traveler needs to refer to a map, it should be done in private. For example, the traveler should study the map in a bathroom stall or another private area. There is nothing more vulnerable than a traveler standing in public reading a map.

- Know the Cardinal points (N-E-S-W; "Never Eat Shredded Wheat") and the traveler's orientation to these points. For example, the sun rises in the east and sets in the west.

Electronic GPS Systems

A traveler may also consider using a hand-held Global Positioning Satellite (GPS) device as a navigational aid during their travels. These GPS devices use a series of satellites to pinpoint their location as well as destination points, often known as waypoints. In effect, the hand-held device can serve as map as well as guide. Many models have sound capabilities that, for example, will instruct a person to "go left 100 yards and then turn right." Depending upon their features, some also have the option to load maps from specific countries and cities into the device, while others have language translators built into them. They can be relatively inexpensive to own, too.

Hand-held GPS devices have some advantages. They are often compact and they can provide detailed maps and directions for the traveler, in addition to a variety of other features, depending upon price and model.

A word of caution is required when using these devices:

- First, the traveler will be taking yet another high-value target with them on their trip.

- Extra batteries or a recharging device will be needed, adding more items needed for the trip.

- Even though these items do provide accurate and detailed directions, the fundamentals of land navigation are still necessary. A person still needs to know where they are.

- Dependence on technology could be dangerous. The device could fail for some reason. Therefore, the traveler should plan for this issue and be prepared to know and apply the basics of map reading, using a traditional paper map to get around.

- The device (like traditional paper maps) should be used in private in order to avoid advertising that a tourist is present.

CLUBS AND RESTAURANTS

Tourists will also frequent clubs and restaurants. While many of the principles of street safety apply in these settings, there are some specific issues that should be addressed.

Of particular concern is the fact that occupancy limits and other safety codes (i.e., alarms, sprinkler systems, fire exits) that are required in the United States may be substandard or not exist at all in many foreign countries. Therefore, the traveler needs to be more diligent regarding their safety and security. Some points to consider are shown below:

- Take a good look at the surroundings – does it make the traveler feel comfortable and safe or does it have a lot of danger signs?

- Immediately identify all emergency exits when entering a facility. Identify the 1st choice and then the 2nd choice exits.

- Check to see if the club/restaurant has smoke detectors, sprinkler systems and extinguishers.

- Always try to sit near an exit (or emergency exits), when possible.

- Always look for clear exit paths. If an emergency should arise, the traveler will need a clear path of departure.

- If and when an alarm sounds, react immediately and leave the building. A common human response to alarms and emergencies is to not immediately evacuate, but to go to friends, assess the situation and then leave. This takes up a valuable amount of time.

- In case of an emergency evacuation, have a pre-planned location where the traveler will meet and assemble with friends outside and away from the establishment.

- Avoid sitting at a sidewalk café table or by a window – this could draw attention. These locations also offer limited protection from flying debris.

- Don't discuss personal matters and travel plans with waiters, etc.

- The traveler should always maintain visual and physical control of their food and drink to ensure that they are not tampered with.

- Be cautious of restrooms. Depending upon the location, drug use and prostitution often occur in these areas. Check the area outside the restroom before using them. Also, check the restroom itself for any suspicious behaviors and/or danger signs. Last, the traveler should always have a partner with them when using these facilities.

ALCOHOL, DRUG USE AND OTHER VICES

Besides location, the traveler also needs to be wary of engaging in certain activities that could be dangerous. Some of these behaviors include alcohol and drug use. Of course, the traveler also needs to be wary of other vices including prostitution and frequenting adult entertainment establishments.

Alcohol Use

It goes without saying that all travelers should be wary of alcohol consumption. Besides impairing the user's decision-making abilities, excessive alcohol use could lead to accidents, or even worse, being targeted for a variety of crimes. Travelers also need to be wary of frequenting places that serve alcohol. Customers in these establishments could also cause a variety of problems for the traveler, ranging from theft to sexual assault.

Travelers also need to recognize that the alcohol content of many beers and other beverages are not consistent with what they may be accustomed to in their home country. As an example, in England there is Strongbow® and Mangers® cider. Unlike cider in the United States, both of these varieties have a high alcohol content, often higher than some beers. Germany, meanwhile, is also known for its plethora of beer. Many of these beers also have a higher alcohol content in comparison to what some travelers may be accustomed to at home.

Combined with the above points, at times it is often difficult to assess the nature and quality of some establishments. As an example, on a trip to England, one of the authors and his English host (who is a police officer) went into a pub for lunch. Even though it was considered to be a safe and clean establishment, a fight erupted between two intoxicated patrons, which resulted in flying glasses and chairs. In order to avoid situations of this nature, the traveler should therefore:

- Scan the establishment. If there are a lot of intoxicated patrons, this should be a danger sign.
- Get an overall feel for the establishment. If it feels or looks questionable, leave.
- Look to see how patrons react to the traveler's presence.
- Leave immediately when some type of problem erupts.

Drug Use

The legalities of drug use and possession vary throughout the world. Some countries will allow drug use in certain controlled areas, or it may be legal to possess types or quantities of certain drugs, but not others. In other countries, meanwhile, drug use and/or possession is considered to be a very serious crime.

Travel Tip

According to the State Department, of the 2,500 Americans arrested overseas annually, 30% of the arrests are drug-related.

Using and purchasing drugs (through legal dispensers and/or illegal dealers) of course, will also expose the traveler to greater levels of danger for a various assortment of crimes. Using drugs also impairs the traveler's judgment and the ability to defend oneself. Therefore, it is strongly discouraged that a traveler should use and/or possess drugs while overseas. The traveler should also avoid drug shops, etc., even if they are legal and in tourist locales. In many cases, these areas are also hotbeds for criminal activities.

Prostitution

Prostitution, legal or not, is found in most major cities. In some cities, there are dedicated areas (i.e., Eros Centers) where prostitution is legal. In fact, in Amsterdam, the Red Light district is actually a popular tourist area. Along with the prostitutes, however, there are other criminals that could prey on the unsuspecting tourist.

Prostitution in some cases may not be readily apparent to the traveler. Sometimes prostitutes will go to great lengths to get a customer, even pretending to be a woman in distress. In other cases, they may meet the person in a club and ask the traveler back to their residence, where the prostitute then solicits the traveler for sex. In countries including Canada and England, the act of prostitution is legal. Public solicitation, however, is not. Therefore, solicitation is done in private.

Besides the risk of being a victim of a crime, there is also the risk of exposure to a variety of sexually transmitted diseases from sex workers. While some "legal" prostitutes may be required to submit to periodic health check-ups, using the services of a prostitute is nevertheless dangerous. Many are unlicensed, victims of human trafficking, or have drug dependency problems. Others, meanwhile, are controlled by pimps who could easily prey on customers.

Adult Entertainment Facilities

Adult entertainment facilities should also be avoided. In many cities (often adjacent to the Red Light Districts), the tourist can find a wide variety of adult entertainment establishments. In some cases they may be well managed and safe. In other cases, however, they could be very dangerous locales. These areas, of course, are also often magnets for con artists and other criminals.

KIDNAPPINGS AND ABDUCTIONS

Believe it or not, kidnappings are also a concern for the traveler. Regardless of age, gender and occupation, all travelers are vulnerable to being kidnapped. In fact, estimates of the "kidnapping business" in foreign countries place its profits at over $500 million per year.[14] If the traveler does not think it can happen to them, think again. A student of the authors was victim to an express kidnapping on Spring Break in Mexico in 2005, where he was ransomed for $250. It happens throughout the world with Central and South America and Eastern Europe the leaders in the "Kidnapping Business." These kidnappings can be individual-based or in some cases, group-based, where there have been documented cases of groups of people (up to 50) being held for ransom.

There are three basic elements to any kidnapping. They include:

- An offender or the hostage-taker;
- The secondary victim or hostage: and,
- A primary victim.

---

[14] Briggs, R. (2001) *The Kidnapping Business*. Foreign Policy Centre. London: England.

The main target of any kidnapping is the primary victim. The primary victim is not the hostage. It is that person or persons responsible for meeting the demands of the hostage taker. The secondary victim is the hostage. These secondary targets are simply the means to the ends, to force the primary victim to meet the demands of the hostage taker(s).[15]

Kidnappers can be terrorists, professional criminals, and opportunistic individuals looking to make some quick money. The primary goal of any kidnapper is money. This money is used for a variety of purposes ranging from personal gain to financing rebel operations.

Kidnappings can be short or long in duration. Two types of short-term kidnappings are:[16]

- *"Secuestro al paso"* or express kidnapping. These types of abductions occur in large cities in Mexico, Colombia, and Brazil. Express kidnappings only last a few hours and can be characterized by an individual being kidnapped and then driven to multiple ATM machines where they are forced to withdraw money and empty their accounts. Then, they are released. Anecdotal evidence suggests that 70 express kidnappings occur every day in Mexico City alone.

- *"Secuestros relampagos"* or lightning kidnappings. These are also known as "fast-food" kidnaps or "mini-kidnappings." In these types of abductions the kidnapper(s) drive the victim around in a vehicle until the ransom is paid. Ransoms range from a few hundred to thousands of dollars. The victim is released soon after their abduction.

There are also the long-term kidnappings. Long-term kidnappings are usually organized by a group of individuals that have staged the abduction. The victim, meanwhile, is held for a

---

[15] Johnson, B.R.; McKenzie, D. and G.L. Warchol. (December, 2003). *Corporate Kidnapping: An Exploratory Study.* Journal of security administration, 46(2), 13-31.
[16] Ibid

long period of time, ranging from several months or over a year, in some instances. Usually, these ransoms are quite large.[17]

Kidnap and Ransom Insurance

In addition to the simple precautionary measures, some travelers have opted to take out Kidnap and Ransom (K & R) insurance. Depending upon the type of policy, some only cover the actual ransom. Others cover the expenses related to the administrative aspects of a kidnap, such as the hiring of consultants and negotiators that deal with all activities associated with the kidnapping, including negotiating the release of the individual(s), to psychological counseling for the family and victim.

K & R agreements can cover four basic hazards. They include:

1) extortion coverage or payment made for the release of individuals;

2) threats that are made against individuals where the individual is not physically harmed;

3) coverage against the threat of physical damage to products or property; and,

4) detention, where an individual is held under duress for any reason and by any individual including legal authorities (which can happen in many countries).[18]

Abductions and Assaults

Besides kidnapping, abductions and assaults are a safety concern. The only way for the traveler to prevent him or herself from being abducted is to never assume that they are safe. The traveler needs to be alert and avoid dangerous situations while also recognizing that abductions are often planned attacks. Therefore, the traveler should be conscious of any types of stationary and mobile surveillance activities against them (people or cars following, suspicious observers around the hotel, etc.).

---

[17]   Ibid
[18]   Ibid

In the context of sexual assault, meanwhile, statistics show that the majority of the victims are assaulted by an acquaintance. Many of these were also planned. Therefore, the traveler needs to be especially diligent on who they associate with, making sure that they are never alone with members of the opposite sex.

DEALING WITH LOCAL AUTHORITIES

The quality and professionalism of the police vary from country to country. Generally, the police in western nations are quite professional and well trained. In other parts of the world, however, the quality of police agencies could be low and staffed by inept and/or corrupt officers. Therefore, it is important that the traveler researches the nature and the quality of the police in their destination country. A general rule of thumb when dealing with the police is to cooperate with them and follow their instructions if it is reasonable and/or logical in nature.

If a Victim of a Crime

If a traveler is a victim of a crime, it is important that it is reported as soon as possible. The general protocol for reporting crimes overseas is to first contact the U.S. embassy, consulate, or consular agency for assistance. Consular personnel are available 24 hours a day, 7 days a week for such emergencies, where they can assist victims in reporting the incident. Consular officials are also familiar with other services or resources that exist in the country that the victim(s) may need. Therefore, it is best to always use consular officials. If, for some reason consular officials cannot be located or contacted, it will then be necessary for the traveler to report the crime on their own. In these situations, it would be best to bring along a trusted person who is from that country (and has knowledge of the criminal justice system). If not from the host country, the traveler(s) should bring along other individuals who can provide support.

Travelers should also request a copy of the incident report for personal and insurance reasons. If the police agency does not provide a copy of the report, at a minimum, the traveler should request an incident report number and note the time, date, and location of where the report was given. Any other information, such as the names of the officers who assisted, could also prove to be useful if additional information is needed by the traveler's insurance company, etc.

If Arrested

If arrested, the traveler has made some enormous errors in judgment. And, to say the least, they are in a serious amount of trouble (and danger) as a consequence of those actions. According to the U.S. Department of State, in those countries where the U.S. has relevant treaties, the arrested person must be told of their right to consular notification and access. The arrested person can then decide whether they want consular representatives notified of the arrest. If the detainee requests representation, then the detaining official must give notice without delay.

In other cases, the U.S. and that particular country may have mandatory notification procedures. Under this type of agreement, mandatory notification must be made to the nearest consulate or embassy "without delay," "immediately," or within the time specified in a bilateral agreement between the United States and the foreign national's country, *regardless of whether the foreign national requests such notification* of the arrest. In either case, the consulate official does not serve as legal counsel. They can, however, notify others of the situation on behalf of the arrested traveler.

When in custody, there are a myriad of safety issues. If possible, a separate cell should be requested to protect oneself against attack. The traveler should also be wary on food sanitation, water quality, and communicable diseases that exist in many jails. Other issues according to Haynes[19] include:

- Always ask immediately for an attorney.
- Request that the nearest embassy or consulate be contacted.
- Do not volunteer information.
- Stay calm and do not provoke anyone.

---

[19] From: Haynes, R. (2001) *Personal security and terrorism awareness.* New York: Writers Club Press.

- DO NOT sign any document unless directed to do so by the consular official or attorney. In all other cases, decline politely.
- Don't accept anyone at face value – always ask for identification and verify when possible.

CONCLUSION

A good sense of what is normal and what is unusual while traveling could be more important than any other type of security precaution taken. Street smarts begins while the traveler is out sightseeing, where care should be taken to avoid the common hazards associated with camera use, knowing the danger areas, being aware of con artists, and knowing what to do if threatened. Being street smart also extends to activities in clubs and restaurants, and recognizing the dangers associated with drug and alcohol use, and visiting vice-related establishments. As this chapter has shown, the traveler also needs to be aware of the risk of kidnappings and abductions while abroad, while also recognizing that in some countries, the quality of law enforcement services may be inferior in comparison to their home country.

GETTING AROUND

M ost likely a traveler is going to use public transportation to some degree or another while abroad. While traveling, there are various forms of public transportation available, including buses, trains and trolleys. Depending upon the country, its public transportation system can be quite effective and safe. In other cases, it can be downright dangerous. Besides public transportation, travelers may also have access to taxis and leased motor vehicles. As is the case with public transportation, there may also be some benefits and risks associated with these forms of transportation.

Planning in advance on what forms of public (or private) transportation will be used is important to ensure a safe and flawless trip. Where to begin to assess the nature and quality of these forms of transportation begins with a review of various sites on the Internet. Travel blogs, the State Department and travel sites can provide a great deal of insight into the nature and quality of the various forms of transportation that exist. Other sources also include talking to previous travelers and travel agents about the safety and reliability of mass transit systems. Upon arrival, meanwhile, it is also important to inquire with hotel staff, police, and other knowledgeable and trusted individuals.

TRAINS, SUBWAYS AND BUSES

A great deal of the information presented in the chapters on Airport Security and Aircraft Safety also applies to using trains, subways and buses. There are, however, some specific issues that need to be addressed when using these forms of transportation.

There are several ways that travelers can make themselves safer when using public transportation:

- Don't travel alone.
- Don't wait long periods of time for the transport.
- Don't wait alone for transportation.

- Don't ride public transportation late at night. There are far less "eyes and ears" around than in the day. Consider spending a little more money on a cab, which is usually safer.

- Purchase a map and timetable to gain an understanding of the public transport system.

- Try to buy tickets in advance. That way, the traveler will not have to stand in line at the stations/terminals, reducing the risk of victimization. Additionally, it is often cheaper to buy tickets in advance.

- Always have the exact fare to speed up purchasing tickets and boarding. Many places also require exact fare.

- A traveler should make sure that they are on the correct platform. Many stations/terminals have multiple level platforms, as well as inbound and outbound platforms.

- Check the time of the last train, bus, or subway to prevent from being stranded.

- Seek local advice when using public transportation, especially when traveling alone and in the evening.

- If possible, purchase a pass. It is usually cheaper to do this, it reduces the amount of time in line, and the traveler doesn't continually have to access their money. Many transit authorities offer daily, weekly, or monthly passes for individuals and even families.

Reading Timetables

All forms of public transportation have a set time schedule and course of travel. This information is often readily available to the traveler in the form of a printed timetable that can be found at local stations and even on the Internet at times. An example of a printed timetable and a detailed description of its major components is shown in Figure 13-1.

Travelers also need to be aware that many train stations also have electronic destination boards that list the arrival time and destination of trains approaching that specific platform. Additionally, these stations may also announce the arrival of each train. Therefore, it is important that travelers pay attention to these boards and announcements for updates and any changes in the platform assignments of their transport.

Usually, most timetables are written using the 24-hour clock, which is commonly referred to in many countries as military time. The main difference between regular and military time is how hours are expressed. Regular time uses numbers 1 to 12 to identify each of the 24 hours in a day. In military time, the hours are numbered from 00 to 23. The 24-hour clock begins with 0000 hours as midnight. Under this system, 1 a.m. is 0100hrs, 1 p.m. is 1300hrs, etc. Minutes (and seconds), meanwhile, do not change. That is, if it is 15 minutes past midnight, the military time equivalent will be 0015hrs. Perhaps the easier way to remember military time is that after noon, the time is higher than 12 (i.e., 4 pm is 1600 hours [12+4=16]). From midnight to noon, meanwhile, the range is from 0-12.

Figure 13-1
Sample Bus Timetable

A

CENTRE - HOSPITAL - LONGLEVENS / ELMBRIDGE CIRCULAR   C ⟶ 6

Stagecoach in Gloucester   ⟵   B

6	Bus Station, London Rd, Great Western Rd, Gloucestershire Royal Hospital forecourt, Great Western Rd, Horton Rd, London Rd, Barnwood Rd, Elmbridge Rd, Cheltenham Rd, Old Cheltenham Rd, Longlevens (Paygrove Ln), Clomoney Way, Greyhound Gardens, Nine Elms Rd, Little Elmbridge, Elmleaze, Meadowleaze, Elmbridge Rd, Barnwood Rd, London Rd, Horton Rd, Great Western Rd, Gloucestershire Royal Hospital forecourt, Great Western Rd, London Rd, Northgate St, Spread Eagle Rd, Bus Station.

D

Monday to Saturday

F

E Service no	6			6	H	6	6 M-F	6 S
Bus Station	0905			05		1405	1505	1505
Royal Hospital	0910			10		1410	1510	1510
Elmbridge Rd	0915			15		1415	1515	1515
Longlevens	0918	Then at		18		1418	1518	1518
Little Elmbridge	0922	these		22	until	1422	1522	1522
Meadowleaze	0924	minutes		24		1424	-	1524
Elmbridge Rd G	0926	past each hour		26		1426	-	1526
Royal Hospital	0933			33		1433	-	1533
Bus Station	0938			38		1438	-	1538
Sunday	No service.							

Bank Holidays etc		No service on Bank Holiday Mondays, Christmas/Boxing and New Year's Days. Contact operator for rest of Christmas/ New Year period. Saturday service on Good Friday.	**I**
Key:	**J**	M-F............Monday to Friday only. S.............Saturday only.	
04.08.07	**K**		

(Adapted from the Integrated Transport Unit, Gloucestershire County Council, Gloucester, England)

A	**Heading** – each timetable has a heading showing the main stopping points of the service.
B	**Operator** – shows the name by the company operating this timetable. Where two or more operators are shown on a timetable there will be another line above the service number, titled operator code, showing a two-letter code for the operator who runs this service
C	**Route Number** – shows the number of the bus route. This number is normally shown on the front of the bus. In most cases, the route number indicates which route the bus will take
D	**Route Description** – a description of towns, villages and roads the bus service runs through, but not individual bus stops. Most bus services will normally stop at all bus stops along the route.
E	**Days of Travel** – shows the days that each section of the timetable operates. In most cases this will either be Monday to Saturday or Monday to Friday. Services that run differently on Saturday and Sunday will each be shown separately. When individual journeys operate on specific days only, this is shown as a code
F	**Code Headings** – these show information on each of the journeys shown. Where different operators are shown on one timetable the service number will show the correct route number and Bus Operator by a two-letter code of the relevant operator running that service. Also, if the days of operation are different from the title, another line will show a code for this: i.e., MW = Monday and Wednesday only. All codes used will be shown in the Key.
G	**List of main stopping points** – only the main stopping points are listed. If your stop is not mentioned in this list, you can calculate the time your bus will stop by looking in the route description and checking where your stop falls between the main stopping points.
H	**Times** – the times are shown from top to bottom, with the left hand side showing the first service of the day and continuing to the last on the right hand side. When a bus service runs at the same time each hour or every 10 minutes, etc., the timetable will show "at these minutes past each hour" then the times for each stop until the last journey to follow that pattern, then returns to showing full times.
I	**Sunday and Bank Holiday information** – additional information on days of operation.
J	**Key** – a full explanation of information shown in the timetable as a one or two-letter code (except bus operator code, which will be shown in brackets next to the operator name).
K	**Start date** – shows the start date of the last change to the timetable.

While at the Terminals/Stations

Stations or terminals can be very interesting places (to say the least) in the context of crime and safety. To reduce the chances of theft and other crimes, a traveler should consider the following points:

- Find that balance between not waiting too long and not missing the transport. As pointed out earlier, the traveler should not wait too long at public areas.

- Look out for the con artists. Con artists abound at many public transportation facilities. For example, official-looking people, with matching jackets and patches similar to legitimate staff, may offer to help purchase tickets and provide other forms of assistance, victimizing the traveler in the process.

- Be wary of crowds – they offer criminals anonymity.

- If the terminal has police, guards and/or CCTV, sit near them.

- Sit near panic buttons, if they are available.

- Be wary of platforms. These are often crowded. A person could be purposely or accidentally pushed off a platform.

- Don't leave any luggage unattended; this causes security alerts and delays.

- When going through turnstiles, a traveler should also be sure to have their luggage in front of them and push it through first. If carried behind, the luggage could become trapped in the door/turnstile. If this were to occur, a criminal could also literally tear it right out of the traveler's control, while the traveler could be trapped on the other side of the gate, unable to get back to the other side and their possessions.

While On Board Transportation

- Watch the door. Some doors on subways and trains are quite strong and when closing, they could push a traveler out of the compartment or cause some other type of injury.

- Sit near exits – the more traffic, the more likely someone is to intervene in a situation. Sitting near an exit also makes it easier to get out of a situation, if one should arise.

- Always try to sit and not stand. In case of an abrupt stop, a traveler is better protected when sitting.

- If the transportation has CCTV, sit near these cameras.

- Sit near the guard or conductor's compartment.

- When seated, keep all bags on the inner side away from the aisle or pathway when possible. That way, it is more difficult for a thief to grab and run away with one's property.

- Don't store personal possessions in aisles or pathways; use the storage areas above the seats, if possible.

- For increased safety and privacy, a traveler could place objects in the seats next to them to prevent people from sitting next to them.

- Try to choose and sit in those seats that are parallel to the wall or the car. That way, a traveler's back is to the wall, and the field of view is increased.

- A traveler should never sleep on public transportation unless they have their own secure compartment, or they are with someone who is, and is willing to stay awake.

- Be prepared to de-board. A traveler should have all of their possessions ready to go. Public transport often has very short stops.

- When de-boarding be aware of any physical hazards (vehicles, platforms, persons and doors).

When on a Train

- If seats are booked in advance, a traveler should make sure that they are sitting in the correct seat in order to avoid a potential confrontation with another traveler.

- Avoid sitting in an empty carriage. Often there is greater safety in numbers.

- Don't stand in open doorways on moving trains. In some countries, passengers can actually do this!

- Consider upgrading to first class. In many situations, upgrades from coach are not that much more expensive (if at all), if done in advance. Unlike airplanes, first class on trains provides more security, since a traveler is in their own compartment.

- Even though sleeper compartments have locks, consider securing the compartment door with an object to prevent it from being forced open. This could be as easy as a belt secured around the door handle or a wedge placed under the door.

USING MOTOR VEHICLES

According to the U.S. Department of State, death and injury from road-related accidents in developing countries are 20 to 70 times higher than those rates in the United States. Therefore, motor vehicle use should be used with caution when traveling.

International Driver's Permits/Licenses

An International Driver's Permit (IDP) or license may be required for renting and/or driving a vehicle overseas. IDP's are not substitutes for an existing license. They are a supplement to an existing license. They can be considered to be an official translation of the traveler's existing license into 10 foreign languages.

While there are many places to obtain an IDP, the State Department has recognized two automobile organizations to issue IDPs. They include the American Automobile Association (AAA), where the traveler can obtain the permit from an AAA local office, or download an application at the AAA website. The second organization is the American Automobile Touring Alliance. Applications for the IDP can be obtained from this organization from its website. Website addresses for both of these organizations are located in Appendix M. The cost of an IDP from these U.S. State Department-authorized organizations is approximately $15.

To apply for an IDP, the traveler must be at least 18 years of age, hold a valid driver's license issued by a state within the U.S., and present two passport-sized photos. The IDP does not require the applicant to take a test. All an applicant has to do is to transfer personal and existing driver's license information to the application, which is then processed and issued to the traveler.

Renting or Leasing Vehicles

Leasing a vehicle is an alternative to public transportation in many countries. Leasing may allow the traveler flexibility in the context of mobility.

Before renting any vehicle, it is very important that the traveler reviews the Road Safety section of the Department of State's Consular Information Sheets. These can be found on the U.S. State Department's website at http://travel.state.gov/travel. The State Department also recommends that travelers check with the *embassy or consulate of those countries* that they will visit in order to learn about requirements for driver's licenses, road permits, and auto insurance.

The traveler also needs to recognize the risks involved in renting any type of vehicle. As pointed out in the Street Smarts Chapter, the risk of injuries related to motor vehicle use can be quite high. The traveler also needs to recognize their limitations. Driving in a different country can be frustrating and confusing. Traffic density at times can be extremely high, and drivers may be more reckless and/or aggressive compared to typical American drivers. Language barriers, combined with signage, may also make driving very difficult. Therefore, the traveler needs to seriously think about these (and many other) issues before getting behind the wheel.

Last, the traveler needs to research what the road system is like in their destination country and/or region. Some questions to consider include:

- Does the country have a road system similar in quality to the United States?
- Does the country have an effective infrastructure and road system (i.e., Autobahn, Expressway, Motorway)?

- Does the country have an adequate support system for motorists (i.e., enough gas stations, rest stops, vehicle assistance)?

- Is the road system similar in function (i.e., right hand drive, multiple lanes)?

Restrictions on Leasing Vehicles

There are often leasing restrictions that vary from country to country and from company to company. In some cases, major leasing agencies such as Avis® and Hertz® will not lease or allow individuals to drive their leased cars to or within certain countries. For example, some car rental agencies strongly discourage and/or prohibit the use of their vehicles in former Soviet Bloc countries. The risk of theft and other related auto-crimes are considered too high in these areas. If a traveler should venture into these countries, usually their supplemental insurance is void, making them fully responsible for any loss or damage that should occur. Other companies, however, may nevertheless lease a vehicle to the traveler for use in these countries. Another common restriction is related to age. Many, if not all leasing agencies have a minimum age of 21 or 25 in order to lease a vehicle.

Insurance Issues

Insurance is also an issue. A traveler needs to make sure that their existing vehicle insurance will cover the loss or damage to the rental car in a foreign country. Policy limitations vary from carrier to carrier, with many companies limiting coverage to the U.S. only. Therefore, a traveler should contact their insurance agent to check for any policy limitations. The traveler should also consider taking out supplemental auto insurance. This can be obtained from the rental company (if not required by them) or from a private carrier. It may be more expensive, but it could save the traveler from a variety of issues if the vehicle should become damaged or stolen.

Other Points on Leasing

- Vehicles should always be reserved in advance so the traveler is not stranded.

- Some leasing companies require supplemental insurance.

- Always rent a vehicle from a well-known international leasing agency. Most likely, these companies will have well-maintained vehicles in their rental fleet.

- Rent a normal looking vehicle that is not "sporty" looking. Also, select a vehicle that is neutral in color.

- Make sure the vehicle has a trunk so any personal property can be stored out of sight.

- Inspect the tires, lights, wipers, horn, and other safety equipment. The traveler should also test the brakes and steering in the rental parking lot to become familiar with the function of the vehicle.

- Write down the vehicle's license plate and VIN number. If the car is stolen, the police will require this information. Be sure not to store this information in the vehicle.

- If the vehicle is leased at the airport: In many situations airports can be a complete nightmare to get out of. Consider hiring a cab to lead the rental vehicle to the main highway.

Using Automobiles

Regardless of whether a car is rented or borrowed:

- Always wear seat belts.

- Don't drink and drive. Alcohol-related laws are very strict in European countries.

- Always keep the vehicle's doors locked.

- Practice driving in a less populated area before attempting to drive in heavy traffic.

- Don't drive at night, especially between cities.

- Certain countries require road permits, instead of tolls. And, authorities will fine those found driving without a permit.

- Always have a map, and know how to get to the destination.

- Never travel alone in a vehicle, if at all possible.

- Instead of using the remote control key fob that may open both the passenger and driver's side door at the same time, use the key. This will prevent somebody from jumping into the car on the opposite side.

- Keep maps and other tourist-identifiers (i.e., luggage) out of sight.

- Store all objects in the trunk. In the case of accidents, loose objects in the vehicle compartment can become projectiles which can cause injuries to the vehicle's occupants.

- Know that nation's traffic laws and international road signs. An example of international road signage can be found in Appendix J.

- Do not pick up strangers while traveling, no matter how much they may appear to need a ride.

- Do not stop for a man, woman, or child who approaches the vehicle. They might be setting the occupants up for an ambush.

- Keep the gas tank at least ½ full at all times. Gas stations may not be as abundant as they are in the U.S.

- If there is car trouble, raise the hood and stay inside the car. If a stranger wants to help, have them call for help. Don't leave the vehicle.

- Know where the safe areas of the city are. Study the local map and know where and how to get to police stations, etc.

- A traveler should always walk with their keys in their hand to the car. Having the keys ready will naturally speed up getting into the car. Keys can also be used as a defensive weapon.

- Always carry an extra set of keys in case the driver should lock him or herself out, or lose them. This extra set should not be kept in the car.

- Always carry the vehicle keys in a pocket (not in a purse or jacket pocket). That way, the driver is always ensured that they will have a key to the auto.

- Travel in convoys when possible. There is increased safety in numbers.

- When at stop signs or lights, always position (or offset) the vehicle so other drivers and passengers in other cars cannot look directly into the vehicle compartment.

- Don't allow the vehicle to be boxed in:

  ▶ When stopped, use the rear and side view mirrors to stay aware of the surroundings.

  ▶ Always keep a large distance from other vehicles. At stop signs, the driver should make sure that they can see the rear tires of the vehicle in front of them, while sitting in the driver's seat. This distance generally allows a driver to maneuver away from the threat, if necessary. Any closer, and the driver will not be able to steer out of the situation. Instead, they may be pinned in.

  ▶ Avoid using center lanes, especially at stoplights and signs. Using outside lanes will allow the driver to prevent themselves from being boxed in – although they may have to drive across a sidewalk or cross into another lane to get away.

  ▶ Be wary of the fake accidents. It is common in many counties for a person to hit a tourist's car and then demand a cash payment for the damages. If someone should hit the vehicle, get a description of the vehicle and driver, its license plate, and report it later to the authorities. If the driver cannot leave for some reason, they should blow their horn until the police or others arrive.

- If the traveler is driving into a gated community, it is best to call ahead to have the gate opened. Otherwise, the driver should wait on the street until the gate is opened before turning in and possibly getting trapped in the driveway.

- Think before stopping to assist in an accident. It may be a set up. It would be much safer to report the accident to the authorities.

Parking Tips

- Before parking, drive around the block to get a feel for the area. If the driver should feel uncomfortable, find another location.

- Always use secure over non-secured parking areas.

- Be especially alert in parking ramps. These are often high-crime areas.

- Look for a location that offers good lighting, is close to the destination, and has a lot of people present.

- When leaving the car at a car park, make sure that the keys are given to the legitimate attendant. A common scam is that criminals will dress similarly to attendants to steal a car.

- A driver should always take the parking receipt/token with them. Without a receipt/token, it will be difficult for a person to steal the vehicle from the secure parking area.

If Followed or Harassed

- A traveler should verify their suspicions. The general rule of thumb is to take three right turns. If the subjects are still following, then the traveler is most likely being followed.

- Try to find the nearest police station, hotel, or other public facility.

- Never lead the threat back to the hotel, etc.

- Never stop and get out and confront a person.

- If a traveler should feel threatened by the presence of nearby strangers, they should lock themselves in the car and blow the horn to attract attention of others.

- Never provoke the threat.

Carjacking

Carjacking is simply stealing a vehicle with the owner/driver present. In most cases the criminal is only after the vehicle. In other cases, however, they are after the vehicle and the driver, and/or other occupants. Carjackers can work alone or in teams. Carjackings are also opportunistic in nature; or, they can be a planned attack. According to the U.S. Department of State, the most likely places for a carjacking include:

- High crime areas.
- Lesser-traveled roads (rural areas).
- Intersections where vehicles must stop.
- Isolated areas in parking lots.
- Residential driveways and gates.
- Traffic jams or congested areas.

All of these areas share the same characteristics: there are motivated offenders present and the car is slowed or impeded in some way, providing the opportunity for the offender(s) to commit the crime.

There are many carjacking methods. According to research by the U.S. Department of State, they include:

- **The Bump** – The attacker(s) bump the victim's vehicle from behind. The victim gets out to assess the damage and exchange information. The victim's vehicle is then taken.
- **Good Samaritan** – The attacker(s) stage what appears to be an accident. The victim stops to assist, and the vehicle is then taken.
- **The Ruse** – The vehicle behind the victim flashes its lights or the driver waves to get the victim's attention. The attacker indicates that there is a problem with the victim's car. The victim pulls over and the vehicle is taken.
- **The Trap** – Carjackers use surveillance to follow the victim home. When the victim pulls into their driveway, the attacker pulls up behind and blocks the victim's car.

If a traveler should become the victim of a carjacking, consider the following points:

- Be calm. Most likely the attackers are wound up and any actions may excite them even more.
- Make no aggressive moves.
- Give up the vehicle and its contents freely.
- Listen carefully to all directions.
- Make no quick or sudden movements that the attacker could construe as a counter-attack.
- Tell the attacker of every move in advance and keep both hands in plain view.
- Let the attacker(s) know that there are others in the car. They may be so focused on the driver that they may not see others, and accidentally drive away with them.
- Keep in mind that they are most likely only after the vehicle. If not, and they are attempting a kidnapping or assault, fight back and make as much noise as possible.
- Try to get a good description of the attacker(s) and the vehicles they are driving.

Taxi Cabs

Many of the same safety and security precautions with vehicles also apply to cabs. However, there are also some specific issues that need to be addressed with taxis.

Gypsy Cabs

"Gypsy" cabs are unlicensed cabs. If not unlicensed, these are cab drivers who violate the conditions of their cab license. For example, by cruising around and picking up passengers on the street, even though their license restricts them to picking up passengers who only call by telephone.

In some countries, the prob lems of gypsy cabs are immense. Depending upon the situation, passengers and drivers can get into physical fights, and in some countries there have even been reports of sexual assaults and kidnappings (Mexico is notorious for kidnapping by cab). Since they are most likely not licensed, the vehicles may also be mechanically dangerous, relative to licensed taxis. In other cases, meanwhile, the gypsy cab driver is an honest person who is simply trying to make a living.

Travel Tip

Black Cabs vs. Mini Cabs in London

In London, travelers can choose between the "Black" and Mini Cabs. The famous Black Cabs are metered, and drivers must pass a rigorous test known as "The Knowledge" (a thorough understanding of the majority of roads in London). With Mini Cabs, the traveler negotiates a quote for the trip. Mini Cab drivers do not take any exams and are not regulated well.

Regardless of the case, these types of cabs should be avoided because of the dangers they pose.

Furthermore:

- Only use official registered or licensed taxis. Some gypsy cabs, even though they may be cheaper, are far more dangerous and not worth the risk.

- Arrange for cabs over the phone. In England, for example, Minicabs that stop in the street may be cheaper, but they are not as safe as those that are arranged by phone.

- Always use a licensed taxi – check the back of the taxi to ensure it carries an official license plate, or in some cases, there are disks, decals, or medallions mounted on the hood or fender of the vehicle.

- Before getting in, make a visual inspection of the cab and check to make sure that the same person who is displayed on the license is the driver. If not, don't get in.

- If possible, a traveler should choose their own taxi and not rely upon other persons to get a cab for them. It could be a set up for a variety of crimes, including kidnapping.

- Travel only in taxis equipped with seat belts, and use them.

- A traveler should also make sure that they have the correct change for the fare. Otherwise, the driver may indicate that they have no change in an effort to defraud the traveler.

- Do not ride in a taxi that already has a passenger in it that the traveler does not know.

- If the taxi does not have a fare meter (which is common in many countries), negotiate the fare before getting in. Ask the driver the approximate total cost of the fare and compare it to other taxis to make sure the driver is honest.

- The traveler should pay the fare while still in the car so the driver doesn't take off with any change that is due.

- Do not put luggage in the trunk until the fare has been decided upon. Otherwise, a traveler's luggage could be held hostage.

- In some cases, a traveler should keep their luggage with them in the back seat. That way, a taxi driver cannot hold the traveler's luggage hostage in the trunk for more money.

- Don't share or split fares with strangers, no matter how well dressed or professional they appear. It could be a set up.

- Before getting in the taxi, make sure that the inside door handle works in case it is necessary to exit quickly.

- A traveler should not exit a taxi until they are sure that they have arrived at their destination.

- Always exit cabs from the curb side, not the street side.

Scooters and Motorcycles

Scooters and motorcycles are another transportation option in many countries. While they are fun to be on, these types of transportation can be very dangerous. Therefore, the authors of this book recommend that travelers avoid using them. If a traveler should nevertheless decide to use this form of transportation (as a passenger or driver), some key points to consider include:

- Always wear a helmet.
- Avoid heavily traveled roads.
- Be very diligent when riding – motorcycles may not be easily seen by other motorists.
- Speed kills.

If they are leased, the same issues reviewed in the section on leasing vehicles applies to scooters and motorcycles.

CONCLUSION

In most cases, a traveler will need to use public transportation while abroad. This transportation may include trains, subways and buses, where it will be important to learn how to read timetables, be safe at stations, and reduce the odds of becoming a victim while on board. In other situations, a traveler may opt to use a motor vehicle, where it is advised to obtain an International Driving Permit. When using vehicles, meanwhile, there are many safety-related issues. Travelers need to be on guard at all times, protecting themselves and their property through awareness and avoidance techniques. This chapter has also reviewed some general safety issues related to the use of taxicabs, especially the risks associated with gypsy or unlicensed cabs that can expose a traveler to a variety of risks.

14
GETTING OUT

onsider the following travel situations in the context of how to get out of them:

In December, 2004, thousands of tourists were stranded after a giant tidal wave slammed into many South Asian countries. The emergency response capabilities of many of these nations were not prepared for such a disaster, leading to an uncoordinated and slow evacuation process. Many tourists were stranded for days until they were rescued – in some cases by U.S. military personnel.

At the peak of rush hour on July 7, 2005, bombs were detonated aboard a London bus and three subway trains by terrorists. Approximately 700 people were injured and 52 were killed. Hundreds of thousands of commuters were stranded, not to mention all of the tourists that also felt the impact of these attacks.

In some situations a traveler needs to evacuate from the host country or particular region of the world for personal reasons, political unrest, disease outbreaks, or natural disasters. If not evacuating from the country, a traveler may need to relocate to safer locations within the host country. Like the other elements of safe travel, there are some key points to consider in order to get out of dangerous situations.

Support in Times of Emergency

If an emergency should arise, there are a variety of support services available to assist the traveler in getting out of the host country. They may include assistance from the host country, the U.S. government, and personal contacts.

215

Local Sources

Depending upon the emergency, local law enforcement, the military, and other emergency services, may be part of that assistance and protection. In many cases, their performance will be fine. In other cases, a traveler should be wary, and assess if there are any risks associated with using these local services. The traveler also needs to assess the quality of services that these agencies could provide in a time of emergency. Many countries, for example, may not have a coordinated emergency response plan. Even if there is a coordinated emergency response plan, it could still fail in the best of nations depending upon the nature and scope of the disaster. Consider Hurricane Katrina and the City of New Orleans, for example, or other major natural disasters. In these types of situations, an emergency response could be uncoordinated or, at best, it could simply consist of a slow recovery process after the event has occurred.

Unfortunately in other situations, emergencies could actually be the result of the actions of local authorities. For example, if the country is experiencing political or civil unrest, the police and military could actually be the perpetrators of these events. In these cases, by going to the police, a traveler could actually expose themselves to greater dangers. Consider, for example, a 2001 incident where 47 British holiday makers were caught up in running a gun battle at Sri Lanka's Bandaranaike International Airport, where government troops attacked and killed 18 rebels. Luckily, none of the British tourists were killed, although they had to flee and hide during the maelstrom.[20]

Overseas Citizens Services

The Overseas Citizens Services (OCS) in the State Department's Bureau of Consular Affairs is responsible for the welfare and whereabouts of U.S. citizens traveling and residing abroad. The OCS has three offices, one of which is the Office of American Citizens Services (ACS). The ACS is divided into geographical regions throughout the world, where ACS officers assist in a variety of matters for Americans abroad including arrests, death cases, financial or medical emergencies, and locating travelers. In

---

[20] BBC News Wednesday, July 25, 2001.

the case of emergencies including plane crashes, hijackings, civil disorder, political unrest, war and natural disasters, the ACS is responsible for coordinating State Department efforts. For example, the Overseas Citizens Services has a call center that can provide up-to-date information to travelers. This service can also be used by the family members of travelers who are trying to seek information on the location and safety of their loved ones. Their phone number can be found in Appendix K.

Embassies and Consulates

In other emergency situations, the local embassy or consulate may be the best alternative. If the emergency is a private matter, the traveler will most likely have to make an appointment in advance. If it is an emergency involving scores of travelers, the embassy will most likely be more accommodating and actually allow individuals onto embassy property or another location without appointments. When approaching a U.S. embassy however, it is not like in the movies where the Marines will simply open up the doors and let a person run in with their luggage. There will most likely be long lines and checkpoints before being admitted. Most likely, luggage and other large parcels will not be allowed on embassy property. Travelers also need to be aware that in some situations, they will not be able to physically access the embassy due to martial law restrictions imposed by the country (i.e., no tourists allowed outside their hotels, house arrest), or because the presence of protestors outside the embassy could physically endanger the traveler.

Personal Contacts

In other cases, the traveler may need to rely upon the good graces of local friends and organizations to assist them in times of emergency. Depending upon the emergency, the best solution could be to "ride the storm out," where the traveler may need to rely upon an institution (i.e., churches, universities, businesses, hotels) or friends for housing, food, and financial support until the situation stabilizes.

PREPARING FOR EMERGENCIES

Throughout this book, the anticipation of risk has been emphasized as the key element to safe travel. Already, the traveler should have a good understanding of their host country and region through their pre-departure planning activities. While traveling, however, the traveler must be aware of and plan for emergency situations.

To Prevent Being Trapped in a Foreign Country

The events (natural or otherwise) that often leave a traveler stranded in a foreign country are not immediate. Instead, there are often some threat indicators present, often days ahead of the "emergency" that should have alerted the traveler of an impending danger. In order to prevent oneself from being trapped, a traveler should therefore:

- Stay informed of and monitor both world and local events to be prepared for any encounters.

- Monitor local weather and news and plan accordingly.

- Keep in mind the ripple effect. That is, a particular event in one country or region could move throughout the country, region, and world fast. Perhaps the best example of the ripple effect was 9/11. The U.S. and many other nations virtually closed their border crossings and skies to air travel, leaving a lot of travelers stranded in foreign countries.

- Know where the closest U.S. Embassy or consulate is. Mark it on a map and be prepared to hike there, if necessary.

- Monitor consular updates on the Internet: Monitor the Department of State, Bureau of Consular Affairs home page and the home page for the U.S. Embassy in the foreign country for up-to-date information about the country and region.

- Get a feel for the area and be aware of any changes that could serve as warning signals. As an example, a former student of one of the authors grew up in Lebanon in the late 1970s. She recalled that residents could always predict when rocket attacks were to occur: an eerie calm would fall over the city, where vehicle and pedestrian traffic would suddenly become minimal.

- Learn to trust one's instincts. If something feels wrong, most likely it is.

- When event(s) have occurred and the traveler has decided, based on the totality of the circumstances, that they need to leave – leave. Don't hesitate. A good example of this is September 11, 2001. A colleague of the authors was attending a meeting in Canada. Immediately after the 1st plane struck, this individual was in his car crossing back into the U.S., just before the borders were closed.

- Review maps, and have an evacuation plan with contingencies. In the earlier London bombing example, a traveler should have had a contingency transport plan and/or alternative routes to evacuate from London in a timely manner.

- Be prepared to walk long distances when evacuating.

- Never evacuate alone. There is usually safety in numbers.

- If in a large group, preplan where the entire group will reassemble in case of emergency or evacuation.

- Reserve transportation on-line or over the phone before leaving for the terminal/station. That way, a traveler will have a ticket and not be stranded at the transportation hub.

Travel Tip

New Zealand publishes emergency advice for its residents living in other countries. They recommend having a backpack (for each person) that contains:

- All personal documents
- A 4-day supply of lightweight ready-to-eat foods
- A flashlight
- Maps
- Stationery
- Seasonal Clothing
- Basic Toiletries
- Water Purification Tablets

From: http://www.nzembassy.com

Evacuation Kits

Escape or evacuation kits should also be considered. At a minimum, the kit should include the passport and money. Depending upon the situation, an escape kit could also include water, clothing, and food. This escape kit should be prepared in advance and constructed from existing items brought on the trip, in addition to food items gathered in the host country. For example, a traveler could keep their carry-on bag packed and ready to go. In case of fire at a hotel, for example, this small shoulder bag could be grabbed on the way out the door. While out walking, however, the escape kit will have to be smaller and simply consist of cash, a credit card and a passport. With these three items, a traveler can acquire transport and leave the country, if necessary. These escape kits are critically important when away on day trips, or when the traveler is far from where they are staying, too; there may not be any time to get back to "home base" to retrieve these items.

IF STRANDED

Depending upon the situation, a traveler could simply become stranded, where they will have to wait for some period of time before evacuation and/or departure. If stranded, some points to consider include, but are not limited to the following points:

- Depending upon the situation, remain as anonymous as possible. Travelers should avoid drawing any attention to themselves.

- Be prepared for communication systems to fail due to the disaster itself, call volume, etc. It may take awhile for the systems to be restored.

- Be wary of whom to trust, depending upon the situation. Foreign sentiment can rapidly change, especially if a local should feel that aiding foreigners could jeopardize his or her own safety.

- If a traveler cannot get out of the country (or it is not necessary), be sure to move to a safer location, away from the threat.

- Find a safe location and stay there. Hopefully, this safe location is the same one that the traveler provided to the embassy/consulate when originally registering the trip.

- Contact the U.S. consulate or embassy as soon as possible (by phone, Internet, short wave, etc.).

- In case of an emergency evacuation, the embassy or consulate will provide instructions on what to do and where to assemble. In many cases, the assembly point may not be at the embassy, but another safe location that can accommodate large groups.

- Maintain an adequate supply of water and food.

- Monitor the BBC, Voice of America or another credible radio station for updates and advice.

- Be prepared to leave behind personal property. Most likely instructions will require evacuees to travel light. As an example, an acquaintance of the authors had to be evacuated from Iran during the Iranian Revolution in 1979. All U.S. citizens were instructed to a hotel in Tehran. This individual made it as far as he could with his vehicle. After that, he parked his car and proceeded on foot, under the cover of darkness to the hotel. He left Iran with the only clothes he was wearing.

- If instructed to go to the embassy and there is no escort available, travel light, leaving luggage behind. Most likely, the embassy will not allow luggage on their property because of the risk of a bomb, etc. A good hotel will store it for a traveler and perhaps ship it later. Walking down a street with luggage is also a blatant indicator that a tourist is present.

- Try to contact family members to update them on the situation in order to calm any fears or concerns that may exist.

- Never give up hope that help is on the way. It is.

CONCLUSION

Emergency situations can occur anywhere and any time. Depending upon the situation, the emergency could require the traveler to relocate or even leave the country or region. The key to getting out of a country, for any reason, is to first anticipate and plan for such events. If an emergency should then occur, the traveler will be better prepared to deal with it, even to the point that if they did not make it out, they will be prepared for a short or long-term stay and the issues associated with the particular event.

15
CULTURE

Throughout this book, the reader has been exposed to a variety of issues related to safe travel. Intertwined within all of these chapters (especially the Blending In and Street Smarts chapters) was the concept of culture.

This chapter will provide the traveler with an overview of culture and the importance of gaining a working understanding of the host country's cultural nuances. Without a good understanding of the host country's culture and knowing how to operate within it, a traveler could inadvertently be exposed as a foreigner, and perhaps jeopardize their safety. At a minimum, a traveler could also cause some degree of embarrassment or even offend their host(s) and/or natives of the country. This, of course, could lead to friction and strife, leading to a depressing travel experience.

What Is Culture?

Culture can be understood as the sum total of the learned behaviors of groups of people. It can also be thought of as the collective programming of the mind that distinguishes the members of one group from another in the context of symbols, language, dress, customs, beliefs, values, food and food preparation, attitudes, religion and other socially transmitted attitudes and behaviors.[21] In effect, manifestations of culture exist everywhere. In the United States perhaps NASCAR, and "baseball and apple pie" are some common cultural manifestations. Grand Prix, football (the U.S. equivalent of "soccer") and croissants, meanwhile, could be European equivalents.

Understanding and adapting to another country's culture can be difficult or frustrating for the traveler. What makes it even more difficult at times is that there are often layers of culture in any given country that include:

- National – attributes that everyone shares
- Regional – ethnic differences and linguistic dialects

---

[21] U.S. Peace Corps. 1997. *Culture Matters: The Peace-Corps Cross-Cultural Handbook/Workbook*. Washington D.C.: Government Printing Office.

- Gender – male and female cultural attributes
- Generational – older traditionalists vs. contemporaries
- Social Class – lower vs. upper class lifestyle differences
- Organizational – differences among employers and the workplace

Even if a country shares a common language, a frequent cultural mistake for many travelers is to assume that "English is English." Just because the foreign country's official language is English, however, does not mean that there will not be any language barriers, especially in the context of vocabulary. In England, for example, if a traveler hears the statement, "I am going to get some fags and then go to the hole in the wall," they might find this statement to be a little peculiar. Translated into American English, this statement simply means: "I'm going to get some cigarettes and then I'm going to the ATM." If not the vocabulary, in some cases, the dialect could often be hard to understand.

Listed in Box 15-1 are just a few examples of cultural differences that exist throughout the world.

Box 15-1
Cultural Differences

♦ **Showing the bottoms of the feet** – Arabs consider the soles of the feet or shoes to be the dirtiest part of the body. Inadvertent display of the bottoms of the feet (i.e., when crossing one's legs) may be considered highly offensive.
♦ **Using the left hand** – In many cultures, the left hand is reserved solely for personal hygiene.
♦ **Simple Gestures** –
  ◊ The yes and no head gestures may be opposite of those used by Americans – In Bulgaria, for example, nodding indicates "no," while shaking indicates "yes."
  ◊ Joining the thumb and the index finger in a circular fashion – most western cultures will accept this gesture as meaning "OK" – the Japanese can perceive it as meaning "expensive," some Arab cultures think it means "I will kill you." In some countries, this sign is used as an offensive gesture: "asshole."
  ◊ Smiling – In some countries this is an indicator of a feebleminded or stupid person.

- ◆ **Pointing with an index finger** – In most Middle Eastern countries and in many other cultures, this is considered offensive. Most Asians point with their palms or thumbs, while some Latin American cultures purse their lips to point.
- ◆ **Taking the shoes off when entering a house** – This may not be the norm in many U.S. households, but it is very important in other cultures.
- ◆ **Shaking hands** – Most Japanese are uncomfortable with touching or shaking hands. They usually bow, unless dealing with westerners.
- ◆ **Table manners** – In Europe two utensils are used simultaneously when eating: the fork is held in left hand and knife is held in the right. Americans usually only use one utensil at a time where the user switches between a fork and knife, when necessary.
- ◆ **Dress** –In Lebanon, it is customary for women to dress scantily. A French tourist in Lebanon, meanwhile, may view them as prostitutes, because that style of dress in Paris is associated with the sex trade.
- ◆ **Personal space** – In many countries, personal space is much smaller in comparison to American standards. To the novice traveler, standing too close to another person or even bumping into them may be a sign of aggressiveness. However, these behaviors and actions are considered normal in their society.
- ◆ **Titles when addressing others** – In America it is common to address others on a first name basis. In other countries, titles are expected to be used (i.e., Mr., Mrs., Sir, Duke, Lady, Lord, Professor) until invited to address the person on a first name basis.
- ◆ **Gender Relationships** – In some countries, fraternization with members of the opposite sex in any manner (i.e., eye contact, holding doors, etc.) is strictly prohibited.

CULTURE SHOCK

Depending upon the destination, in some cases the traveler will also experience culture shock. Culture shock can be described as a sense of confusion, anxiety, and uncertainty when the traveler is exposed to an alien culture or environment.[22] According to many authors, there is usually a three-stage process that a traveler will go through.[23]

---

[22] *Merriam Webster Dictionary* (2001).
[23] Rohrlich, B.F. (1986). *There and back again. and Kohls, R.L. Survival kit for overseas.* Intercultural press.

Stage 1 – The Honeymoon/Euphoria Stage

In this stage, the traveler finds differences to be exciting, novel, and positive. The traveler may also find that things are not too different from at home. The traveler may be interested in seeing all of the tourist-related sites, tasting novel foods and meeting interesting people.

Stage 2 – Dislocation/Unease/Irritation and Hostility

In this stage, the traveler begins to experience culture shock. The differences that were discovered in the honeymoon phase now become irritable distractions that cause some distress. The traveler also begins to notice more and more dissimilarities that can cause some discomfort, frustration, and confusion that leads to negative feelings about the people and the culture of the host country. These frustrations could range from language barriers, problems using public transportation, or longing for things from home.

During this stage the traveler may become homesick and bored. The traveler may also exhibit other stress responses ranging from excessive sleeping, compulsive eating or drinking, medical problems, and hostility toward the locals and other travelers. The nature and extent of culture shock varies with the traveler and of course, the cultural differences that exist. Existing research, for example, has been conducted on the cultural distance between Britain and other foreign countries. Countries such as Australia, Canada, New Zealand and Germany have been found to be somewhat similar while countries such as Pakistan, Tibet, India and China have ranked higher on cultural distance indexes.[24]

Coping With Culture Shock

In order to cope with culture shock, a traveler needs to anticipate, accept, and manage any cultural differences that should arise. The following reviews these issues in detail:

---

[24] Mumford, D.B. (March, 2000). *Culture shock among young British volunteers working abroad: Predictors, risk factors and outcome. Transcultural psychiatry, 37*(1), 73-87.

- *Anticipation*

One of the most important coping strategies is to be prepared for, and anticipate that there will be cultural differences. Therefore, research and education is key. The traveler must try to find out as much as possible about the host country.

Some topics that should be researched include, but are not limited to:

- Food and Food Preparation
- Greetings – Social Etiquette
- Gender Relationships
- Body Language
- Communication Patterns – volume and tone
- Clothing/Dress
- Conduct in Public
- Dining Etiquette

As was the case with the other topics in this book, contacting former travelers, experts on the country or region, and searching the Internet will provide a great deal of useful information. Upon arrival at the host country, perhaps one of the best things that a traveler can do is to sit and watch and be attentive, identifying the small cultural nuances that exist. Prior to venturing out, for example, it would be wise for the traveler to simply sit and watch the everyday activities of the citizenry of the country.

- *Acceptance*

The traveler must also learn to accept the culture of the host country. One common mistake often made by the traveler is the imposition of their cultural beliefs on the host country. While often it is difficult to prevent this from happening because culture is ingrained, fighting against or resisting the host nation's culture will simply result in increased levels of frustration, and an unpleasant experience. When considered in the context that the purpose of travel is to experience a foreign culture, it makes no sense to resist cultural differences. It is much better to "go with the flow." The traveler must also recognize that acceptance may require a great deal of tolerance and patience. For example, the foods in many counties can be dramatically different in the context of preparation, presentation, flavor, and portion size. Personal conduct can also differ, too. For example, in some countries women are treated much more differently than they are accustomed to in the United States. In fact, some female travelers may construe how they are treated as sexual harassment and/or gender discrimination, based on the misogynistic behaviors (perhaps both the males and females) of the residents in the host country. In their perspective and cultural experiences and expectations, from the U.S., unfortunately it is. Nevertheless, in the foreign country, it may actually be part of its culture where conduct of that nature is accepted. Therefore, instead of reacting negatively to the situation and making a scene, it will most likely be better in many cases to treat it as a cultural learning experience and develop appropriate coping and avoidance techniques.

- *Management*

Box 15.2 provides some tips to cope with and manage culture shock. By using some of these tips and developing other appropriate coping strategies, over time, culture shock will become manageable, where it may be recognized that cultural differences are in actuality, not that different from one another. Eventually, the traveler accepts their surroundings and situation, adapting to the new culture. In effect, what has happened at this stage can be considered as cultural learning. The traveler has learned to negotiate social situations and has now begun to feel comfortable in the host country.

Management also includes avoiding cultural faux pas. Even though the traveler has conducted a thorough analysis of the host country's culture prior to departure, and has developed a comprehensive understanding of the host country's culture, mistakes can still occur. Usually, it is readily apparent when these mistakes are made. In these situations, it is best to apologize for the faux pas and adjust behaviors accordingly so they do not occur again.

Box 15-2
Coping with Culture Shock

♦ Learn to speak the host country's language as soon as possible.
♦ Find a place that is comfortable and spend time there.
♦ Do not associate with fellow Americans who are also experiencing culture shock – their culture shock and complaining could serve to exacerbate the traveler's own culture shock.
♦ Talk to friends and counselors as a means to improve existing coping mechanisms.
♦ Try to engage in the same hobbies and interests done at home, while abroad.
♦ Find someone who understands both the U.S. and host country's culture. Ask them questions related to any frustrations that exist.
♦ If depressed, ask: "What were my expectations, were they reasonable, what can I do to make them come true, or how can I make the best use of my time?"
♦ Adopt a culture friend or guide from the host country to teach, explain, and interpret the new culture.

Stage 3 – Reverse Culture Shock

Reverse culture shock occurs when the traveler has returned home. As a result of the overseas experience, the traveler has now returned home with a new outlook. The traveler will want to share their experiences with others who may not understand or be interested in their experiences. In combination with this, the traveler may miss certain cultural elements and friends from the host country, leading to frustration and a sense of loneliness. Foreign travel may have also changed the traveler's attitudes and perspectives toward certain customs in their home country, where these new ideas and beliefs now cause some personal conflicts with the traditional customs at home. In an effort to reconcile these differences, the traveler may try to find like (or internationally)-minded people to bond with, which could be further frustrating if none are available. According to some experts, reverse culture shock often is worse than culture shock.

CONCLUSION

A host country's culture can be quite different in the context of language, dress, and custom. In other cases, there can also be some cultural differences that are not readily apparent to a traveler. Consider, for example, Winston Churchill's famous quote, "We are two countries separated by a common language," noting how American English differs from the "Queen's English." In order to be safe and have a positive trip, the host country's culture must be as understood as good as possible prior to departure. Even though the traveler will have a good understanding of the host country's culture, they should nevertheless be prepared for and anticipate, accept, and manage the effects of culture shock. A traveler should also be aware that they may also experience reverse culture shock when getting home, where similar coping methods used while traveling will assist in their readjustment to life at home.

16
SPECIAL NEEDS

When the term "Special Needs" is used, it is generally a term used in clinical diagnostic and functional development to describe individuals who require assistance for medical-related disabilities, mental health issues, and/or psychological disorders that may relate to phobias of people, places or travel (fear of flying, etc.). In the context of this travel book, a much more inclusive definition is used where special needs includes any form of assistance or modifications to the trip that a traveler will need in order to reach their travel destination without physical or mental discomfort, and to enjoy their stay in their chosen location(s).

These special needs can exist on a spectrum of seriousness and include the following:

◆ Acute and Chronic Diseases and/or Illnesses	◆ Travel with Medical Devices/Hidden Needs (Pacemakers, Prosthetics)
◆ Traveling with Infants and Children	◆ The Need for Mobility Devices
◆ Age-Related Mobility Issues	◆ Communicable Diseases
◆ Visual Disabilities	◆ Traveling while Pregnant
◆ Hearing Problems	◆ Various Injuries

These are just a few examples of special needs that exist. Inasmuch, developing a comprehensive understanding of how to deal with special needs is important for **all** travelers. For example, travelers with specific special needs may find that the usual methods of support and assistance may not be available during their travel and vacation period. Besides those who have special needs, those travelers without special needs also need to recognize that they will be traveling with others who have special needs. In this context, it is important for these individuals to be cognizant of these special needs, and be prepared to assist and intervene in some manner, if and when necessary. Last, a person may develop special needs (i.e., broken bones, sickness) during their travels which will require them to modify the remainder of their trip to some degree by considering and using the information provided in this chapter.

Already, this book has provided the traveler with a wealth of information for planning a safe trip. A great deal of this information, especially from the Getting Ready and Healthy Travel chapters apply to planning for special needs, too. While it is beyond the scope of this book and chapter to specifically address every special need that exists, this chapter provides the reader with a general understanding of some of the key points to consider when traveling with a special need.

PLANNING FOR AND ASSESSING SPECIAL NEEDS

Already, Chapter 2 of this book has recommended that the traveler construct an Emergency Contact Information Form that can be found in Appendix C. In those cases where the traveler has special needs, additional planning will be required, beginning with an assessment of existing (and even potential) special needs. In the context of existing special needs, the traveler needs to critically review any medical-related special needs. They also need to consider non-medical special needs that could include mobility-related issues due to age and even height and weight related issues that could impact the outcome of a trip.

Shown in Box 16-1 is a Special Needs Assessment form that a traveler can use to reflect upon their special needs in the context of their travels (an example of a traveler who has bad knees, provides some insight on how to use this form). In the first column, the traveler should list their condition that requires some modification to the trip. Next, the traveler then needs to reflect upon this special need/condition in the context of the limitations that this special need will impose on their travels. Last, the traveler needs to reflect upon what accommodations they will require. An additional form is located in Appendix K.

Box 16-1
Special Needs Assessment Form

Special Need	Limitations	Required Accommodations
Bad Knees	Walking up stairs and inclines, uneven surfaces. Walking for long periods of time	Elevators/escalators; places to rest, hotel rooms, etc. on the lower floor; more time between points of travel; mobility assistance in airport; more time to board aircraft

Next, the traveler needs to plan for each of the special needs that were identified. Planning for the special need, in some cases, can be relatively simple. Accommodations for the special need could simply include providing for enough time between stops. Or, it could require locating (in advance) restrooms or privacy areas for changing dressings or taking medications. In other cases, however, planning for the special need(s) may reveal that there may be too many barriers to having an enjoyable trip based on the activities and/or location. This does not mean that a traveler should simply give up and not travel. Instead, the traveler should consider what other options they have at their disposal in order to optimize their travel experience in light of their special need(s). For example, one alternative may be to explore structured trips that specifically cater to individuals with special needs.

As shown in Box 16-2, a traveler needs to review their special need(s) with the activities they are going to engage in. Following the identification of these activities, the traveler then needs to identify organizations and individuals that can assist them in planning for their special needs. Part of this assessment, meanwhile, is to properly identify what a specific person or organization can do for the traveler. It is also important to determine any

limitations in meeting the accommodations for the special need
and to determine if their needs can be met. The case of a traveler
with bad knees is also used as an example in this form, where
this fictitious person completed the form (with fictitious
information), based on their specific activities, etc. An additional
copy of this form can be found in Appendix L.

Box 16-2
Special Needs Inventory

Need: Bad Knees	Contact Info	Description of Accommodations	Any Limits w/Accommodations	Needs Met? Y	N
Transportation					
United Airlines	1-800-555-1212 (Jay Smith x333)	Will provide wheelchair and boarding assistance	None	X	
Taxis	Black Cab Co.	Have large cabs	None	X	
Busses	Double Decker Busses...	Have seating on 1st level	None	X	
Lodging Facilities:					
The Kings Inn	011-555-1212 123 Jones Way www.info	Have elevators and rooms at lower levels	None	X	
Lions Head	011-555-1212 123 Jones Way www.info	Too old – have no acomm's at all	Can't meet needs		X
Organized Tours:					
HMS Belfast	011-555-1212 123 Jones Way www.info	Only have ramp to main deck	Yes – can't go to lower decks		X
Imp War Museum	011-555-1212 123 Jones Way www.info	Fully Accessible		X	
Westminster	011-555-1212 123 Jones Way www.info	Have Wheelchairs if necessary	Might be some limits due to stairs	X	
Tower of London	011-555-1212 123 Jones Way www.info	Some access	Limited to grounds....	X	
Specific Locales...					
Stonehenge	011-555-1212 123 Jones Way www.info	Very Limited	Uneven Terrain		X
Cliffs of Dover	011-555-1212 123 Jones Way www.info	Very Limited	Can see from road and/or carparks	X	

Other Issues

There are a variety of other issues that also need to be considered when traveling with special needs. Some of these are shown here.

- **Travel Companions** – In some cases, travelers may consider bringing along a service companion for their trip. In their capacity as a service companion, this individual can provide a vast array of services beginning with planning the trip prior to departure and ensuring that all special needs are met while traveling. A service companion could simply be a friend or family member. In other cases, these individuals could actually be hired to accompany a person on their trip.

- **Service Animals** – Service animals can include dogs and perhaps monkeys. Travelers should be aware that some countries have restrictions on service animals traveling through or within their country. Therefore, it is important to check for any restrictions with the embassy or consulate of each country of travel. Information of this nature can be found at http://travel.state.gov, at each country's respective web page, or by contacting the country's embassy or consulate in question. If service animals are permitted, it is important to check to see what restrictions exist regarding the quarantine of animals and proof of vaccination. A traveler should also be well-versed in the security screening of service animals. Information related to the screening of service animals in the U.S. can be found on the www.tsa.gov website.

- **Special Diets** – If special diets are necessary, it will also be important to gain an understanding of the local foods in the destination countries and plan for such occasions. As well as researching the foods in the host countries, it would also be wise for the traveler to carry a sufficient amount of food with them in order to prevent any food-related incident. As an example, if a traveler is hypoglycemic, it would be wise to carry protein-rich foods with them in case appropriate foods are not readily available while on their various side-trips in the host country. If there are other dietary needs that may be difficult to meet in another country, a traveler may also consider finding lodging facilities that offer cooking facilities, or even locate restaurants that could meet the traveler's special needs.

- **Continued Medical Treatment** – In some cases, a traveler may need to continue with their therapeutic regime while traveling (i.e., hemodialysis). In these situations, it is very important that the traveler meets with their doctor and schedules all of these therapies in the host country prior to departure. It is also important to have all information regarding the medical treatment facility (i.e., name of facility, location, phone number, name of contact medical personnel). It is also strongly encouraged that the traveler also has a backup plan and/or location in case any issues should arise.

- **Keep Routines Similar** – Depending upon the special need, it may be important to keep the same routines when traveling as they were at home (i.e., meals, sleep). This could serve to reduce anxiety and stress.

- **Allow for More Time** – Many special needs simply require a little more time to get from point A to B. Therefore, it would be wise to allow for more time between flights, trains, etc. in order to ensure a smooth trip.

- **Don't Over-Program** – The U.S. Department of State provides a good tip: the additional physical activity undertaken during travel can be quite strenuous, and sudden changes in diet and climate can have serious health consequences for the unprepared traveler. Therefore, make sure the travel schedule is not too hectic.

- **Know the Needs of Other Travelers** – It is also important to know one another's special needs and share this information with others on the trip to ensure that other travelers are aware of and are prepared to assist and deal with any issues that may arise.

TRAVELING WITH SPECIAL NEEDS

As already pointed out, overcoming obstacles related to a special need can be achieved through in-depth planning. The following section will provide some ideas in the context of legislation that protects the rights of special needs travelers. This section also provides information and ideas regarding what a person with special needs has to do and expect on various forms of transport, at lodging facilities and at specific tourist locations.

Disability-Related Laws

Organizations in the United States must comply with the Americans with Disabilities Act (ADA) that protects the civil rights of persons with disabilities. The ADA sets forth mandatory compliance standards that private and public sector organizations must follow, including airports and other forms of transportation. Accessibility guidelines for airports (as well as other locales and forms of public transport) can be found in the "Accessibility Guidelines for Buildings and Facilities" (at http://www.access-board.gov/adaag/html/adaag.htm). The guidelines encompass a wide range of regulations that cover accessible handicap parking, traveler aid stations, signage, as well as accessibility to ticketing booths, shuttle vehicles, baggage areas, and aircraft. In addition to ADA standards, airlines must follow standards set forth under the Air Carrier Access Act. The Act sets forth requirements that airlines must follow that are related to all types of disabilities (i.e., mobility, hearing and vision impairments) in regard to the access of tickets, gate assignments, scheduling, luggage claims, etc. The Air Carrier Access Act can be found at http://www.dotcr.ost.dot.gov/asp/airacc.asp.

In other countries, meanwhile, accommodations for disabilities may be more limited. In fact, some countries may not have mandatory laws governing accessibility to individuals with disabilities. Therefore, it is advised that the traveler investigates each destination country and consult with travel agents and other individuals in order to determine what types of accommodations are available, specific to the special need(s).

Chapter 16

The Airport

Perhaps one of the more difficult places a traveler will have to navigate in is at airports. Nevertheless, any challenges and barriers can be readily overcome and managed through careful planning. This planning begins with reviewing the accessibility of the airport, followed by airport screening issues. The planning stage should also include researching the specific airline that will be used for the journey.

Airport Accessibility

Although airports in the United States comply with existing laws and regulations regarding the accommodation of travelers with disabilities, they can still nevertheless be a challenge. This can be attributed to the simple fact that airports are large, confusing, and are often heavily congested. In order to prevent any issues, it is important that the traveler contacts the airport well in advance of arrival to ensure that they have the available resources (i.e., shuttles). The same point applies to any connecting airports that will be used on the trip. Specific questions to ask include:

- Any available terminal transport (i.e., skycaps, moving walkways, trams).
- The best time to use the airport based on the number of flyers and density.
- What airport entrance to use to minimize travel distance.
- The most direct route from the airport entrance to ticket counters and screening.
- Curbside check-in of baggage (if available).
- Accessibility issues (if any) in the airport, including restrooms.

In many cases, the airport website can provide a great deal of information to a traveler. For example, O'Hare International Airport's website has a specific location titled "ADA Friendly Services," that provides helpful tips. This site also includes specific phone numbers for the traveler if they have additional questions.

Airport Screening

Already, this book has reviewed the airport security screening process in "The Airport" chapter. In the context of a person with special needs, the screening process may take a little longer and perhaps it could be a little more complicated, depending upon the traveler's special need(s). Some points to consider include, but are not limited to the following:

- An individual with a disability must undergo the same security screening as any other member of the traveling public. In those cases where a person with a disability cannot pass through the normal screening procedures as reviewed in "The Airport" chapter, different screening procedures will be used.

- Be sure to bring along any documentation regarding the disability. This will speed the process up and serve to clarify any issues that may arise at the screening stage.

- Let TSA screeners know your ability levels (i.e., cannot walk unassisted, inability to remove shoes).

- Be sure to notify TSA screening personnel of any medical implant, prosthetic device, hearing and/or vision issues, or other disabilities.

- If a traveler is wearing an exterior medical device (i.e., brace) and they are uncomfortable with going through the metal detector, they can request to be hand-wanded, or they can request a pat-down search.

- Under the provisions of the Air Carriers Access Act, non-traveling individuals can assist a person with a special need beyond the security checkpoint. These individuals must present themselves at the airline's check-in desk, where they can receive a pass allowing them to go through security screening without a boarding pass or ticket.

- Security personnel are free to examine any assistive device (i.e., wheelchairs, canes) that they believe is capable of concealing a weapon or other prohibited item. If an individual with a disability is unable to pass through the system without activating it, the person will be subject to further screening in the same manner as any other passenger activating the system.

- Security screening personnel at some airports may employ a hand-held device (a metal detector wand, for example) that will allow them to complete the screening without having to physically search the individual. If this method is still unable to clear the individual and a physical search becomes necessary, then at the passenger's request, the search must be done in private.

- A traveler can request a private area for their personal search. TSA personnel can also provide a disposable paper drape for additional privacy, if a pat down search is required.

- The TSA website also provides additional information on the screening of persons with disabilities. The TSA also has a Call Center (1-866-289-0673). Questions can also be e-mailed to them at tsa-contactcenter@dhs.gov.

- It would also be wise to research the security measures at airports in other foreign countries, since there will most likely be differences in the security measures and procedures used.

Airlines

It is also important to check with airlines regarding any special needs. Airlines will be quite helpful in answering a variety of questions related to the airport itself and what specific services they can provide to the special needs traveler. A review of the Airline's Website will also be helpful in gaining an understanding of any services that are offered. Some (but not all) questions the traveler should ask include:

- Seat assignments (and perhaps seats) that can accommodate the special need.

- The type of aircraft that is scheduled for the flight, and if that aircraft is suitable for accommodating the special need(s).

- Any special accommodations needed (on-board chairs, assistance in using restrooms).

- The need for a wheelchair, if necessary, and/or airport courtesy wheelchair assistance.

- Policies on the handling of mobility aids and assistive devices.

- Assistance in making a connection.

- Assistance in the baggage claim area.

- Traveling with medical or assistance devices.

- Traveling with service animals.

- The use of oxygen and/or Portable Oxygen Concentrators (POC's).

- Assistance in boarding and deplaning.

- Alternative boarding procedures.

- What or how flight attendants can assist the special needs traveler.

Airlines do not require advanced notice of a person with a disability traveling UNLESS a traveler requires certain accommodations that require preparation time on behalf of the airlines.

> **Travel Tip**
>
> Assistive devices brought into the aircraft cabin by an individual with a disability do not count toward a limit on carry-on items.

For example, airlines may require at least 48 hours advanced notice for the transportation of an electric wheelchair or an oxygen hookup. If assistance is required, it is important to contact the airlines and advise them of any assistance that may be required. The airline will ask for the confirmation number, so have this readily available.

In some cases, airlines can refuse transportation on the basis of a disability if that disability should pose a danger to other passengers or the overall safety of the flight. Depending upon airline policy, some medical equipment or services are not authorized, where the airline can refuse service. For example, some airlines can refuse service to persons who are stretcher bound, need incubators, require power from the aircraft's electrical supply, or need oxygen. In other cases, an airline may allow oxygen as long as it is provided by them (for an additional fee). In other cases, an airline may work with an outside medical company. This outside medical company (i.e., Med Link) will contact the traveler by phone to further discuss any issues and coordinate the travel with the person's physician. Other airlines may also have specific forms that will need to be completed by the traveler's physician several days prior to departure. Requirements vary from carrier to carrier, so it is again strongly advised the traveler contact their airline well in advance to ensure that there are no delays (or even cancellations) of their ticket.

Attendants and Air Travel

Some airlines may also require that the special needs traveler have an attendant who will provide personal service to the special needs traveler. According to guidelines set forth under the U.S. Department of Transportation[25] a carrier can require an attendant when:

- A person is traveling on a stretcher or in an incubator.
- A person, because of a mental disability is unable to comprehend or respond appropriately to safety instructions from carrier personnel.
- A person with mobility impairment so severe that the individual is unable to assist in his or her own evacuation from the aircraft.
- A person who has both severe hearing and severe vision impairments which prevent him or her from receiving and acting on necessary instructions from carrier personnel when evacuating the aircraft during an emergency.

An attendant can be an off-duty employee of the airline, or a volunteer from among other passengers. The carrier could even provide a free ticket to a person designated as an attendant. The airline, however, is not required to find or furnish an attendant. In those cases where the passenger and airline disagree about the use of an attendant, this issue can be brought forward to the Complaints Resolution Officer (CRO) who is available at each airport. Each flyer is entitled to talk with the CRO to resolve any

---

[25] *New Horizons: Information for the Air Traveler with a Disability* (February, 2004). U.S. Department of Transportation

complaints on behalf of the carrier. The CRO is required to provide the passenger with a written statement summarizing the facts and reasons for the decision.

The activities of flight personnel are also limited. According to the Air Carrier Access Act, personnel are required to assist a passenger with a disability to:

- Move to and from seats as a part of the boarding and exiting process.
- Open packages and identify food (assistance with actual eating is not required).
- Use an on-board wheelchair (when available) to enable the passenger to move to and from the lavatory.
- Move to and from the lavatory, in the case of a semi-ambulatory person (as long as this does not require lifting or carrying by the airline employee).
- Load and retrieve carry-on items, including mobility aids and other assistive devices stowed on board the aircraft.

Personnel, meanwhile, are not required to provide assistance:

- Inside the lavatory.
- With personal hygiene.
- In providing any medical-related services.

Medical Certificates for Air Travel

In some cases, travelers will also need to present a medical certificate to the airline. A medical certificate is simply a written statement from the traveler's doctor stating that the passenger is capable of flying without the requirement of extraordinary medical care. A disability itself is not grounds for a medical certificate. A medical certificate will be required if:

- A person is on a stretcher or in an incubator (and the airline offers such services).

- A traveler needs oxygen (and the airline offers such services).

- If the traveler has a communicable disease.

- The traveler has some other condition that causes the airline to have reasonable doubt that the passenger will not be able to complete the flight without extraordinary medical assistance during the flight.

Rail Transportation

As is the case for air travel, there may be some specific regulations and issues related to rail transport. Therefore, it is important to check to see if there are any restrictions or issues. For example, AMTRAK has restrictions on oxygen use and size restrictions for wheelchairs. AMTRAK (like other rail providers) will also provide accommodations for travelers. It is important for the traveler to contact rail transport providers well in advance of the trip to ensure that they can meet any disability-related accommodation. Of course, what a rail provider is required under their country's laws vary from country to country. Therefore, it is important to research each rail carrier based on the country that they are operating in.

Water Transportation

Perhaps the most common forms of water transport are cruise ships. For those ships operating in U.S. waters (regardless of whether they are a foreign registry), a U.S. Supreme Court decision has determined that all ships must comply with ADA requirements. In other countries, however, foreign ships will most likely have different laws and guidelines. Therefore, taking a cruise ship in another country might lead to issues, depending upon the special needs of the traveler. Like other means of transportation, it is important to:

- Check with the travel agent and/or the cruise line itself regarding the special need and if the ship can accommodate those needs (be sure to get the answers in writing, if a problem should arise later).

- If the special need is related to a physical impairment, verify that there are ramps, if decks can be accessed without assistance, and if dining facilities and other locations are barrier-free.

- Request a cabin that is designed for persons with disabilities, or a cabin that is in close proximity to activities, etc.

- Research the Internet to see if the cruise line caters or accommodates travelers with special needs.

- If in a foreign country, be sure to explain the special need and verify that the ship will be able to accommodate those needs.

- Research what types of special accommodations exist at various ports of call.

A traveler should also keep in mind that there are other forms of water transportation. They may include ferry boats and hovercraft that are used in the English Channel and Mediterranean. As is the case with cruise ships, it is important to check with the transport companies to ensure that no problems will be encountered.

Other Public Transportation

It is also important to make sure that available transportation in the host country can accommodate the special needs of the traveler. In some cases, public transportation may not be able to accommodate the traveler's special needs. A traveler may have to opt for and select other forms of semi-private or specialized transport including taxis that may be better-suited for the traveler's special needs. Therefore, it will be important to plan and call ahead to ensure that such forms of transport will be available.

Lodging Establishments

Lodging establishments may also be a challenge for persons with special needs. While lodging establishments in the United States must conform to the regulations and standards set forth under the ADA, in other countries, those standards related to the reasonable accommodations of persons with disabilities may be lacking. In order to avoid any potential problems with the selected lodging facility, the following points should be considered:

- Select U.S. Owned Lodging Facilities. Most likely, their standards will be very similar to those found in the U.S. However, do not assume – call and/or write to verify that they can accommodate the special need.

- Try to book reservations in newer hotels. Older facilities, by their construction alone, may physically impede some travelers.

- Make sure that the facility has a working elevator if the special need is based on a physical disability.

- Try to get rooms closer to the ground floor in order to avoid any strenuous walks up stairs, etc.

- Always check to make sure that doors are wide enough – at both the main entrance and the guest room.

- Always ask about the room layout and any disability-related devices that may exist in the room.

- Ask about any physical barriers outside of the hotel (curbs, etc.).

- Ask if there is staff available to assist in accommodating the traveler's needs.

- If there is a diet-related need, check to see if the facility's restaurant can accommodate the need for special diets.

- Check to see if the establishment has an on-call physician who is readily available.

Tourist Destinations

As pointed out in the planning section of this chapter, it is also very important for the traveler with special needs to thoroughly research every tourist-related site they wish to visit in their destination country. In doing so, it is important to work with individuals from the tour group, guides and persons from the specific site. In some cases, depending upon the special need, the traveler may not be able to engage in that specific activity due to the inaccessibility of certain locales. For instance, in Europe, many castles and other buildings may be partially or fully inaccessible to a person with a mobility-related special need. Furthermore, there may be no curb cuts (ramps), while the streets and sidewalks in some areas may be narrow and uneven. Therefore, it is important to research each travel destination in detail to ensure that any special needs can be met.

TRAVELING WITH MEDICAL EQUIPMENT

Travelers may also have to travel with medical equipment. This medical equipment may include: Insulin Pumps, CPAP (Continuous Positive Airway Pressure), oxygen concentrators, canes, walkers and wheelchairs. In order to prevent any issues, the traveler should research any restrictions that may exist by reviewing appropriate websites, contacting officials, and consulting with their physicians. The traveler should also carry any medical certificate(s) that explains their need for such devices. Some specific issues to consider are listed below:

- **Security Restrictions** – Already, this chapter has pointed out that medical devices will be searched at the airport screening stage. These devices may also be screened at other public transport facilities and even at some tourist locations, depending upon security regulations. Unfortunately, in some cases, certain types of medical equipment could be banned from tourist locales.

- **Power Sources** – Check to make sure that power sources are compatible and if there is a need to bring along any back-up power supplies.

- **Check with all Couriers** – Check to make sure that all forms of transport will allow for, or accommodate the medical device to be used in their specific form of transport.

- **Consider Renting/Leasing** – In some cases, a traveler might be able to rent medical equipment. That way, the traveler can be assured that the device will not be damaged in transit and work with that country's electrical supply. It will also reduce the number of items carried. Renting/leasing will require some advanced planning. If this decision is made, it will be important to locate medical vendors in the host country. It is also important to verify the integrity of these companies and have a back-up vendor, if an issue should arise.

- **Always Find a Back-Up Source** – For essential devices, it will be important to find a company in the host country that could provide repair and/or renting of such equipment if the device should fail. Otherwise, a traveler should plan in advance with their vendor at home to see if they could rapidly ship a replacement device. Therefore, it is important that a traveler locate vendors in the host country that could provide back-up equipment and/or repair if the primary device should fail.

- **Electrical Converters** – Appropriate and high-quality electrical converters will also be needed in many foreign countries. Or, in some cases, the medical device itself could be set to another voltage and plug assembly. This will require contacting the vendor and/or company to ensure that conversion is done appropriately, and that it will work.

- **Carry all Devices** – It is best to carry all devices to ensure that they will not suffer from the abuses of the handling process by airline personnel, hotels, and other locales. These should be properly carried in sturdy and secure cases.

- **Documentation** – Be sure to have a letter or certificate from a physician explaining the need for the medical device(s).

- **Be Sure that the Devices Work** – In some cases, security personnel will want to see that the device works. In those situations where the device operates on a battery source, be sure to have the battery charged and ready to go in case of inspection. Also, have the power cords readily available, too.

- **Batteries** – Restrictions on batteries may vary from carrier to carrier and location. For example, airlines require gel packs to ensure that a battery will not leak in stowed luggage or in the passenger compartment of the aircraft. It is important to check with all of the transportation companies, and specific locales to make sure that batteries are allowed and what, if any, procedures for handling batteries exist.

- **Properly Pack the Devices** – If the decision is made to stow the medical devices, they must be properly packaged in sturdy and secure cases. There are many manufacturers that make high-impact cases with closed foam inserts that can be custom-fit to the specific device. One manufacturer of such cases is Pelican Brands (http://www.pelican.com). In some cases where the equipment is stowed, airlines may require that the item be properly labeled as a medical device. Therefore, it is important to check with the airlines and other carriers for any restrictions or requirements on transporting medical devices.

- **Maintenance Checks** – Consider having a maintenance check done on the device(s) to ensure that everything is in working order before departure.

- **Weight and Size Limitations** – Some common carriers and locations may have weight and size restrictions.

- **Don't Forget the Equipment** – In the hustle and bustle of traveling don't leave the medical equipment behind (at airports, hotels, etc.).

CONCLUSION

Throughout this book, we have dealt with the issues that some travelers may face. One particular issue, as reviewed in this chapter, is traveling with a special need. Traveling with a special need adds another layer of planning and an added challenge to the trip. As this chapter has pointed out, the recognition and planning for the special need(s) is very important. Regardless of the special need, there are a series of procedures that a traveler should follow.

Some of the major points include:

- Conducting a self-assessment of any special needs that exist.

- Consulting with your physician regarding the special need(s).

- Conducting a special needs inventory by speaking with a number of individuals and organizations that can provide detailed and accurate information and accommodations for the special need.

- Thoroughly researching all forms of transport, accommodations, and tourist sites.

- Recognizing any and all limitations that exist regarding the transport and use of assistance devices.

The fact that a traveler has identified that they have special needs should not be viewed as a negative, but as a challenge that can be overcome with planning. With the information contained in this chapter, in combination with other information found throughout the other chapters of this book, a special needs traveler can have a safe and worry-free journey.

Appendix A
COUNTRY SAFETY CHECKLIST

Information from Travel Warnings:

☐ _____   ☐ _____
☐ _____   ☐ _____
☐ _____   ☐ _____
☐ _____   ☐ _____
☐ _____   ☐ _____
☐ _____   ☐ _____

Information from Consular Sheets:

☐ _____   ☐ _____
☐ _____   ☐ _____
☐ _____   ☐ _____
☐ _____   ☐ _____
☐ _____   ☐ _____
☐ _____   ☐ _____

Other Relevant Information on Country:

_____
_____
_____
_____
_____
_____
_____
_____
_____
_____
_____
_____
_____
_____
_____
_____

COUNTRY SAFETY CHECKLIST

Information from Travel Warnings:	
☐ _____	☐ _____
☐ _____	☐ _____
☐ _____	☐ _____
☐ _____	☐ _____
☐ _____	☐ _____
☐ _____	☐ _____

Information from Consular Sheets:	
☐ _____	☐ _____
☐ _____	☐ _____
☐ _____	☐ _____
☐ _____	☐ _____
☐ _____	☐ _____
☐ _____	☐ _____

Other Relevant Information on Country:

_____

_____

_____

_____

_____

_____

_____

_____

_____

_____

_____

_____

_____

_____

_____

_____

Questions	Answers
What is the nature and extent of their travel experience?	
How do they handle stress?	
What is their level of emotional maturity?	
What are their strengths?	
What are their weaknesses?	
How will they correct these weaknesses?	
Are they a leader or follower?	
What are some of their greatest concerns with this trip?	
How will they ensure the success of the trip?	
Other Points...	

TRAVELER ASSESSMENT FORM

Questions	Answers
What is the nature and extent of their travel experience?	
How do they handle stress?	
What is their level of emotional maturity?	
What are their strengths?	
What are their weaknesses?	
How will they correct these weaknesses?	
Are they a leader or follower?	
What are some of their greatest concerns with this trip?	
How will they ensure the success of the trip?	
Other Points...	

Appendix C
EMERGENCY CONTACT
INFORMATION*

Traveler Information:
Full Name _____
D.O.B _____
SSN: _____
Passport # _____

Flight Information:
Airlines: _____
Flight #'s _____
_____

U.S. Emergency Contact:
Name _____
Address _____
City, State _____
Telephone _____
E-mail _____
Relationship _____

Primary Care Physician:
Name _____
Address _____
City, State _____
Telephone _____
E-mail _____

Health Insurance
Policy # _____
Name _____
Address _____
City, State _____
Telephone _____
E-mail _____

Dental Insurance
Policy # _____
Name _____
Address _____
City, State _____
Telephone _____
E-mail _____

Overseas Contact:
Name _____
Address _____
City, State _____
Telephone _____
E-mail _____
Relationship _____

Known Medical Conditions:
_____
_____
_____

Prescriptions
_____
_____

Detailed Daily Itinerary:
_____
_____
_____
_____
_____
_____

* Be sure to leave copies of your passport and any other travel documents with your emergency contacts.

EMERGENCY CONTACT INFORMATION

Traveler Information:
Full Name _____
D.O.B _____
SSN: _____
Passport # _____

Flight Information:
Airlines: _____
Flight #'s _____
_____
_____

U.S. Emergency Contact:
Name _____
Address _____
City, State _____
Telephone _____
E-mail _____
Relationship _____

Primary Care Physician:
Name _____
Address _____
City, State _____
Telephone _____
E-mail _____

Health Insurance
Policy # _____
Name _____
Address _____
City, State _____
Telephone _____
E-mail _____

Dental Insurance
Policy # _____
Name _____
Address _____
City, State _____
Telephone _____
E-mail _____

Overseas Contact:
Name _____
Address _____
City, State _____
Telephone _____
E-mail _____
Relationship _____

Known Medical Conditions:
_____
_____
_____

Prescriptions
_____
_____
_____

Detailed Daily Itinerary:
_____
_____
_____
_____
_____
_____
_____
_____

* Be sure to leave copies of your passport and any other travel documents with your emergency contacts.

Destination Country: _____

Region of the World: _____
Characteristics of
Neighboring Countries: _____

Form of Government: _____
Location of
Embassy/Consulate: _____
Major Religion(s):
Health Risks?   _____

Size: _____

Population Density: _____

Overall Stability of Region: _____

                                _____

Overall Stability of Country: _____
Other Points:

                                _____

                                _____

                                _____

                                _____

                                _____

                                _____

                                _____

COUNTRY CHARACTERISTICS FORM

Destination Country: _____

Region of the World: _____
Characteristics of
Neighboring Countries: _____

Form of Government: _____
Location of
Embassy/Consulate: _____
Major Religion(s):
Health Risks?   _____

Size: _____

Population Density: _____

Overall Stability of Region: _____

Overall Stability of Country: _____
Other Points: _____

                               _____

                               _____

                               _____

                               _____

                               _____

                               _____

Appendix E
TRANSPORTATION CHECKLIST

Form of Transportation	Risks

TRANSPORTATION CHECKLIST

Form of Transportation	Risks

TRAVEL EXPENSE FORM

Nature of Activity	Cost
Pre-Departure Expenses	
Clothing Necessities	
Luggage	
Passport/Passport Photos	
Medical (Exams, Inoculations, etc.)	
Toiletries and Sundries	
Tickets	
Others (Itemize Accordingly)	
Destination-Related Expenses	
Room Rates x No. Days	
Breakfast x No. Days	
Lunch x No. Days	
Dinner x No. Days	
Snacks and Beverages x No. Days	
Souvenir/Gifts/Postcards x No. Days	
Entertainment x No. Days	
Tips x No. Days	
Other Travel Expenses x No. Days	
Activity Fees x No. Days	
Others (Itemize Accordingly)	
EXPENSE TOTAL	

TRAVEL EXPENSE FORM

Nature of Activity	Cost
Pre-Departure Expenses	
Clothing Necessities	
Luggage	
Passport/Passport Photos	
Medical (Exams, Inoculations, etc.)	
Toiletries and Sundries	
Tickets	
Others (Itemize Accordingly)	
Destination-Related Expenses	
Room Rates x No. Days	
Breakfast x No. Days	
Lunch x No. Days	
Dinner x No. Days	
Snacks and Beverages x No. Days	
Souvenir/Gifts/Postcards x No. Days	
Entertainment x No. Days	
Tips x No. Days	
Other Travel Expenses x No. Days	
Activity Fees x No. Days	
Others (Itemize Accordingly)	
EXPENSE TOTAL	

Appendix G
RISK CHECKLIST

Event	Risk Priority	Risk Reduction Strategies (reduction, avoidance, transfer, spreading)

RISK CHECKLIST

Event	Risk Priority	Risk Reduction Strategies (reduction, avoidance, transfer, spreading)

	U.S. Dollars (USD)		
U.S. Dollars (USD)	1.0		

	U.S. Dollars (USD)		
U.S. Dollars (USD)	1.0		

	U.S. Dollars (USD)		
U.S. Dollars (USD)	1.0		

	U.S. Dollars (USD)		
U.S. Dollars (USD)	1.0		

CURRENCY CONVERSION CHARTS

	U.S. Dollars (USD)		
U.S. Dollars (USD)	1.0		

	U.S. Dollars (USD)		
U.S. Dollars (USD)	1.0		

	U.S. Dollars (USD)		
U.S. Dollars (USD)	1.0		

	U.S. Dollars (USD)		
U.S. Dollars (USD)	1.0		

Appendix I
LUGGAGE INVENTORY FORM

LUGGAGE INVENTORY CHECKLIST						
Item(s)	Qty.	Size/ Color	Maker	Age	Condition	Approx. Price
SUITCASE						

CONTACT INFORMATION	
Name:	
Address:	
E-mail Address:	
Home Address:	Destination Address:
Home Ph.:	Dest. Ph.:
Special Instructions:	

LUGGAGE INVENTORY FORM

LUGGAGE INVENTORY CHECKLIST						
Item(s)	Qty.	Size/Color	Maker	Age	Condition	Approx. Price
SUITCASE						

CONTACT INFORMATION	
Name:	
Address:	
E-mail Address:	
Home Address:	Destination Address:
Home Ph.:	Dest. Ph.:
Special Instructions:	

Priority Road
You Have the
Right of Way

Priority Road Ends
Yield to Traffic
from Right

Ring Road

**Passenger Drop-Off
or Pick-Up Only**
During Times Shown

Truck Route
(Or Other Vehicle
Type Depicted)

**Approaching
Road Construction
and Lane Crossover**

**Approaching
Town of Wilster**
Implies Reduced
Speed Zone

**Leaving
Town of Wilster**
Implies End of
Reduced Speed Zone

Minimum Speed

One Way

Keep Left
(Keep Right on
Right Arrow)

Turn Left
(Turn Right on
Right Arrow)

**No Passing
Zone Ends**

**Speed Limit
Zone Ends**

Derestriction Sign
(Multiple Diagonal Lines)

**National
Speed Limit Applies**
(Single Diagonal Line)

Danger

Yield

Curve

S-Curve

Uneven Road

Crossroads or Junction
Yield to Traffic from
the Right

**Two-Way
Traffic**

**Railroad Crossing
with Barriers**

Special Need	Limitations	Required Accommodations

SPECIAL NEEDS ASSESSMENT FORM

Special Need	Limitations	Required Accommodations

Appendix L
SPECIAL NEEDS INVENTORY FORM

Need: _____	Contact Info	Description of Accommo-dations	Any Limits w/Accom-modations	Needs Met? Y	N
Transportation					
Lodging Facilities:					
Organized Tours:					
Specific Locales...					
Other...					

SPECIAL NEEDS INVENTORY FORM

Need: _____	Contact Info	Description of Accommo- dations	Any Limits w/Accom- modations	Needs Met?	
				Y	N
Transportation					
Lodging Facilities:					
Organized Tours:					
Specific Locales...					
Other...					

L isted below are some private sector and governmental websites that provide additional information on safety and security-related issues. In the left hand column are symbols related to the primary information that each site provides.

Legend

✈	**Transportation Information**
🌐	**Geography**
$	**Financial Issues**
🛟	**Safety and Security**
⚕	**Health Information**

Resource	Organization and Description
✈	**Air Transport Association:** http://www.air-transport.org This site details airline accidents and fatalities records, as well as information on how airline maintenance and security programs work, how airline employees are trained, and joint efforts between the government and air carriers to improve airline safety.
⚕ ✈	**The Air Carrier Access Act:** http://www.dotcr.ost.dot.gov/asp/airacc.asp This site provides information on flying with special needs. It provides in-depth information on the legal obligations that airlines have toward customers with special needs/disabilities.

275

Resource	Organization and Description
	American Automobile Association: http://www.aaa.com Travelers can obtain an IDP permit from an AAA local office, or download at application from this site.
	American Automobile Touring Alliance: http://thenac.com/international_driving_permit.pdf Applications for the IDP can be obtained from this organization.
	Australian Department of Foreign Affairs and Trade: http://www.smarttraveller.gov.au This site is a joint initiative between the travel industry and the government of Australia.
	Canadian Consular Affairs Bureau: http://www.voyage.gc.ca This is the Canadian government's equivalent to the U.S. Dept of State. It provides a wealth of information on safe travel.
	CIA World Factbook: https://www.cia.gov Information on geography, people, government, transportation, economy, communications, etc.
	Embassy.org: http://www.embassy.org/embassies/ This site provides a list of all foreign Embassies in Washington, D.C.

Resource	Organization and Description
	Foreign and Commonwealth Office (FCO): http://www.fco.gov.uk This official government website from England provides a range of information to help British travelers overseas.
	International Student Travel Confederation: http://www.istc.org The International Student Travel Confederation (ISTC) is a not-for-profit organization, founded in 1949 by the travel departments of a group of national student unions, to explore the needs of the growing numbers of student and youth travelers, etc.
	National Transportation Safety Board: http://www.ntsb.gov You'll find accident statistics compiled monthly and annually, as well as reports on airline safety issues here at the National Transportation Safety Board's Website.
	New Zealand Ministry of Foreign Affairs and Trade: http://www.safetravel.govt.nz The official governmental site for New Zealand citizens for safe travel.
	Overseas Advisory Council (OSAC): http://www.osac.com This is a U.S. Government inter-agency Web site managed by the Bureau of Diplomatic Security, U.S. Department of State. It provides links to non-government websites as a public service only.

Resource	Organization and Description
	Student Air Travel Association: http://www.aboutistc.org/sata/index.html The Student Air Travel Association (SATA) is an international membership association of student travel agencies who share a commitment to provide affordable and accessible travel to young people.
	U.S. Department of State: http://travel.state.gov This is perhaps the most comprehensive resource for Americans to obtain travel information and conditions throughout the world.
	U.S. Department of State– Office of Overseas Citizens Services (OCS): The Department of State's Office of Overseas Citizens Services (OCS), in the Bureau of Consular Affairs, has established a Washington, D.C.-based call center to provide general information to the public. The call center will refer case-specific calls directly to the appropriate OCS country officer (or to a special task force in a crisis) and non-Consular calls to the appropriate agency or office. The call center has direct access to the most recent Consular Information Sheets, Travel Warnings and Public Announcements. The OCS call center normally operates from 8:00 a.m. to 8:00 p.m. U.S. Eastern Daylight Time (8:00 p.m. to 8:00 a.m. in Hong Kong and Macau), Monday through Friday (except U.S. federal holidays; check the Consulates holiday schedule for reference). The center will run 24-hours-a-day as needed during a crisis. It has a 24-hour a day hotline at (202) 647-5225 or at 888-407-4747 for American Citizens Services.

Resource	Organization and Description
	U.S. Center for Disease Control and Prevention: http://www.cdc.gov/travel/ This site provides information on disease and health issues throughout the world. The Centers for Disease Control and Prevention (CDC) maintains a toll-free number for public inquiries about travel-related health issues. The number is 877-394-8747.
	U.S. Department of Homeland Security: http://www.dhs.gov Provides information on travel security and procedures.
	SafeCanada: http://www.safecanada.ca This site maintained by the Government of Canada provides information on travel safety. This site is similar to the U.S. Department of State website.
	Transportation Security Administration: http://www.tsa.gov The TSA is a component of the Department of Homeland Security that is responsible for security of the nation's transportation systems.
	The United Nations: http://www.un.org This site provides information on human rights, economic and social development, security situations, etc. regarding world events.
	World Health Organization (WHO): http://www.who.int/en/ WHO is the directing and coordinating authority for health within the United Nations system. This site provides reports and brochures related to health throughout the world. This website provides up-to-date reports on disease outbreaks and specific health conditions. Additional information about the

Resource	Organization and Description
	risks of communicable diseases associated with travel is available in the WHO yearly publication "International Travel and Health."
$	**The World Bank:** http://worldbank.org This site provides information regarding the economic health of countries and regions of the world.

Index

Specifically designed to be a functional workbook, *Safe Overseas Travel* allows you to create a "trip strategy" that allows you to more thoroughly–and safely–enjoy your trip!

Safe Overseas Travel is a comprehensive, easy-to-use guide for both the novice and the experienced traveler who must navigate the myriad security complexities of modern-day travel. It not only helps you to safely arrive at your destination, it also deals with the numerous security issues that await you regarding lodging, money matters and blending in with (and standing out from) host country cultures.

This nifty guide also includes information on passport and visa matters, healthy travel issues, navigating foreign transportation systems and educates you on things to watch for when you get to your destination and, most importantly, what to do if things go wrong. It's an excellent primer for overseas travel, covering preparation activities, critical transportation issues, and cultural and security hazards in foreign lands. Many of the security practices shared in this book were developed by protective services professionals for VIPs and are made easy for "the rest of us" to use.

– Robert T. Meesig Ph.D., Lt. Col.,
USAF Criminal Investigation Branch (Ret.)

This book is ideal for people who advise and orient others for overseas travel: study abroad providers, university study abroad officials, travel agents, tour leaders. It is essential reading for professionals who organize and lead pre-departure orientation for study abroad students, and is a great resource for policy makers in deciding if orientation practices and study abroad policies are sound.

-- Mark Schaub
Executive Director, Padnos International Center
Grand Valley State University, MI

This is a very comprehensive how-to guide to safe and hassle-free travel written by two professionals in the fields of criminal justice, security, and terrorism. It carefully details the steps of preparation for the trip, embarking on the trip, and making a safe return home. The recommendations in this book are germane to both foreign and domestic travel. In the kind of world we inhabit, this book is a must-read for every traveler.

– Richard Grossenbacher
Adjunct Criminal Justice Professor
and U.S. Secret Service (Ret.)